AF323037

The Arrow and the Olive Branch

THE ARROW AND THE OLIVE BRANCH

Practical Idealism in U.S. Foreign Policy

JACK GODWIN

Foreword by Leon E. Panetta

The Ethics of American Foreign Policy
David A. Welch and Robert G. Patman, Series Editors

PRAEGER SECURITY INTERNATIONAL
Westport, Connecticut · London

Library of Congress Cataloging-in-Publication Data

Godwin, Jack.
   The arrow and the olive branch : practical idealism in U.S. foreign policy / Jack Godwin ;
   foreword by Leon E. Panetta.
      p. cm. — (The ethics of American foreign policy, ISSN 1939–0203)
   Includes bibliographical references and index.
   ISBN-13: 978–0–313–34820–4 (alk. paper)
1.   United States—Foreign relations. I. Title
E183.7.G653   2008
327.73—dc22   2007038904

British Library Cataloguing in Publication Data is available.

Library of Congress Catalog Card Number: 2007038904
ISBN-13: 978–0–313–34820–4
ISSN: 1939–0203

First published in 2008

Praeger Security International, 88 Post Road West, Westport, CT 06881
An imprint of Greenwood Publishing Group, Inc.
www.praeger.com

Printed in the United States of America

The paper used in this book complies with the
Permanent Paper Standard issued by the National
Information Standards Organization (Z39.48–1984).

10 9 8 7 6 5 4 3 2 1

To my mentors
Richard Chadwick of the University of Hawaii
Edwin Duerr of San Francisco State University

Contents

Foreword

In March 2006, members of Congress took action to create the bipartisan Iraq Study Group to conduct an independent assessment of the situation in Iraq and make forward-looking recommendations. Cochaired by James A. Baker III and Lee H. Hamilton, members of the Iraq Study Group included Lawrence S. Eagleburger, Vernon E. Jordan Jr., Edwin Meese III, Sandra Day O'Connor, William J. Perry, Charles S. Robb, Alan K. Simpson, and myself.

For more than eight months, we explored four broad policy areas: the strategic environment in Iraq and the region; key challenges regarding Iraq's internal security; political challenges facing Iraq's newly elected government; and Iraq's economy and reconstruction. We convened several plenary sessions, interviewed numerous current and former U.S. government officials, military officers, intelligence officers, diplomats, legislators, academics, journalists, and other experts. We traveled to Iraq and interviewed dozens of Iraqi government officials and representatives to assess U.S. policy in Iraq, its impact on the surrounding region, and potential consequences for U.S. interests.

In December 2006, we issued our official report, *The Iraq Study Group Report: The Way Forward—A New Approach.* The report recognizes the realities of the situation on the ground and makes seventy-nine specific recommendations necessary to overcome those realities and achieve our goals. The report's findings and recommendations are neither a magic formula nor a guarantee of success, but the best alternative to "give Iraq an opportunity for a better future, combat terrorism, stabilize a critical region of the world, and protect America's credibility, interests, and values." Most important, the report reflects the bipartisan consensus of the study group. While it may not seem very extraordinary, the ten members of the study group (five Republicans, five Democrats) worked very hard to reach across the aisle and do the right thing.

There is an old adage worth repeating: when it comes to foreign policy, party politics should end at the water's edge. Anyone who believes this nation is at its best when our leaders work together to find solutions will find *The Arrow and the Olive Branch* to be an invaluable resource. The book opens on September 11, 2001 the day nineteen men hijacked four commercial jets and turned them into weapons of mass destruction. Then it travels back in time to September 17, 1796, the day George Washington gave his farewell address and advised us to refrain from foreign entanglements. Building on this first principle, Jack Godwin tracks down every foreign policy precedent set by every president since Washington. He reconstructs the doctrine of practical idealism and guides the reader on a journey to rediscover the historic, timeless, bipartisan ideals of the American school of diplomacy. Although practical idealism is open to interpretation, and full of complexities and contradictions, Godwin's research reveals a surprising degree of continuity over time, across changes of power from one party to another, through adversity and numerous adjustments imposed by events.

In 1823, James Monroe and his secretary of state John Q. Adams proclaimed the Monroe Doctrine, which nominally forbid future European colonization in the Western Hemisphere. At the end of the nineteenth and beginning of the twentieth century, William McKinley and Theodore Roosevelt redefined the Monroe Doctrine and expanded its geographic scope beyond the Western Hemisphere. The United States defeated Spain, occupied Guantánamo Bay in Cuba, acquired the Philippines and Hawaii, and began construction of the Panama Canal. Following the horrors of WWI, Woodrow Wilson envisioned a new world order based on universal principles of openness, justice, and of course self-determination. Anyone who believes Wilson's idealism was exceptional may be surprised to learn every president elected since Franklin Roosevelt (Republicans and Democrats alike) has expressed their support for self-determination.

One of the most enduring aspects of practical idealism (and certainly relevant to current and future challenges) comes from an unlikely source, Ulysses S. Grant. In 1875, Grant refused to intervene in Cuba's insurrection against Spain and advocated using American power with restraint. In 1950, following Grant's precedent, Harry Truman chose to fight a limited war in Korea. In the 1960s and early 1970s, Lyndon Johnson and Richard Nixon fought the Vietnam War as a limited war. In 1992, George H.W. Bush described the limited objectives of the mission in Somalia. In 1994, Bill Clinton described the limited objectives of his intervention in Haiti. In the early months of the Iraq War, George W. Bush tried to limit the duration of the Iraq War by using what he believed was decisive force.

The Arrow and the Olive Branch makes an important contribution not because of George Santayana's warning that those who cannot remember the past are condemned to repeat it. Rather, it is important because of Winston Churchill's advice to study history, because history is the receptacle for the secrets of statecraft. For those not well versed in history, the problems we face today may seem unprecedented. For those not well versed in history, the idea that conservatives and liberals could work together, let alone reach unanimous agreement, may seem unthinkable.

In 1941–1942, the United States and Great Britain were recovering from a series of military disasters. President Franklin Roosevelt and Prime Minister Winston Churchill communicated frequently with each other and their constituents as they developed their war plans and prepared for the difficult days ahead. These two great leaders believed people would respect their candor if they told the truth about the realities they faced.

In *The Hinge of Fate*, volume four of Churchill's massive WWII history, he said there was no worse mistake in public leadership than to give people false hope. People could endure hardship if they had to, but bitterly resented being deceived or discovering their leaders were deceiving themselves. Decades later, it is instructive to remember Churchill's advice and follow Roosevelt and Churchill's example. It is equally instructive to consider the advice of George Washington and his successors. In the years and decades to come, we should be mindful of the full range of foreign policy options available to us, skeptical of false historical analogies and vigilant in defense of America's credibility, values, and interests.

Leon E. Panetta
June 2007
The Leon & Sylvia Panetta Institute for Public Policy
CSU Monterey Bay, Seaside, California

Acknowledgments

Thanks to all my colleagues at California State University, Sacramento, particularly Monica Freeman and Eric Merchant, as well as Edmundo Aguilar, Matt Altier, Patrick Cannon, Kevin Cornwell, Tracey Culbertson, Bob Curry, David Earwicker, Ruedi Egger, Leo Evangelista, Buzz Fozouni, Spencer Freund, Donald Gerth, Larry Glasmire, Sho Hayashigatani, Kim Harrington, Lori Harrison, Celene Harwell, Cristy Jensen, Terry Manns, Pam Milchrist, Kathy Mine, Jennifer Narodzonek, Kim Nava, Daniel Orey, Sam Parsons, Roberto Pomo, Janis Silvers, Preston Stegenga, Don Taylor, Donna Thomason, Leonard Valdez, Miki Vohryzek-Bolden, David Wagner, Mlima Wells, and Len Wycosky.

Thanks to Patti Garamendi, Susan Grivas, Markos Kounalakis, John Morris, and Marsha Vande Berg formerly of the California State World Trade Commission.

Thanks to David Satterwhite and everyone at the Japan-United States Educational Commission.

Thanks to Brooks Ohlson of the Sacramento Center for International Trade Development.

Thanks to Gwen Robinson and Eugene Robinson Jr. of Sacramento, California.

Thanks to Michele Gault of the Northern California World Trade Center.
Thanks to Eduardo Bermudez and Brett Perkins of Kaiser Permanente.
Thanks to Ken Brown of the California State University, Long Beach.
Thanks to Susanne Stirling of the California Chamber of Commerce.
Thanks to Roberto Sainz of the University of California, Davis.
Thanks to Lee Fritschler of George Mason University.
Thanks to Frank Malaret of Sacramento City College.

Thanks to Jock O'Connell of the Clark Street Group.
Thanks to Hilary Claggett and everyone at Praeger.
Thanks to Anne Beer and N. Magendra Varman at BeaconPMG.
Thanks to Jeffery McGraw of the August Agency.
Thanks to Steffan and Margarita Todorov.
Special thanks to Eme and Audrey.

Preface

If George Washington were alive today, would you consult him about the Middle East? How about Ronald Reagan or Franklin Roosevelt? If you could, would you ask Richard Nixon about China? Would you ask Dwight Eisenhower about strategic defense? Would you ask Harry Truman about weapons of mass destruction? Would you ask him about Korea? If you were the current incumbent, facing all these problems—some inherited, some self-inflicted—whose advice would you ask? Whose example would you follow?

In the American system of government, the power to conduct foreign policy belongs to the president, commander-in-chief according to Article II, Section 2. The Constitution places a few specific limitations on the president's authority, for example, requiring the president to get the Senate's advice and consent on political appointments and a two-thirds majority on treaties. The Constitution also gives Congress the power to regulate international trade, appropriate funds for the armed forces, and declare war. However, that is the full extent of the Constitution's language regarding the conduct of foreign policy, and *The Federalist Papers*—the instructions Alexander Hamilton, James Madison, and John Jay wrote explaining how the Constitution should work—add little clarification.

Presidents rarely suffer from too little advice. There are thousands of pundits, lobbyists, and scholars (some of them former speechwriters) and others offering their expert advice. Very few of them ever sat in the big chair, and those who have are often ignored, reluctant to speak or deceased. With this in mind, my goal was to write a reference book for foreign policy practitioners, a cross between *The Federalist Papers* and *The Prince,* Niccolò Machiavelli's sixteenth century treatise on statecraft.

My research entailed tracking down every major presidential statement on foreign policy from George Washington to George W. Bush, and studying thousands of speeches, transcripts, press conferences, and other primary documents. This included extensive research of secondary sources in order to provide the case history for significant foreign policy events, but excluded anything presidents communicated before or after their term of office. What I wanted was the executive perspective—the view from the big chair—not campaign promises, private diaries, or self-serving memoirs.

What did all this research reveal? In John Kennedy's 1961 annual message, he said, "On the Presidential Coat of Arms, the American eagle holds in his right talon the olive branch, while in his left he holds a bundle of arrows. We intend to give equal attention to both."[1] This is the symbol of *The Arrow and the Olive Branch: Practical Idealism in U.S. Foreign Policy.* On one side, there is an eagle ready to defend American ideals such as freedom of speech, freedom of religion, democracy, human rights, the rule of law, and equal justice. On the back, there are several ugly reminders: world war, cold war, limited war, proxy war, secret war, preemptive war, and holy war.

Part I covers the late seventeenth century and most of the eighteenth, from George Washington to the end of Grover Cleveland's second term. Highlights include James Monroe's 1823 declaration the United States would oppose new European colonies in the Western Hemisphere, a variation on Washington's advice to limit European influence in North America. Decades later, Ulysses Grant would set another precedent, introducing the concept of restraint in the use of American power. In 1875, Grant refused to intervene in Cuba's fight for independence from Spain because he did not consider the Cuban insurrection a full-fledged revolution. This relatively brief section, subtitled *Purchase, Annexation and Conquest,* lays the foundation for the rest of the book.

Part II, subtitled *Two Oceans and Two World Wars* begins with William McKinley's presidency, the war with Spain, acquisition of the Philippines and Hawaii, and the Open Door policy in China. This section covers the presidency of Theodore Roosevelt, who strongly supported construction of a new canal across Panama connecting the two oceans and expanding the geographic scope of the Monroe Doctrine. This section also includes many observations from Woodrow Wilson, who led the United States to victory in World War I and envisioned a new world order based on open diplomacy, free navigation, free trade and of course, self-determination. Every president elected since Franklin Roosevelt has cited self-determination to support a wide range of policies, a testament to its durability. Finally, this section concludes with Franklin Roosevelt, who led the great alliance to victory over Nazi Germany and Imperial Japan in World War II.

Part III begins with the eventful presidency of Harry Truman, who set several precedents beginning with his order to attack Hiroshima and Nagasaki with nuclear weapons. This was followed by the Marshall Plan; the National

Security Act that created the Central Intelligence Agency, Department of Defense, Joint Chiefs of Staff, and National Security Council; the Berlin airlift; Executive Order 9981 which desegregated the military; and the creation of NATO (North Atlantic Treaty Organization). Harry Truman also introduced the concept of limited war in Korea, a variation of Grant's emphasis on using power with restraint. Subtitled *Cold War and Limited War,* this section covers the United States' involvement in Southeast Asia, beginning with Dwight Eisenhower, with particular emphasis on Lyndon Johnson and Richard Nixon. This section ends with the presidencies of Jimmy Carter and Ronald Reagan, the Iran Hostage crisis and the Iran-Contra affair.

Part IV covers the prudent foreign policy of George H. W. Bush during the fall of the Berlin Wall, Iraq's invasion of Kuwait, the end of the Cold War, and collapse of the Soviet Union. It also covers the presidency of Bill Clinton, whose foreign policy dealt mostly with international trade and a few regional crises. Finally, this section covers George W. Bush's first term in office and part of his second term, the invasion of Afghanistan, the Iraq disarmament crisis, Iraq War and occupation. Subtitled *Global Supremacy and Global Stewardship,* this section takes us from the last days of the Cold War to the first years of the Global War on Terror.

To understand the doctrine of practical idealism with all its complexities and contradictions, you should read the book from start to finish. This approach is instructive because you can follow practical idealism chronologically as presidents uphold, overturn, redefine, or disregard precedents set by their predecessors. Occasionally, you can even hear them arguing with each other. If you wish, you may open the book to any chapter and hear each president plead his case before the court of public opinion, analyzing, rationalizing, and economizing on the truth.

To those who hope to succeed the current incumbent, I recommend you reread Bill Clinton's 1995 address to the Iowa State Legislature. Speaking a few days after the Oklahoma City bombing in which more than one hundred sixty people died, including several children, Clinton asked people to exercise their freedom of speech responsibly because *words have consequences.* "If words did not have consequences, we wouldn't be here today," he said, "We're here today because Patrick Henry's words had consequences, because Thomas Jefferson's words had consequences, because Abraham Lincoln's words had consequences. And these words we hear today have consequences—the good ones and the bad ones, the ones that bring us together, and the ones that drive a wedge through our heart."[2]

To those who would take everything presidents say literally, I recommend you turn your information filter up to full volume. Americans are human, so practical idealism would be incomplete without pride, greed, envy, conceit, vanity, racism, hypocrisy, and most other human failings. To those who would dismiss everything presidents say as empty rhetoric, let me remind you: a single speech may be empty, but a thousand is a data mine, full of useful information to identify complex relationships and patterns, discover anomalies, and forecast trends. Words have consequences. And so it is with *The Arrow and the Olive Branch: Practical Idealism in U.S. Foreign Policy*.

Introduction

On September 11, 2001, members of the fundamentalist Islamic group al-Qaeda hijacked four commercial jets and crashed two of them into the twin towers of New York's World Trade Center. They crashed a third plane into the Pentagon building across the Potomac River from Washington and a fourth into a field in rural Pennsylvania. The attacks killed approximately three thousand people, including more than three hundred firefighters. A few weeks later, the United States launched a war on terror, invaded Afghanistan and overthrew the Taliban, Afghanistan's al-Qaeda-friendly religious dictatorship.

In George W. Bush's 2002 annual message a few months later, he pledged the United States would pursue two primary objectives. First, the United States would destroy terrorist camps, prevent terrorists from executing their plans, and bring terrorists to justice. Second, the United States would prevent terrorists and rogue nations from threatening the United States and the world with weapons of mass destruction. He said the United States would work closely with its allies to prevent terrorist organizations and their state sponsors from acquiring the materials, technology, and expertise to develop weapons of mass destruction. In particular, Bush said North Korea, Iran, and Iraq were threatening world peace, and called them "an axis of evil."[1]

In September 2002, about a year after the 9/11 attack, Bush released his NSS (National Security Strategy), which explained the justification for preemptive action. According to the NSS, because terrorists could launch a surprise attack against the United States with weapons of mass destruction, the United States had the right to take preemptive action in self-defense. Furthermore, the NSS said preemptive action is consistent with international law, which does not require countries to wait for an attack before they can lawfully defend themselves. In the past, a threat was "imminent" if armed forces were visibly mobilizing and preparing to attack. Because rogue states and terrorists have acquired new capabilities, new weapons, and tactics—and could launch an attack on the United States's civilian population using weapons of mass destruction—it is imperative to act against emerging threats before they are fully formed, in other words before they become imminent. According to the NSS:

> The United States has long maintained the option of preemptive actions to counter a sufficient threat to our national security. The greater the threat, the greater is the risk of inaction—and the more compelling the case for taking anticipatory action to defend ourselves, even if uncertainty remains as to the time and place of the enemy's attack. To forestall or prevent such hostile acts by our adversaries, the United States will, if necessary, act preemptively.[2]

In addition to the doctrine of preemptive action, the NSS includes of a wide range of initiatives around which the U.S. government organizes its military power, homeland defenses, law enforcement, intelligence, diplomacy, and foreign aid. These include strengthening alliances, diffusing regional conflicts, removing weapons of mass destruction, stimulating global economic growth, promoting democracy, and restructuring America's national security institutions. In the cover letter to the NSS, Bush said American principles such as human rights, the rule of law, freedom of speech, freedom of religion, equal justice, respect for women, respect for religious and ethnic diversity, and respect for private property are all nonnegotiable. Taken as a whole, the NSS presents a comprehensive and coherent foreign policy balancing pragmatism and idealism.

In the cover letter Bush said, "The events of September 11, 2001 taught us that weak states, like Afghanistan, can pose as great a danger to our national interests as strong states." (He repeated this assertion in his 2006 annual message.) He also said the nexus of terrorism and high technology creates new threats—and the task of protecting America has changed dramatically. Finally, Bush said the United States was at a crossroads, and had the best opportunity to spread peace, prosperity, and freedom "since the rise of the nation-state in the seventeenth century."

That was 1648 to be specific, when the Treaty of Westphalia formally ended the Thirty Years War.[3] The immediate impact of this treaty was to resolve a bitter religious dispute in Europe between Catholics and Protestants. The treaty also laid the foundation of the modern nation-state, and is considered the birth date of the international system that survives to this day. One of the characteristics of the international system is that nation-states have sovereignty, meaning power over a geographic territory, which other nation-states recognize. This was a radical departure from the system of overlapping political and religious affiliations, which was the case before the Treaty of Westphalia. This is why terrorism and international terrorist organizations such as al-Qaeda, with their overlapping political and religious affiliations, represent a historic foreign policy challenge.

•••

More than 350 years later, historical context and political precedent were on George W. Bush's mind when he delivered a speech to commemorate the sixtieth anniversary of the United States's victory over Japan. He likened the 9/11 attacks to Pearl Harbor and WWII.[4] He said the fundamental principle that guided him—*never underestimate the power of freedom*—was the same one that guided Franklin Roosevelt to victory. Unfortunately, on the day before this speech Hurricane Katrina devastated the Central Gulf Coast region and eclipsed everything he said.

A few weeks later, Bush used a different analogy. This time, he compared the war on terror to the cold war, noting the similarities between the leaders of communism and the leaders of Islamic radicalism. Both belonged to an elitist, self-appointed vanguard with contempt for human life, justice, and morality. Aided and abetted by anti-Semitic elements of the Arab news media, Bush said Islamic radicals would not hesitate to murder Jews, Christians, Hindus, or Muslims to achieve their "endless ambitions of imperial domination." Although Islamic radicals chose their victims indiscriminately, their ultimate goal was to establish an Islamic empire from Spain to Indonesia. To accomplish this, Islamic radicals sought to end American influence in the Middle East, acquire weapons of mass destruction, and gain control of moderate Muslim governments such as Egypt, Saudi Arabia, Pakistan, Jordan—and of course Iraq.

Based on this troubling premise, Bush rejected appeasement as an option. In his words:

> Over the years these extremists have used a litany of excuses for violence—the Israeli presence on the West Bank, or the U.S. military presence in Saudi Arabia, or the defeat of the Taliban, or the Crusades of a thousand years ago. In fact, we're not facing a set of grievances that can be soothed and addressed. We're facing a radical ideology with inalterable objectives: to enslave whole nations and intimidate the world. No act of ours invited the rage of the killers—and no concession, bribe, or act of appeasement would change or limit their plans for murder.[5]

With popular support for his policies plummeting, Bush delivered a series of speeches to outline his strategy for victory in Iraq, beginning late in 2005. This coincided with the release of a document called the *National Strategy for Victory in Iraq*, an unclassified version of the strategy the government had been pursuing since 2003.[6] The document was important because it showed, "how we look at the war, how we see the enemy, how we define victory, and what we're doing to achieve it." In terms of *how we see the enemy*, Bush said most of the insurgents by far were "rejectionists," mostly Sunni Arabs and "ordinary Iraqis" who enjoyed privileged status under Saddam Hussein's regime and rejected any political structure in which they were not the dominant group. In terms of how we define victory, Bush said our goal was to leave behind a democracy capable of governing itself, sustaining itself, and defending itself.

He refused to withdraw the U.S. troops until his definition of victory— based on a set of political, economic, and security milestones, not an artificial timetable—was complete. "To retreat before victory would be an act of recklessness and dishonor, and I will not allow it," he said.[7]

The most important—and mostly overlooked—element of these speeches was Bush's persistent rejection of appeasement as a policy option. This may seem unremarkable, but there was once a time when appeasement was a legitimate instrument of British diplomacy to settle international disputes. The point was to acknowledge grievances, negotiate and compromise— and thus avoid armed conflict. Ever since British prime minister Neville Chamberlain surrendered the Sudetenland to German chancellor Adolf Hitler in the 1938 Munich Agreement, however, appeasement has become synonymous with weakness, and thus irreconcilable with practical idealism. By persistently rejecting appeasement, Bush defended a relatively long-standing (albeit nonbinding) political precedent that Franklin Roosevelt, Harry Truman, and others consistently upheld.

•••

Although presidential pronouncements are not equivalent to constitutional amendments or legally binding judicial opinions, presidents live in the shadow of foreign policy precedent as much as legal precedent. Thus, we must read each one chronologically, beginning with the 1793 Proclamation of Neutrality, issued by the only American president without precedent, George Washington.[8] France was at war with Great Britain and her allies: Austria, Prussia, Sardinia, and the Netherlands. From his office in Philadelphia, Washington said it was in America's best interest to remain neutral in the war, even though one of the belligerents was France, America's first ally. In 1778, France signed a treaty of "commerce and friendship," and sent ships and troops—including the nineteen-year-old major general Marquis de Lafayette—to fight alongside Americans during the Revolutionary War.

For George Washington, neutrality was synonymous with free navigation of the seas. He asserted America's neutrality and the right to free navigation again in 1794, with the notorious Jay Treaty, which gave Britain most favorable trading status in return for Britain agreeing to withdraw its troops from North America.[9] Washington wanted to clear up some unfinished business from the treaty that ended the American Revolutionary War, particularly Britain's military posts in northwestern U.S. territory. Part of the fallout from the Jay Treaty, however, was the French government's petulant refusal to receive Washington's minister to France. Shortly after Washington left office, another episode took place, the so-called XYZ affair, in which French authorities solicited a bribe as a precondition for a meeting between the American envoy and the French foreign minister.

In his 1796 farewell address, Washington shared a few of the timeless principles of international relations, such as avoid permanent alliances, avoid permanent enemies, and always build foreign relations on a foundation of commerce as well as politics. He also offered his successors a few suggestions, which would become the foundation of the doctrine of practical idealism. Of course, he counseled neutrality—though he knew that neutrality by itself was not enough. Because Washington appreciated the geopolitical significance of late eighteenth century sea power, he knew it would take a powerful navy to keep commercial shipping channels open and ensure free navigation.[10]

Although there is no Washington Doctrine so-called, there might as well be, because it is still in force. It is the doctrine of practical idealism. Of course, it also lives on in the minds of those who take Washington's advice literally, and would apply his principles meticulously. Strict adherence to Washington's first principle—beware of foreign entanglements— would become difficult a few short years later, in October 1800, when France and Spain signed the secret Treaty of San Ildefonso, which would eventually lead to the reacquisition of the Louisiana Territory by America's old ally France.[11]

PART I

Purchase, Annexation, and Conquest, 1796–1895

1

European Influence and Monroe Doctrine

Louisiana Purchase; European Influence; Free Navigation; Annexing Texas; Mexican-American War; Gunboat Diplomacy

In the 1796 presidential election, Vice President John Adams defeated Secretary of State Thomas Jefferson. Shortly after Adams took office it became apparent that refraining from foreign entanglements would be easier said than done. French authorities solicited a bribe as a precondition for a meeting between the French foreign minister and Adams's envoys in the XYZ affair. Less than a year later, France passed a law giving itself permission to seize a neutral vessel if any portion of its cargo contained British-made goods. Adams considered the law an "unequivocal act of war." In 1798, Congress retaliated. First, they suspended trade with France, then passed a law permitting American merchant vessels to defend themselves against such "depredations and outrages," and eventually nullified all treaties with France.[1] The "quasi-war" would continue until 1800, when the two parties negotiated a settlement that restored friendly relations and resurrected the historic alliance.[2]

In the 1800 presidential election, Thomas Jefferson unseated incumbent John Adams. Jefferson said little regarding foreign policy in his first inaugural address, except to pledge "honest friendship with all nations [and] entangling alliances with none."[3] In his 1801 annual message, he mentioned he deployed a squadron of frigates into the Mediterranean to keep piracy under control along the Barbary Coast. From 1786 to 1836, the United States negotiated several treaties with the North African city-states of Morocco,

Algeria, Tunis, and Tripoli. Because the fledgling U.S. Navy could not protect American merchant ships from pirates along the Barbary Coast, the United States agreed to pay tribute to (bribe) the governors. In November 1796, the United States negotiated a treaty with the Bey (provincial governor) of Tripoli. According to Article 11 of the treaty:

> *As the government of the United States of America is not in any sense founded on the Christian Religion*—as it has in itself no character of enmity against the laws, religion or tranquility of Musselmen [Muslims]—and as the said States never have entered into any war or act of hostility against any Mehomitan [Muslim] nation, it is declared by the parties that no pretext arising from religious opinions shall ever produce an interruption of the harmony existing between the two countries.[4]

In 1801, the Bey of Tripoli reneged on the treaty and demanded a larger tribute to protect American merchant ships, which is what prompted Jefferson to send the squadron of frigates into the Mediterranean. Thus, the pretext that interrupted the harmony between the two countries was not religion; it was business.

In his 1802 annual message, Jefferson reported the Louisiana Territory had changed hands, and observed the event called for "a change in the aspect of our foreign relations."[5] There can be no doubt that Washington's warnings about European ambition and foreign influence were on Jefferson's mind when he learned about the terms of the Treaty of San Ildefonso. In particular, he worried France would restrict free navigation of the Mississippi River and the Port of New Orleans, which would pose a constant threat to the nation's economic security. Thus, Jefferson dispatched future president James Monroe to France as his special envoy to negotiate navigation and landing rights and possibly purchase New Orleans outright. What emerged from the negotiations, of course, was the Louisiana Purchase Treaty, which France and the United States signed in Paris in April 1803.[6] Although the treaty did not specifically define Louisiana's geographic boundaries, the territory consisted of almost one million square miles—about five times the area of France, and included all of what would become Missouri, Arkansas, Iowa, Minnesota, North and South Dakota, Nebraska, and Oklahoma, and parts of Kansas, Colorado, Wyoming, and Montana.

The Louisiana Purchase is significant because it sets three precedents. First, it was a practical application of the Monroe Doctrine—twenty years before the Monroe Doctrine appeared. Second, it signaled the United States' systematic acquisition of territory for the rest of the nineteenth century. Third, by securing the departure of all French and Spanish troops, it was an excellent example of practical idealism. For a few million dollars, Jefferson guaranteed free access to the Mississippi River and Port of New Orleans, secured the departure of all French and Spanish troops from the territory, and assured the dominance of the United States in North America.

In his 1805 annual message, Jefferson reported Native Americans were discovering that "the earth yields subsistence with less labor and more certainty than the forest." Based on his perceptions at least, relations with the Indians seemed quite friendly. In 1806—as Jefferson was reading and digesting reports from the Lewis and Clarke expedition—he said, "We continue to receive proofs of the growing attachment of our Indian neighbors, and of their disposition to place all their interests under the patronage of the United States."

The Louisiana Purchase and relations with Indian Nations were not the only foreign policy issues on Jefferson's mind. By 1805, pirates were harassing American commercial shipping, capturing, plundering, and sinking friendly ships. Some pirates abandoned the crews in lifeboats on the open sea or on desert shores with no food or shelter. As a result, Jefferson sent the navy and marines several times to North Africa (the "Barbary Coast") to protect American merchant ships. He equipped a small fleet of gunboats, a precursor to the Coast Guard, to arrest pirates and bring them to justice. Jefferson also took action to reinforce forts and land batteries with heavy cannon to defend against warships approaching the coast.

In June 1807, the British attacked the frigate Chesapeake in American territorial waters, killing several crewmembers and kidnapping others. Britain refused to admit any wrongdoing for the attack on the Chesapeake, and refused to pay reparations claimed by the United States for the murder and kidnapping of American merchant seamen. In response, Jefferson signed a bill banning all exports from American ports, but enforcing the law was difficult, and even when it was enforced it hurt American merchants more than anybody else, particularly those in trade-dependent New England. The only thing the embargo accomplished was to hurt the American economy—and antagonize France and Britain more than ever. This was followed by the 1809 Non-intercourse Act, which lifted the embargo, except to France and Britain. Equally unsuccessful, it too was lifted after a year.

•••

In November 1808, James Madison won the presidential election. In his 1809 inaugural address, he listed four broad foreign policy goals. First, he would promote peace and goodwill toward all nations who would do likewise. Second, he pledged to resolve differences through negotiation rather than fighting. Third, he would maintain a standing military force, adequately armed and trained. Fourth, he would maintain neutrality in the conflicts between European nations.

As stated, neither Britain nor France recognized the United States' neutrality, regardless what claims we made. Britain and France were locked in a struggle for world domination that would not stop until June 1815, when British forces under the Duke of Wellington defeated Napoleon Bonaparte in the Battle of Waterloo. (The enthusiasm with which France recognized America's independence from Britain is evidence—the American Revolution was a theater in that epic struggle.)

By the middle of Madison's second term, however, the Napoleonic Wars were winding down. The French Empire under Napoleon had already reached its pinnacle, and Napoleon had made the long retreat from Russia. With the situation in Europe beginning to settle, the United States hoped to persuade Britain to come to the negotiating table. Madison sent instructions to London communicating his willingness to negotiate an armistice, but with certain requirements, particularly that the British release the American seamen they kidnapped, and that Britain put an end to the indiscriminate seizure of American merchant ships. Britain ignored Madison's offer.

The British-American War of 1812 began in June of that year when Congress agreed to Madison's request to declare war. Madison deployed volunteers and regular army members from Ohio to the Michigan Territory, to intercept British forces attacking from Canada. American forces took the offensive, but were beaten back. Madison ordered the navy to retaliate against British forces near Detroit. Troops from the New York Militia attacked British forces near Niagara—and appeared to be victorious—but were later overwhelmed by British regulars and their Native American allies. American naval forces on Lake Erie were more successful. They captured a superior British force and enabled American ground forces to drive the British completely out of Michigan.

The key engagements took place in 1814, when the British fleet occupied Chesapeake Bay and used it to stage numerous raids, most notably into the city of Washington, setting fire to the White House and Capitol building, and forcing James Madison to evacuate. The British then turned against Baltimore, first overland and then from the water. It was during Britain's attack on Fort McHenry in Baltimore Harbor when Francis Scott Key wrote his famous poem, which was later set to music and became the national anthem.

In March 1814, the charismatic general Andrew Jackson led a combined force of army regulars, Tennessee militia and Cherokee Indians against the Creek Indians allied with Britain. Jackson's troops then moved toward New Orleans, where Jackson successfully defended the city in a series of engagements. In late December, while American and British commissioners were negotiating a peace treaty in Ghent, Belgium, Andrew Jackson fought the Battle of New Orleans. After two decisive American victories in the first days of the New Year, British forces withdrew into the Gulf.

The peace treaty—the Treaty of Ghent—stipulated that all Native American Tribes or Nations "shall agree to desist from all hostilities against the United States of America." The treaty included provisions for follow-up negotiations on disarmament, which resulted in both the United States and Britain reducing naval forces in the Great Lakes region. All prisoners of war taken by either side were released. All territory and possessions seized during the war, including "slaves or other private property," were restored. Finally, the two signatories agreed the international slave trade was "irreconcilable with the principles of humanity" and pledged to abolish it.[7] This section of the peace treaty would become prominent decades later, when the British Navy detained and boarded several American vessels they suspected of transporting a cargo of African slaves for sale in the New World.

•••

James Monroe won the 1816 presidential election and was reelected in 1820. Monroe announced the Monroe Doctrine in his 1823 annual message. He said, "the occasion has been judged proper for asserting, as a principle in which the rights and interests of the United States are involved, that the American continents, by the free and independent condition which they have assumed and maintain, are henceforth not to be considered as subjects for future colonization by any European powers."[8]

The Monroe Doctrine defined the geographic boundaries of what Americans should consider their sphere of influence. Because the United States did not have the military strength to enforce it, success depended on the absence of a coalition of European nations to challenge it. As a result, the great European powers tacitly gave the United States—a regional power—autonomy to take regional action as long as it did not upset the global balance of power. This was an early example of a practice that would become common decades later. In 1908 for example, when Japan invaded Korea, Theodore Roosevelt did not protest because he believed that Korea (the relatively weaker power) belonged in Japan's sphere of influence.

The Monroe Doctrine arose, in part, from the insurrections in Spain's South American colonies. Before Monroe took office in 1817, several South American colonies rejected Spanish authority after Napoleon's brother Joseph Bonaparte was installed on the Spanish throne. By 1815, the fight for independence gained force under the leadership of Simón Bolívar, among others. After several defeats, Bolívar led rebel armies to victory in Venezuela and Colombia, and later in Ecuador.

Naturally, the Monroe administration took an interest in who won, even though neutrality was the official policy, just as it was between Britain and France. Monroe pledged all parties would have access to American ports, and no one would receive any aid or special treatment. Monroe's policy of "strict impartiality" extended to arms sales as well, because all parties "enjoyed an equal right to purchase and export arms, munitions of war, and every other supply."[9]

•••

There was another issue closer to home, in the Florida Territory. In his 1818 annual message, Monroe reported on the state of increasing lawlessness and anarchy in the parts of Florida under Spanish authority. Monroe asserted that Spain had lost control of Florida, and it had fallen into the hands of "adventurers connected with the savages." With Spain's South American colonies in a state of full rebellion, Monroe was worried American security interests were threatened. As American forces under Andrew Jackson defeated Florida's Seminole Indians in a series of engagements, it was clear that Spain had allowed their authority over Florida to deteriorate.

Monroe gave great importance to the possibility of acquiring the Florida Territory because of its strategic location. It would provide access to the ocean from neighboring states, and establish a security buffer against powerful Indian tribes, the Seminoles in particular. Florida had several excellent harbors in the Gulf of Mexico large enough to accommodate the county's fleet of warships, which were strategically located to protect the Port of New Orleans and the Mississippi Delta. Eventually Spain realized it could not govern Florida while they were trying to suppress their rebellious South American colonies, and agreed to cede the Florida Territory in the Adams–Onís Treaty of 1819.

Under the terms of the treaty, Spain ceded to the United States all the territories east of the Mississippi River in Florida. The territory west of the Sabine River, south to the Gulf of Mexico (approximately) belonged to Spain. Similar to the terms of the Louisiana Purchase, Spain agreed to withdraw its troops within six months; the treaty guaranteed the inhabitants would become American citizens, and be free to practice the religion of their choice or move back to Spain if they so desired. The U.S. government generously agreed to pay costs to transport the Spanish troops to Cuba, and permitted Spanish ships to continue to trade in Florida with most favorable trading terms.[10] This treaty would resolve some, but not all the unfinished business of the Treaty of San Ildefonso.

In Monroe's 1822 annual message, he told his audience Europe's recent history demonstrated that America's policy of neutrality was no longer the best way to guarantee America's national security. Monroe understood that George Washington's advice on neutrality was just a tactic useful for a specific case, but the long-term strategy was to limit foreign influence in North America. Monroe warned his listeners that a love of peace coupled with a defenseless position would invite the United States's enemies to attack. Foreshadowing sentiments Ronald Reagan would express more than a hundred fifty years later, Monroe said the surest way to avoid war is to prepare for it.

●●●

In the 1824 presidential election, no candidate received a majority in the Electoral College, and the House of Representatives voted in favor of

John Quincy Adams, son of the second president who previously held a variety of ambassadorships in Europe and served as secretary of state in the Monroe administration. In his 1825 inaugural address, Adams listed his predecessor's foreign and defense policy successes. The United States acquired Florida, and several of Spain's former colonies won their independence. The United States' coastal defenses had been fortified, and the navy was strengthened in order to suppress the African slave trade. In his 1825 annual message, Adams also reported the United States recognized the sovereignty of the Republic of Colombia, and he would soon be presenting a treaty to Congress. Similar treaties with all the other newly independent South American states were in the works.

In his 1825 annual message, Adams said, "Our relations with the numerous tribes of aboriginal natives of this country...dependent even for their existence upon our power, have been during the present year highly interesting." Congress recently passed legislation appropriating funds to pay expenses to implement treaties with several Indian tribes east of the Mississippi River. One agreement authorized construction of a road from Missouri to New Mexico. Another defrayed expenses related to establishing boundaries and keeping the peace between the Sioux, Chippewa, and other tribes. "The first and last objects of these acts have been accomplished," said Adams. The first object was to secure "pledges of permanent peace between several tribes which had been long waging bloody wars against each other," while the second—evidently—was to make "large and valuable acquisitions of territory."[11]

Here is a blunt statement of the government's Indian policy, from John Quincy Adams's fourth and final annual message:

> As independent powers, we negotiated with [the Indians] by treaties; as proprietors, we purchased of them all the lands which we could prevail upon them to sell; as brethren of the human race, rude and ignorant, we endeavored to bring them to the knowledge of religion and letters. The ultimate design was to incorporate in our own institutions that portion of them which could be converted to the state of civilization...we have been far more successful in the acquisition of their lands than in imparting to them the principles or inspiring them with the spirit of civilization.[12]

Breathtaking though it is to read the above quotation, the worst was yet to come. The 1828 presidential election was a rematch of the 1824 election between John Quincy Adams and Andrew Jackson, the hero of the Battle of New Orleans and the First Seminole War. This time Jackson won. In his first inaugural address, Jackson said, "It will be my sincere and constant desire to observe toward the Indian tribes within our limits a just and liberal policy, and to give that humane and considerate attention to their rights and their wants which is consistent with the habits of our Government and the feelings of our people."[13] Despite Jackson's pledge of a just and liberal policy, the United State' relations with the Indian Nations would reach a new low during his administration.

•••

In Andrew Jackson's 1829 annual message he said, "It has long been the policy of Government to introduce among [the Indians] the arts of civilization, in the hope of gradually reclaiming them from a wandering life."[14] Unfortunately, this policy was incompatible with another U.S. policy, the purpose of which was to help the Indians "civilize and settle" themselves. As the government purchased Indian Tribal lands at every opportunity, it pushed the Indians farther and farther away from their ancestral homelands. The government was not settling them, but forcing them to be nomads and creating the impression—perhaps inadvertently—that the American people were indifferent to their fate. Whatever one's assessment of America's treatment of the Indians, Jackson's analysis is unusually candid. The government was indeed defeating its own policy.

It was too late to reconsider the United States' policy to include the Indians and their tribal lands within the boundaries of the new states. There was no way to turn back the clock, no way to restrict the power of Congress to draw the boundaries of newly admitted states, and no way to rewrite the constitution. It was not too late, however, to ask if the government could do something to preserve the "much-injured" Indian people in a way that did not violate states' rights. What Jackson suggested was to set aside a parcel of land west of the Mississippi River beyond the boundaries of any established state, and then give it to the Indians as a land grant. Each tribe would occupy and control a designated portion of the land grant, and exercise self-government without interference from the U.S. government.

In 1830 the following year, Jackson signed the Indian Removal Act, which offered land west of the Mississippi to the Indians in exchange for agreeing to migrate away from approximately one hundred million acres of their tribal lands in the east.[15] In addition to the land grant, the government also agreed to provide subsistence payments to the tribes upon their arrival at their new location. Emigration to the land west of the Mississippi would be voluntary, Jackson said, because it would be cruel "to compel the aborigines to abandon the graves of their fathers and seek a home in a distant land."[16] The United States paid the Indians to abandon their land, just as they paid the French to abandon Louisiana and the Spanish to abandon Florida.

•••

Martin Van Buren, Andrew Jackson's loyal vice president, won the 1836 presidential election. In Van Buren's 1837 inaugural address, he laid out a few simple principles for the conduct of foreign affairs. Van Buren said that international relations should be regulated by "the approved principles of private life." Among those principles were equal rights, justice, candor, directness, and sincerity. Added to this list was *the gentlemanly code:* never yield to force and never seek to acquire anything by force. Van Buren argued the United States should cultivate friendship with all nations, decline alliances with all nations, develop commercial relations on equal terms, conduct foreign relations with openness and sincerity, maintain neutrality in all controversies, refuse to meddle in disputes, and never to permit a wrong to go unpunished.

We can see George Washington's influence in Van Buren's rules, and we can see concepts that would reappear some seventy years later under Woodrow Wilson. Van Buren even admitted his policy was nothing but a faithful continuation of Washington's. He said, "Our course of foreign policy has been so uniform and intelligible as to constitute a rule of Executive conduct which leaves little to my discretion." Van Buren was as certain as Andrew Jackson that forcing the Indians to migrate to the other side of the Mississippi was justified. It started during the Jefferson administration, it was adopted by every succeeding administration, and has become he said "the settled policy of the country." Of course, Van Buren's *gentlemanly code* applied only to European nations. There was a second code for the Indian Nations, and a third for former European colonies, as Mexico would soon discover.

•••

Although Mexico won its independence from Spain in 1821, the Mexican government had almost no control over the country outside of Mexico City, and in 1823, the provinces of Guatemala and Central America seceded. From 1821 to 1867, Mexico had too many constitutions, governments, provisional governments, presidents, dictators—and one emperor—to count. In 1862, France invaded Mexico in the hope of taking control of the former Spanish colony while the United States was preoccupied with the Civil War and thus unable to enforce the Monroe Doctrine. In 1864, a group of Mexican conservative monarchists with the support of French troops installed Maximilian I, a member of Austria's royal family, as Emperor of Mexico, but Mexican liberals led by President Benito Juárez refused to recognize the puppet regime. In 1867, following years of stubborn resistance, the French withdrew their troops from Mexico, Maximilian was executed and Juárez became president again.

At the time of independence in 1821, Mexico's territory extended from Panama northward to the Oregon Territory. In 1823, because the Texas territory was so sparsely populated, the Mexican government awarded a huge land grant to Stephen Austin (an American who immigrated to Texas with his father), to encourage immigration from America. The idea was so successful that hundreds of American families began colonizing the territory, and the Mexican government tried to prohibit further emigration several years later. In 1832, Austin and his settlers began fighting back, and in 1836—after Sam Houston's forces routed Santa Anna's army at the Battle of San Jacinto—Texas won its war for independence, though Mexico refused to recognize it. In 1845, the United States annexed Texas, and a few months later, the Mexican-American War began.

By then, John Tyler was president. In the 1840 election, William Henry Harrison defeated Van Buren, but Harrison died very shortly after taking office in 1841 and Tyler succeeded him. In Tyler's 1842 annual message, he reported receiving a complaint from the Mexican foreign minister that the United States was permitting Americans to help white settlers in Texas in the ongoing conflict between Texas and Mexico. Bands of skirmishers from both sides were keeping tensions high along the border, and the long-term consequences were troubling. Later in the same speech, in the section with the financial update, however, Tyler reported that the costs associated with preserving the United States' neutral relations with Texas and keeping the Indians "in check" would continue so long as circumstances made it necessary.

Although the United States and several European nations had recognized Texas's sovereignty, Mexico had not, and Tyler was concerned Mexico intended to reconquer it. Tyler pointed to the good example set by Britain during the American Revolution—who did not waste its energies trying to subdue the American colonies—but had the wisdom to acknowledge their independence. After seven years of fighting, Mexico failed to force Texas into submission, and Tyler argued Mexico would do well to imitate Britain's example. Tyler warned if the war went on much longer, it would deplete the resources of both Mexico and Texas. Both nations would be weakened, and perhaps vulnerable to takeover by one of the European powers.

Britain and France both wanted to check the spread of American influence in the hemisphere—and both recognized Texas as a sovereign nation shortly after the Battle of San Jacinto. The British government opposed the annexation of Texas so vehemently it urged Mexico to recognize Texas's sovereignty if the United States promised not to annex Texas. Mexico agreed and offered to recognize Texas's sovereignty on those terms, but Tyler refused. He denounced Britain and said this was exactly what George Washington means when he warns against foreign influence and European ambition.

In Tyler's 1844 annual message, he speculated again that unless the United States acted, one of the European powers would intervene—surely on Mexico's behalf. There was no alternative, he said "but to take advantage of the well-known dispositions of Texas and to invite her to enter into a treaty for annexing her territory to that of the United States." Mexico had no right, according to Tyler, to jeopardize "world peace" [sic] by carrying on a war she had no hope of ever winning. The United States had a duty to intervene in the "useless and fruitless contest" because the American families of the Texas immigrants could not restrain themselves much longer. Finally, Tyler said the United States should intervene to protect Mexico from Texas! The longer the war went on, the stronger Texas might get, and if the

United States did not settle the boundary between Texas and Mexico now, Texas could start annexing neighboring provinces in Mexican territory. In Tyler's words:

> Mexico requires a permanent boundary between that young Republic and herself. Texas at no distant day, if she continues separate and detached from the United States, will inevitably seek to consolidate her strength by adding to her domain the contiguous Provinces of Mexico. The spirit of revolt from the control of the central Government has heretofore manifested itself in some of those Provinces, and it is fair to infer that they would be inclined to take the first favorable opportunity to proclaim their independence and to form close alliances with Texas.[17]

In November 1844, James Polk won the presidential election. In his 1845 inaugural address, he said that the question over Texas annexation was between America and Texas, and warned Mexico not to interfere. Polk said this was not annexation but a reunification of what was once American territory. "Texas was once a part of our country—was unwisely ceded away to a foreign power," he said referring to the Adams–Onís Treaty of 1819, in which the United States acquired the Florida Territory. In fact, the Spanish conquistadores landed in Texas well before the English settled the Atlantic Coast. Spanish rather than English (or French for that matter) was the first European language spoken in Texas. Spain occupied Texas for more than a hundred years before Mexico won its independence in 1821, which the American government under James Monroe recognized immediately. Long before that, the Spanish built numerous presidios, roads, and dozens of Catholic Missions, particularly the mission at San Antonio, which became the first formal municipality in Texas, and since 1772 was the seat of government until shortly after Mexican independence.

In his 1846 annual message, however, James Polk presented a different account of events, as follows:

> Texas constituted a portion of the ancient Province of Louisiana, ceded to the United States by France in the year 1803. In the year 1819 the United States, by the Florida treaty, ceded to Spain all that part of Louisiana within the present limits of Texas, and Mexico, by the [1821] revolution which separated her from Spain and rendered her an independent nation, succeeded to the rights of the mother country over this territory.[18]

Polk said, "The Texas which was ceded to Spain by the Florida treaty of 1819 embraced all the country now claimed by the State of Texas." The treaty in question, however, ceded Florida to the United States and settled a border dispute over a relatively small section of territory between Northern Texas and Louisiana. It is an overstatement to say the United States ceded Texas to Spain. But the pivotal issue is that Spain's Central and South American colonies were in full revolution by then, and Mexico won its independence in 1821, a mere two years after the Florida settlement. In other words, the United States' deal was with Spain, not Mexico.

In April 1846, U.S. forces under General Zachary Taylor fought a series of battles against Mexican troops in South Texas between the Rio Grande and Nueces Rivers. In May, the United States and Mexico both declared war. General Taylor led his troops south across the Rio Grande, and defeated the Mexicans in the Battle of Monterrey (September 1846) and the Battle of Buena Vista (February 1847). Meanwhile, Polk ordered General Winfield Scott to make an amphibious landing near Veracruz, on the Gulf of Mexico 225 miles east of Mexico City. Scott's army of twelve thousand surrounded the city and forced the garrison to surrender. From there, Scott fought his way toward Mexico City, winning battles at Cerro Gordo and Chapultepec.

In mid-September 1847, General Scott's troops entered Mexico City, effectively ending the war. In Polk's 1847 annual message, he said the only way Mexico could reimburse the United States for the cost of the war was by ceding a portion of her territory. He boldly repudiated what he called—with unintended humor—the "doctrine of no territory," and flatly refused to sign any treaty that did not compel Mexico to relinquish a generous portion of land.[19] Polk was proud of the United States' "spirit of liberality," meaning it would not seize everything it conquered, only enough territory to offset the monetary value of Mexico's war reparations. Naturally, Polk was interested in the territory near the American border, especially the contiguous Provinces of New Mexico and California.

Polk compared the acquisition of California to the Louisiana Purchase in terms of its economic and strategic value. If the economic potential and strategic advantages of California were apparent to Polk—they were apparent to the Europeans as well. Polk presented his 1847 annual message to Congress in December that year, a few weeks before James Marshall discovered gold at Sutter's Mill in California. If the United States did not make an aggressive move to acquire the territory, Polk said one of the European powers probably would, and speculated on the possible scenarios. Because Mexico was not powerful enough to defend California, it could be conquered. Because Mexico had no money, the government might be tempted to sell California to somebody else. Because Mexico could not govern California, a group of revolutionaries might try to establish an independent state there, which would be vulnerable to European conquest. For Polk, all these possibilities violated the Monroe Doctrine—and the risk of any one of them occurring was too high.

•••

With the exception of Ulysses Grant, none of Polk's immediate successors added any precedents to the doctrine of practical idealism. The essential goal of Abraham Lincoln's foreign policy was the same as George Washington's, which was to limit European influence in North America. Specifically, Lincoln did not want the European powers to intervene in the Civil War or recognize the Confederacy. In November 1861, an American warship fired on and boarded the British merchant vessel *Trent* sailing in international waters. American sailors searched the *Trent* and arrested two Confederate representatives onboard. Congress and American public opinion approved, but the British government was outraged at the violation of free navigation of the seas. After the British threatened to go to war, the United States apologized and released the Confederate commissioners. Because the captain of the American ship was not acting on orders from the government, releasing the commissioners was consistent with Lincoln's policy of neutrality.

In 1869, Ulysses Grant became president. In his 1869 annual message, he stated the guidelines he would follow for the use of American military power. Because of the United State' colonial origins, said Grant, the United States had the right to intervene on behalf of a people struggling for their independence. This was not an abstract theory Grant developed, but had concrete policy implications in Cuba, a Spanish colony fighting a war of independence for more than a year.

In Grant's mind, Cuba was the most recent instance of a Spanish colony struggling for freedom, part of a struggle going on since 1821, when Mexico won its independence from Spain. The people of the United States, said Grant, had the same sympathies for the people of Cuba as they had for the rest of Spain's former colonies. However, Grant was not convinced that the Cuban insurrection merited classification as a full-fledged revolution because the Cuban rebels had no "de facto political organization" sufficient to justify recognition under international law. In his 1875 annual message, Grant said because the rebellion had not risen "to the fearful dignity of war," the United States should not intervene in the conflict. With this contribution to the doctrine of practical idealism, Grant set an important precedent: *restraint in the use of American power.*

In Grant's 1870 annual message, he reported the Senate failed to ratify a treaty to annex the Republic of Santo Domingo. Grant was convinced that annexation would have been economically beneficial to the Dominican people and politically beneficial to the United States particularly because of its proximity to what would later be the eastern approach to the Panama Canal. In Grant's words:

> The acquisition of San Domingo is desirable because of its geographical position. It commands the entrance to the Caribbean Sea and the Isthmus transit of commerce. It possesses the richest soil, best and most capacious harbors, most salubrious climate, and the most valuable products of the forests, mine, and soil of any of the West India Islands. Its possession by us will in a few years build up a coastwise commerce of immense magnitude, which will go far toward restoring to us our lost merchant marine. It will give to us those articles which we consume

so largely and do not produce, thus equalizing our exports and imports. In case of foreign war it will give us command of all the islands referred to, and thus prevent an enemy from ever again possessing himself of rendezvous upon our very coast. At present our coast trade between the States bordering on the Atlantic and those bordering on the Gulf of Mexico is cut into by the Bahamas and the Antilies. Twice we must, as it were, pass through foreign countries to get by sea from Georgia to the west coast of Florida.[20]

Applying the same rationale as James Polk regarding California (that is, if the economic potential and strategic advantages were apparent to us, they were apparent to Europeans), Grant said if we did not take action, someone else would. He tried to assure Congress that officials in Santo Domingo knew what they were getting themselves into and sought annexation voluntarily.

Grant listed the political and economic rationale for annexation. Politically, Grant said annexation would enhance America's national security consistent with the Monroe Doctrine. He believed Santo Domingo's free labor market would pressure Puerto Rico and Cuba (and perhaps even Brazil) to abolish slavery. He also hoped annexation would encourage a peaceful resolution of the insurrection in Cuba. Economically, the country was an attractive market for American goods and could supply American consumers with commodities such as sugar, coffee, tobacco, and tropical fruits. In general, Grant saw annexation as one way to balance the nation's trade deficit—a novel approach. With some prescience Grant said, "it is not so easy to see how this result is to be otherwise accomplished."

In 1871, Grant reported to Congress about the breakdown in negotiations with Britain over settlement of claims dating back to the Civil War, when Britain harassed American commercial shipping. After letting the dispute go unresolved for several years, Grant finally proposed to negotiate a treaty with Britain to resolve the differences between the two nations through arbitration. Following a joint request from the United States and Britain, the Geneva Arbitration Tribunal was created, and the king of Italy, the president of the Swiss Confederation, and the emperor of Brazil each named arbiters to the tribunal. When the tribunal reached their decision in 1872, they found England in violation of international law and ruled in favor of the United States.

In Grant's last annual message in 1876, he summarized the accomplishments of his eight-year presidency and restated his support for the annexation of Santo Domingo. He did so not in the hope the Senate would revisit the issue, but to "vindicate" his position. Despite the "united opposition of one political party" and "strong opposition from the other," Grant remained convinced—for the reasons listed above—the Senate's rejection of the annexation treaty was a mistake.[21]

•••

Before Grant left office, the Union Pacific and the Central Pacific Railroads would meet in Northern Utah in 1869, and complete the transcontinental railroad. For the rest of the nineteenth century, settlers moved west across the Great Plains, and the United States fought battle after bloody battle with numerous Indian Tribes, including the Apache, Arapaho, Cheyenne, Comanche, Lakota, Modoc, Navajo, and Sioux.

In 1893, Grover Cleveland reported the United States' foreign affairs were uneventful, and that the country faced no challenge it could not overcome with "the spirit of fairness and love of justice which, joined with consistent firmness, characterize a truly American foreign policy." Although Cleveland's views on foreign policy were not particularly original, he enforced the Monroe Doctrine to the letter. In 1895, the Venezuelan government asked Cleveland to arbitrate a border dispute with Britain. When Britain hesitated, Cleveland interpreted it as a violation of the Monroe Doctrine. In response, Cleveland sent a threatening diplomatic note to London—known as the Twenty-Inch Gun Dispatch. Setting the precedent of gunboat diplomacy, he then deployed American ships into the Caribbean to ensure "the attitude of the United States was fully and distinctly set forth."[22] Though the British initially refused Cleveland's offer of "friendly and impartial arbitration," they eventually agreed to accept arbitration.

Two Oceans and Two World Wars, 1896–1945

2

Monroe Doctrine II and Dollar Diplomacy

Panama Canal; Spanish-American War; Acquiring the Philippines; Acquiring Hawaii; Open Door Policy in China

In 1896, William McKinley, Civil War veteran and former governor of Ohio won the presidential election largely by staying home and speaking to crowds from the front porch of his Canton, Ohio home. In his 1897 inaugural message, McKinley said the United States has remained free from foreign entanglement and "cherished the policy of noninterference with affairs of foreign governments wisely inaugurated by Washington." He pledged to pursue a firm, dignified, and impartial foreign policy, which would guard the United States' national honor and enforce the rights of American citizens abroad. "We want no wars of conquest; we must avoid the temptation of territorial aggression," he said. Along with parroting George Washington's admonition to avoid foreign entanglements, McKinley concurred with Ulysses Grant that arbitration was the best method to settle international differences.

In his 1897 annual message, McKinley said the United States' relationships with Spain and Cuba were its most important problems. Unrest and discontent in Cuba, dating back decades continued to fester. It was twenty-two years since Ulysses Grant said the United States sympathized with Cuba's desire for freedom and self-government, but chose not to intervene because the Cuban insurrection was not well organized enough to merit American or international recognition. It was seventy-four years since James Monroe declared the United States would consider any attempt by the Europeans to extend their system in the Western Hemisphere a threat to American national security.

The insurrection then taking place in Cuba broke out in 1895, and the Spanish were becoming more ruthless and more desperate to suppress it. The United States made several overtures to mediate between Spain and Cuba, as far back as Ulysses Grant, and as recently as Grover Cleveland. By 1897, McKinley was growing more and more apprehensive as he received reports of atrocities committed by both sides. Reports about the Spanish army destroying homes, depopulating the countryside, and forcing farmers and peasants to relocate to garrisoned towns shocked McKinley, who said, "It was not civilized warfare. It was extermination." Based on these reports, McKinley sent an official protest to the Spanish government, along with another offer to mediate. McKinley had no wish to cause Spain any embarrassment, but did expect a speedy resolution.

In reply, the Spanish government said it appreciated McKinley's gesture of goodwill, acknowledged America's interests, and declared the Spanish government was committed to a change of policy to establish peace in Cuba. With some skepticism, McKinley reported Spain began to initiate political reforms leading to the autonomy of Cuba—while maintaining Spanish sovereignty over the island—even as military operations against the rebels continued. Under Spain's reform plan, a local council would govern Cuba while Spain would control the court system, the army, navy, and all foreign trade.

Though the United States was officially neutral, Cuban insurgents were privately receiving assistance from American citizens. Despite this, McKinley was outraged that Spain's diplomatic note did not acknowledge the United States was in full compliance with international law, and not a single military expedition or armed vessel departed American shores to intervene in the Cuban crisis. In other words, McKinley believed—like Ulysses Grant before him—the United States had the right to intervene in Cuba. The fact that Spain's diplomatic note did not acknowledge Cuba was in the American sphere of influence was offensive to McKinley. Not only was the policy of neutrality not working, Spain was becoming insolent, he said. Clearly, McKinley was losing his patience and wanted to begin exploring alternatives. First, he would have to decide on the legitimacy of the insurgency. If he gave official recognition to the rebellion, he would have no choice but to take their side against Spain.

By the end of the nineteenth century, Cuba and Puerto Rico were all that remained of Spain's former colonial empire in the Caribbean. In the Pacific Ocean, the Philippines and a few other island chains were all that remained. After the legendary Cuban writer and revolutionary José Martí died in 1895, many in Congress believed that Cuban independence was inevitable. In 1896, Congress passed a concurrent resolution pressuring McKinley to act, but McKinley, perhaps wisely, deferred to the Grant Doctrine. The United

States' colonial heritage gave it the right to intervene, he said, but not until the rebels earned international recognition. In McKinley's opinion, however, recognition of Cuba was both unjustified and impractical. No matter how dreadful and devastating the conflict was, no matter how much pressure McKinley was under to defend U.S. interests on the island, it did not pass Grant's test. Although American companies owned millions of dollars worth of land in Cuba, and trade in sugar, tobacco, and iron was significant, McKinley chose to monitor events and reserved the right to intervene.

In his 1898 annual message, McKinley said the only reason the United States had not yet intervened in the Cuban crisis was that he wanted to see if the reforms Spain began to implement were having any positive effect. With Cuba under martial law, however, there was no real progress. The Cubans had rejected the bogus reforms, and though outnumbered and outgunned, were holding their own against Spanish forces. McKinley was disgusted with Spain's atrocious depopulation and relocation policy, and with good reason worried it was deteriorating into genocide. There was an alarming increase in the number of Cuban civilians killed; conservative estimates from Spanish sources estimated the mortality rate was more than 40 percent since Spain's "reconcentration" decree was enforced.

In January 1898, McKinley sent the USS *Maine* to Havana to defend American interests in Cuba. In February 1898, the *Maine's* forward gunpowder magazines exploded, sinking the ship and killing three-quarters of her crew. Although a naval board of inquiry could not conclusively determine the cause of the explosion, the newspaper chains of Joseph Pulitzer and William Randolph Hearst—and popular opinion—placed the blame squarely on Spain. The suspicious nature of the catastrophe, McKinley said in his 1898 annual message, "stirred the nation's heart profoundly." By this time, relations between the US and Spain had reached a crisis, and the findings of the board of inquiry hardly mattered. In April 1898, McKinley ordered a blockade of Cuba's northern coast and Congress issued a formal declaration of war.

In his 1898 annual message, McKinley enumerated several goals: to end the hostilities between Spain and Cuba, to establish a stable government on the island, and to ensure the security of American citizens. He asked Congress for the authority to use military force as necessary, and to provide emergency relief to the Cuban people. Congress responded quickly to McKinley's request by overwhelmingly passing a joint resolution in both houses demanding Spain withdraw its forces and relinquish its authority in Cuba. When the Spanish government received the news, it immediately broke off diplomatic relations.

Based on these goals, McKinley said the only option consistent with American traditions and values was to intervene in Cuba *as a neutral to stop the war*. McKinley listed the grounds that justified his decision.

First, American intervention was in "the interests of humanity." Second, his duty was to protect the lives and property of U.S. citizens in Cuba. Third, Spain's depopulation and relocation policies were devastating the island and damaging American commercial interests. Fourth, he wanted finally to remove, "the constant menace and the burdens entailed upon our Government by the uncertainties and perils of the situation caused by the unendurable disturbance in Cuba."

Thus, McKinley applied the Grant Doctrine, but in reverse. In McKinley's 1897 annual message, he praised the "wise utterances" of Ulysses Grant, and quoted a long passage from Grant's 1875 annual message. Grant decided not to intervene on behalf of the rebels because even after years of fighting, the Cubans still had no de facto political organization either capable of governing the island or recognizable under international law. McKinley said that Spain, after years of fighting had failed to put the insurrection down. Like Mexico's decade-long failure to retake Texas, this proved that Spain was incapable of governing the island.

•••

The first engagement did not take place in the Caribbean Sea or the even Atlantic Ocean, but in Manila Bay. In early May 1898, American naval forces entered Manila Bay from the South China Sea at dawn. By noon on the first day of battle, Spain had lost ten battleships. American forces captured the Bay and crushed Spain's naval power in the Pacific—without losing a ship and with very few American casualties. In Guam, the Spanish governor surrendered, unaware his country was even at war. In June, several hundred American troops landed at Cuba's Guantánamo Bay. A month later, American troops attacked the San Juan Heights, where Theodore Roosevelt and the Rough Riders made their famous cavalry charge. The decisive battle occurred in July, when an American squadron routed the Spanish fleet, destroyed several ships, ran others to ground, captured 1,300 prisoners, including the Spanish admiral, and killed six hundred.

American casualties in the Spanish-American War—in the Caribbean and Pacific theaters—were extremely light. The navy fought in two major battles and transported more than fifty thousand men. American casualties for the army and navy totaled approximately sixteen hundred killed and wounded. No Americans were taken prisoner, and only one ship was lost. The war lasted two months. According to the terms of the formal peace treaty signed in December, Cuba became an independent nation, Puerto Rico became American territory, American forces occupied the Philippines, and Spain had to evacuate its island territories in the Caribbean. Finally, the United States agreed to purchase the Philippines from Spain for twenty million dollars.[1]

McKinley wanted the United States to acquire the Philippines in order to control the eastern and western approaches to the forthcoming Panama

Canal. The United States' strategic and commercial interests in the canal demanded control of the shipping channels from the east and west. By defeating Spain and forcing it to withdraw from the Caribbean, the United States controlled the eastern approach. By acquiring the Philippines, the United States controlled the western approach, which consisted of a triangle with apexes at Panama, the Philippines, and Hawaii. Within a few weeks of the peace treaty formally ending the Spanish-American War, the United States annexed the Hawaiian Islands.

When the King of Hawaii, David Kalakaua died in 1891 while traveling in San Francisco, his younger sister Liliuokalani became queen. In 1893, the descendants of the large and influential missionary families living in Hawaii were dissatisfied with the queen's autocratic style. They took aggressive action to depose her and establish a provisional government. An American steamship arrived in Honolulu the day they deposed the queen, and a small force of men landed, ostensibly to protect the lives and property of American citizens. In 1894, the Republic of Hawaii was established, and the provisional government moved swiftly to negotiate a treaty of annexation with the United States, which the Senate ratified and McKinley signed in 1898. In his 1898 annual message, McKinley said the annexation of the Hawaiian Islands would lead to the expansion of American influence and commerce in the Pacific—and made the construction of "a maritime highway" connecting the two oceans more important than ever. McKinley urged Congress to take prompt action to ensure that the United States would control access to the canal.

In his 1899 annual message, McKinley spoke at length about the responsibilities of empire. With the acquisition of the Philippines, it was up to Congress to resolve the civil rights and political status of the native inhabitants of the recently acquired territories. In McKinley's words:

> The future government of the Philippines rests with the Congress of the United States. Few graver responsibilities have ever been confided to us. If we accept them in a spirit worthy of our race and our traditions, a great opportunity comes with them. The islands lie under the shelter of our flag. They are ours by every title of law and equity. They cannot be abandoned. If we desert them we leave them at once to anarchy and finally to barbarism.[2]

McKinley said the United States' legal ownership of the Philippines was not only in accord with both houses of Congress, it was also was in accord with the wishes of the Filipino people. McKinley pledged the American government would do everything in its power to advance the islanders' interests, and tried to reassure them the United States came "not as invaders and conquerors, but as friends to protect the natives in their homes, in their employments, and in their personal and religious rights."

In January 1899, McKinley sent a team of special envoys to Manila to help facilitate and expedite the transfer of sovereignty. McKinley was sure the reputation of the envoys would be sufficient to communicate the United States' good intentions. Before the team of envoys arrived in Manila, however, a story began to circulate that an American military officer promised one of the leaders of the Filipino insurgents that if the insurgents allied with the Americans to defeat the Spanish, the U.S. government would grant their independence. Although the story is certainly believable—perhaps it was wishful thinking—McKinley insisted it was a complete fabrication and attributed it to the "sinister ambition" of a few Filipino leaders.

Just like the Cubans, the Filipinos had been fighting to throw off the Spanish for years, but the quick work of the United States' powerful military gave the Filipinos other ideas. "No sooner had our army captured Manila than the Filipino forces began to assume an attitude of suspicion and hostility," said McKinley, an attitude which American officers could do nothing to change. Shortly before the Senate was due to ratify the peace treaty with Spain, which from the Filipino point of view resembled nothing but a transfer of authority from one colonial power to another, the Filipinos launched an attack. Whatever the future of the Philippines might have been, said McKinley, there was only one option now: to beat the insurgents into submission. Over the next three years, thousands of American troops, Filipino guerillas and civilians died—far more than were killed during the Spanish-American War.

With Spain defeated and sovereignty of the Philippines in American hands, the United States became a power in Asia. Then as now, the Asian market most interesting to American traders was China, a major terminus on the maritime highway McKinley envisioned. The major European powers and Japan, however, were dividing China into spheres of influence and threatening to exclude American trading firms. In 1899, McKinley instructed Secretary of State John Hay to propose what became known as the "open door" policy, which would ensure American traders would have access to China, and limit the advantages of others with well-established spheres of influence. Hay knew American public opinion would not support the use of force so soon after the Spanish-American War, so he decided to try diplomacy. He circulated diplomatic notes among the major European powers (Britain, France, Germany, Russia, and Italy) and Japan to gain formal recognition of the open door and persuade the other powers to respect China's territorial integrity. Though all the countries Hay approached gave him noncommittal replies, he triumphantly announced that an agreement had been reached.

According to McKinley's 1900 annual message, the United States' official policy was to preserve China's territorial integrity and promote the United States' commercial interests in China. While the United States was trying to open China to foreign trade, Chinese nationalists were trying to close it to foreigners, culminating in the Boxer Rebellion, an uprising against Western (and Japanese) commercial and political influence in China. In June 1900, the conflict came to a head when organized armies of Boxers, joined by elements of the Imperial army, attacked foreign compounds in Tianjin and Peking (Beijing) in an effort to end what they saw as foreign occupation. The Boxers surrounded legations in Peking and began a two-month siege. An international force, which included American sailors and Marines, fought its way inland, overwhelmed and crushed the rebellion. More than 230 foreigners, thousands of Chinese Christians—who the Boxers saw as agents of foreign influence—and an unknown number of rebels were killed.

•••

In early September 1901, slightly more than a year after the Boxer Rebellion was crushed, McKinley was visiting the Pan-American Exposition in Buffalo, New York. When an alleged anarchist shot and killed McKinley, Vice President Theodore Roosevelt, veteran of the Spanish-American War became president. In Roosevelt's first annual message in 1901, a few short weeks following his ascension to the presidency, and seventy-eight years since Monroe announced the doctrine bearing his name, Roosevelt asserted the Monroe Doctrine would continue to be the "cardinal feature" of the United States' foreign policy.

Roosevelt went a little further than Monroe intended, however, when he said this should also be the foreign policy of every other nation in the Western Hemisphere. What Roosevelt means by this is every North and South American nation should respect their neighbors' territorial rights. The nineteenth century political maps of Europe were redrawn with such frequency there was hardly time for the ink to dry, and Roosevelt wanted to safeguard the independence of the smaller Central and South American countries. Roosevelt expanded the Monroe Doctrine to include the basic premise of the open door policy, which would ensure equal access of every American nation to every American market. In principle, Roosevelt's conception would establish a hemispheric free trade area, not to acquire exclusive rights for U.S.-made goods, but to guarantee "the commercial independence of the Americas."

Meanwhile, the United States negotiated a treaty with Columbia in 1902 to acquire control of a six-mile-wide strip of Columbia's isthmus, or "Panama Territory." In consideration, the United States agreed to pay Colombia ten million dollars, plus an annual payment of two hundred fifty thousand dollars for a 100-year lease. Soon afterward, Panama declared its independence from Colombia and sought recognition from the United States. In 1903, the United States recognized Panamanian independence, and signed another treaty, this time with the newly sovereign Republic of Panama. According to the terms of the 1903 treaty, the United States agreed to guarantee the independence of the Republic of Panama, and Panama gave the United States a monopoly for the construction, maintenance, and operation of the canal; railroad; and any system of communication across its territory between the Caribbean Sea and the Pacific Ocean—in perpetuity.[3] Roosevelt appointed one chief engineer, who resigned, and then another, who also resigned. Then he put construction of the canal under American military authority. Despite monumental logistical challenges and chronic medical problems afflicting the workers (particularly yellow fever and malaria, as well as tuberculosis, cholera, diphtheria, and smallpox), the Panama Canal was completed in 1914, and stands as one of the greatest engineering projects in history.

By asserting the United States' right to market access in China, establishing strong defensive positions in the Caribbean and Pacific Ocean, and achieving a dominant position in Central America, Presidents McKinley and Roosevelt redefined the scope of the Monroe Doctrine. They expanded the geographic scope of vital American interests, particularly commercial interests, from the Western Hemisphere to include every region of the world. For Roosevelt, the Monroe Doctrine had been gradually evolving since 1823. The way to keep the doctrine alive was to adapt it, to reassert it as forcefully as the new situation required, and then recommit the country to its consequences. This was especially true regarding the construction of the Panama Canal. In Roosevelt's 1905 annual message, he said, "As a mere matter of self-defense we must exercise a close watch over the approaches to this canal; and this means that we must be thoroughly alive to our interests in the Caribbean Sea."

Although Roosevelt was fulfilling his constitutional duty to report to Congress, he was also sending a message to the United States' new neighbors in Central America. As stated, the United States recognized the sovereignty of the Republic of Panama in 1903. Roosevelt's highest priority was to get the canal built. In a spectacular display of circular logic, Roosevelt promised not to invade any of the countries of neighboring Panama unless they "invited" the United States to do so through their inability or unwillingness to control their borders.

Roosevelt believed that asserting the Monroe Doctrine, specifically liberating Cuba and Panama, and opening China to free trade, was in the United States' own best interest as well as the interest of all humanity. Rather than dismiss Roosevelt's naiveté or cynicism, it is possible to assume he was sincere. Roosevelt said Americans had enough of their own problems, including corruption, crime, violence, and racial prejudice, without worrying about conditions in other countries. In his 1904 annual message, Roosevelt cautioned against hypocrisy and paraphrased the New Testament when he said, "There must be no effort made to remove the mote from our brother's eye if we refuse to remove the beam from our own." In his 1906 annual message, he elaborated on this theme, as follows: "In many parts of South America there has been much misunderstanding of the attitude and purposes of the United States towards the other American Republics. An idea had become prevalent that our assertion of the Monroe Doctrine implied, or carried with it, an assumption of superiority, and of a right to exercise some kind of protectorate over the countries to whose territory that doctrine applies. Nothing could be farther from the truth."[4]

One of the precepts of classical realism is that politics drives international relations, and the moral standards that apply to the lives of individuals do not apply to nation-states. However, in Roosevelt's 1905 annual message he said, "The Golden Rule should be, and as the world grows in morality it will be, the guiding rule of conduct among nations as among individuals." In his 1906 annual message, Roosevelt flatly contradicted classical realism: "Good manners should be an international no less than an individual attribute." In his 1908 annual message, he made an assertion that revealed similar thinking: "This nation's foreign policy is based on the theory that right must be done between nations precisely as between individuals."

Roosevelt considered the formation of the international tribunal at The Hague a good omen and said establishing a permanent institution to resolve international disputes was preferable to creating a one-time arbitrator every time a specific case arose. (The Permanent Court of Arbitration known as the Hague Tribunal was founded in 1899 in the Netherlands.) Years before Woodrow Wilson, the somewhat impractical idealist behind the League of Nations, Roosevelt said arbitration should replace war to resolve disputes between civilized nations. In his 1905 annual message, Roosevelt said he saw evidence that relations between countries were becoming closer—and the establishment of the Hague Tribunal was the best indication. Roosevelt was optimistic about the Hague Tribunal, and hoped settling international disputes through arbitration would eventually become customary. To further the new closeness in international relations—years before Wilson— Roosevelt offered a suggestion: "Our aim should be from time to time to take such steps as may be possible toward creating *something like an organization of the civilized nations,* because as the world becomes more highly organized the need for navies and armies will diminish."[5]

In his 1901 annual message, Roosevelt said, "The American people must either build and maintain an adequate navy or else make up their minds definitely to accept a secondary position in international affairs, not merely in political, but in commercial, matters." In his 1902 annual message, he asserted American foreign policy, particularly the Monroe Doctrine, made it imperative to maintain a first class navy. It was important for Roosevelt to be able to project American power wherever and whenever necessary— to deploy the battle fleet from one ocean to the other easily—and there was no more effective instrument than the navy and the Panama Canal together as a single integrated system. Thus, Theodore Roosevelt surpassed George Washington in the practice of geopolitics, particularly managing the relationship between geographic space, political power, and sea power.

In his 1903 annual message, Roosevelt quoted a remark Monroe made in his 1824 annual message: "The Navy is the arm from which our Government will always derive most aid in support of our rights." In his 1907 message, Roosevelt went farther—perhaps too far—when he said, "The only efficient use for the Navy is for offense." Roosevelt's belief that the nation's foreign policy was inseparable from its defense policy was the rationale behind his desire to control Hawaii and the Philippines. Roosevelt argued that having a naval base at Subig Bay would be "desirable" in peacetime and "indispensable" in wartime. Toward the end of his presidency, work began on a naval base at Hawaii's Pearl Harbor. In his 1905 annual message, he said Hawaii was the most important point in the Pacific in terms of American interests, and urged Congress to take immediate action to fortify it. In his 1908 annual message, he urged Congress to appropriate funding sufficient to make the Hawaiian Islands "practically impregnable." It would be useless to develop Hawaii's commercial and military infrastructure unless we could ensure its safety from foreign attack.

In Roosevelt's 1904 annual message, he said:

> There is no more patriotic duty before us...than to keep the Navy adequate to the needs of this country's position. We have undertaken to build the Isthmian [Panama] Canal. We have undertaken to secure for ourselves our just share in the trade of the Orient. We have undertaken to protect our citizens from proper treatment in foreign lands. We continue steadily to insist on the application of the Monroe Doctrine to the Western Hemisphere.[6]

Roosevelt argued that when we considered America's foreign policy—particularly America's role in the world—it was necessary to factor in the use of armed forces. It was impossible to separate the country's foreign policy from its willingness to use force. Our army and navy, said Roosevelt, were the vehicles through which the country expressed its power, regardless of whether the power served our own interest or the interest of others. It was unwise, and even contemptible, for a nation to take a position unsupported with threat of force.

●●●

William Howard Taft—who served as commissioner of the Philippines and then secretary of war in the Roosevelt administration—won the 1908 presidential election. Historically squeezed between Theodore Roosevelt and Woodrow Wilson, Taft served only one term as president and never faced a major international crisis except for sending two thousand American troops to stabilize political unrest in Nicaragua. The handful of observations he made suggest he believed it was a turning point for the United States' foreign policy.

In his 1909 inaugural address, Taft urged Congress to increase military spending so the United States could defend its trade interests. He reiterated everything Theodore Roosevelt said about the importance of maintaining a strong navy—including the ability to project power and influence in

international affairs. Taft specifically asked Congress to fund an expeditionary force to defend the Monroe Doctrine, prevent the colonization of the
Western Hemisphere, and protect the United States' new overseas territories.
In his 1909 annual message, he announced the establishment of a naval base
at Pearl Harbor, fortification of the island of Corregidor and adjacent
islands near the entrance to Manila Bay, and postponement of a naval
station at Subig Bay in the Philippines. He reiterated the importance of the
base at Guantánamo to protect the eastern approach of the Panama Canal.

In his 1912 annual message, Taft said his highest foreign policy
priority was to increase American exports, "substituting dollars for bullets."
Opening the canal signaled a new era in American foreign policy, and
nowhere was the Monroe Doctrine more vital than in the Canal Zone.
Taft said it was time for Congress to join the realist school, because the
country was not only full grown, but standing "at the threshold of our
middle age as a Nation." In decades past, Americans could afford to be
self-centered and concerned exclusively with domestic matters, but now it
was time to adapt the "great guiding principles" laid down by George
Washington to the conditions of today.

3

World War I and New World Order
Intervention in Mexico; Free Navigation; the Special Relationship; Expeditionary Force; Treaty of Versailles; League of Nations

In 1912, when the Republican Party renominated Taft, Theodore Roosevelt quit the party and ran as the Progressive or "Bull Moose" candidate. With the Republican Party split, Democrat Woodrow Wilson easily won the presidential election. In his 1913 annual message, Wilson displayed his tendency toward wishful thinking. "The country, I am thankful to say, is at peace with all the world, and many happy manifestations multiply about us of a growing cordiality and sense of community of interest among the nations, foreshadowing an age of settled peace and good will."[1]

Wilson admitted there was "one cloud upon our horizon," and it was hanging over Mexico. The dark cloud that troubled Wilson was Victoriano Huerta, Mexico's military dictator, whose rise can be traced back to 1910, when political activist Francisco Madero called for Mexican president Porfirio Diaz to renounce power and not seek reelection. The Mexican government arrested and jailed Madero shortly before the 1910 election—which Diaz easily won—and then released him soon afterward. Madero then fled to Texas where he denounced the fraudulent election and declared himself Mexico's provisional president. When Madero returned to Mexico, he called on Diaz again to step down. This coincided with widespread peasant uprisings in the north under Pancho Villa, and in the south under Emiliano Zapata. In the spring of 1911, the rebels won what would prove to be the decisive victory of the revolution by capturing Ciudad Juarez, forcing President Diaz to step down and sending him into exile.

In June 1911, Francisco Madero entered Mexico City and became president, and then won an election held in October, giving his presidency a veneer of legitimacy. The quality of life for most Mexicans, however, was no better under Madero than it was under Diaz. Madero's resistance toward land reform led to an open break with Emiliano Zapata. Madero sent troops to disarm Zapata, which only succeeded in increasing Zapata's popularity throughout the country. By 1912, Madero lost the support of Mexico's peasants and the elite, as well as the U.S. government. Thousands of American troops were stationed on the border threatening to invade.

At this moment, Victoriano Huerta was planning a coup to overthrow Madero—with the enthusiastic cooperation of the American ambassador. Huerta's forces attacked the presidential palace, and Huerta assumed a military dictatorship, dissolved the legislature, and arrested more than a hundred legislators. Madero resigned and was murdered a few days later.

Though Victoriano Huerta was a skilled military strategist, he is widely considered Mexico's worst president. Woodrow Wilson refused to recognize Huerta's government, and urged Huerta to resign. In Woodrow Wilson's 1913 annual message, he said unequivocally, "Mexico has no Government." Wilson's refusal to recognize Huerta's presidency made getting loans from American banks—and weapons from American manufacturers—nearly impossible. In April 1914, after receiving information that a German freighter loaded with weapons was heading toward Veracruz, Wilson sent the navy into the Gulf of Mexico and ordered occupation of the city—which would last almost seven months.

Wilson decided that force was the only way to oust Huerta, and began supplying weapons and money to the anti-Huerta forces. After suffering one defeat after another in throughout 1913 and 1914, the various revolutionary factions came together against Huerta. Realizing he was defeated, Huerta resigned and fled Mexico City. In August 1914, Venustiano Carranza was installed as provisional head of the new government, though bloodshed in Mexico would continue for several more years, and the orderly succession of presidents would be a chronic problem. In 1916, after Pancho Villa's force crossed into New Mexico and raided the town of Columbus, Wilson sent General John Pershing on an expedition to kill or capture Villa. Although Pershing chased Villa and his band for almost a year, he never caught up with him and the expedition returned to the United States, but not for long.

•••

In summer 1914, following Archduke Franz Ferdinand's assassination in Sarajevo, Horatio Kitchener, Britain's secretary of war (under Prime Minister Herbert Asquith) called for a hundred thousand men to join the British Army. Britain and Japan declared war on Germany. Germany declared war on Russia and France. German forces invaded Belgium and penetrated deep into French territory. French and British forces counterattacked—in the first Battle of Marne—halting the invasion and saving Paris. Germany retreated and both sides dug in. Four years of slaughter and stalemate followed, dozens of countries waged war on each other, and millions of people died. In the span of a few years, empires that stood for centuries would exist only in memory.

As soldiers in Europe died on an unprecedented scale, Woodrow Wilson found inspiration for his foreign policy in George Washington: stay neutral, offer friendship to all, do not threaten anyone and do not overthrow anyone. His defense policy was a continuation of the eighteenth and nineteenth century tradition of opposing the maintenance of a large standing army. Wilson admitted the United States was unprepared to put a large, well-trained army in the field. "Of course we are not ready to do that" he said, "and we shall never be in time of peace so long as we retain our present political principles." As 1914 ended, Wilson was adamant about not overreacting to a war he thought had nothing to do with the United States merely because "some amongst us are nervous and excited."[2]

By 1915, German U-boats were attacking not just warships, but also unarmed freighters, merchant ships, and at least one hospital ship. The Germans used poison gas for the first time in January, against the Russians in the Battle of Bolimow, and used it again—more effectively—against the Canadians in April at Ypres. In February 1915, Wilson sent his first written warning to Germany of the consequences of sinking merchant vessels from neutral countries.[3] In May, German U-boats sank the British ocean liner *Lusitania*. Following the *Lusitania* incident, Wilson sent another message to Germany protesting the deaths of more than a thousand passengers and crew, including more than a hundred Americans.[4]

In April 1915, forces from Australia and New Zealand landed in North Western Turkey on the Gallipoli Peninsula in an effort to capture Constantinople and break the stalemate in Western Europe. The Australians and New Zealanders met stiff resistance from the Turks, and after dozens of battles and hundreds of thousands of casualties, the Allied forces withdrew in late December. With these events setting the stage, Wilson opened his 1915 annual message with the following statement:

> Since I last had the privilege of addressing you on the state of the Union the war of nations on the other side of the sea, which had then only begun to disclose its portentous proportions, has extended its threatening and sinister scope until it has swept within its flame some portion of every quarter of the globe, not excepting our own hemisphere, has altered the whole face of international affairs, and now *presents a prospect of reorganization and reconstruction such as statesmen and peoples have never been called upon to attempt before.*[5]

Wilson reminded his audience the United States played no part in starting the war and was still officially neutral. The United States' neutrality, said Wilson, was a product of our "habitual detachment from the politics of

Europe." Nonetheless, the country had no choice but to remain conscious of its duty to the international community. The United States did its duty on behalf of its neighbors to the south, according to Wilson, "even without invitation from them." Wilson's definition of duty helps explain his interpretation to the Monroe Doctrine: the United States was the guardian of the Western Hemisphere. In fact, Wilson was baffled that the people whose freedom the United States was trying to protect sometimes called the United States' motives into question. It was difficult, he said, to maintain the role of guardian without offending anyone's pride. In Wilson's words:

> The moral is, that the states of America are not hostile rivals but cooperating friends, and that their growing sense of community or interest, alike in matters political and in matters economic, is likely to give them a new significance as factors in international affairs and in the political history of the world. It presents them as in a very deep and true sense a unit in world affairs, spiritual partners, standing together because thinking together, quick with common sympathies and common ideals.[6]

Wilson believed the United States was destined to play a special mission in international affairs, and he would later promote Pan-Americanism as a model of "reorganization and reconstruction" during the Paris peace conference. Although he was sure the country was in no immediate danger, Wilson had two goals as 1915 ended. One was to prepare the country to defend its own security. The other was to make sure the country had as much freedom of movement as possible. Anticipating the imminent crisis, Wilson proposed creating a defense advisory board consisting of business executives, particularly from the transportation and manufacturing industries. Wilson also asked Congress to increase federal funding for industrial and vocational education, increase farm subsidies, and conserve natural resources.

●●●

In February 1916, the Battle of Verdun took place in northeastern France. German forces launched a massive artillery barrage against the French, and advanced through France's network of trenches, but failed to capture Verdun. The losses were staggering for both sides, with hundreds of thousands of troops killed or wounded. In May, British and French diplomats signed the Sykes-Picot Agreement, establishing their respective spheres of influence in the postwar Middle East.[7] Also in May, battleships from the Royal Navy and the German fleet met in the North Sea and fought the Battle of Jutland, the war's greatest naval battle.

The Allies' Somme offensive would go from July to November and result in more than a million casualties on both sides. Allied forces had hoped to break through German lines, but had not learned the futility of making a frontal assault against a heavily fortified position, a harsh lesson from the

American Civil War. The first day of battle would be particularly traumatic for the British, who suffered nineteen thousand dead and thirty-five thousand wounded. The British used the tank for the first time in this battle, but advanced only six miles by the time it was over.

•••

With the Somme offensive still underway, foreign policy would be a major issue in the 1916 presidential election. Wilson continued to push for military preparedness and economic mobilization. Publicly committed to neutrality, Wilson campaigned on the slogan "He kept us out of war," and narrowly won reelection over Charles Evans Hughes, the former governor of New York and associate justice of the Supreme Court.

In Wilson's 1917 inaugural address, he called on the country to stand firm "in armed neutrality," though he knew the United States was neutral in name only. In January 1917, Arthur Zimmerman, German foreign minister, wrote a communiqué suggesting Mexico ally itself with Germany if the United States entered the war. Zimmerman hoped to neutralize the United States and force Britain to sue for peace. In case Germany's submarine warfare was unsuccessful, he proposed an alliance with Mexico. He even offered to help Mexico regain the territory it lost following the Mexican-American War.[8] British naval intelligence intercepted and decrypted the communiqué, forwarded it to the British foreign secretary, who forwarded it to the British embassy in Washington, and then to the White House. Wilson reacted furiously, of course, but the gesture cemented the special relationship, which was exactly what the British wanted. From that day forward, Britain would be America's indispensable ally. When the press published the telegram, many people thought it must have been a hoax perpetrated by the prowar lobby. Then, Zimmerman himself authenticated the telegram! When Wilson severed diplomatic relations with Germany in February, he knew there could be no turning back, and the United States was going to war ready or not. Wilson was still angry about the episode nine months later, and in his 1917 annual message said Germany's "sinister and secret diplomacy has sought to take our very territory away from us and disrupt the union of the states."

In January 1917, a few months before Wilson asked for a declaration of war, he shared with the Senate his vision of the postwar "peace without victory." This was two years before the Treaty of Versailles, and decades before the consequences of the punitive peace would become so well known. In Wilson's words:

> Victory would mean peace forced upon the loser, a victor's terms imposed upon the vanquished. It would be accepted in humiliation, under duress, at an intolerable sacrifice, and would leave a sting, a resentment, a bitter memory upon which terms of peace would rest, not permanently, but only as upon quicksand.

> Only a peace between equals can last, only a peace the very principle of which is equality and a common participation in a common benefit.[9]

This brief quotation is an accurate description of the years 1919–1939. Wilson knew no peace treaty could guarantee peace. He also knew he would have to transform the war from a struggle for a new balance of power, into a war for principle. In April 1917, Wilson addressed a special session of Congress and requested a formal declaration of war. Because of Germany's recent actions—including the Zimmerman communiqué—Wilson said the country was already at war, and Congress should take immediate steps to put the country on a war footing. Our quarrel was not with the German people, for whom most Americans had feelings "of sympathy and friendship," said Wilson. A small group of ambitious men were misleading the German people and using them as pawns and tools. In Wilson's words:

> The world must be made safe for democracy. Its peace must be planted upon the tested foundations of political liberty. We have no selfish ends to serve. We desire no conquest, no dominion. We seek no indemnities for ourselves, no material compensation for the sacrifices we shall freely make. We are but one of the champions of the rights of mankind. We shall be satisfied when those rights have been made as secure as the faith and the freedom of nations can make them.[10]

In addition, Wilson referred to the "wonderful and heartening" events in Russia, which deserves some explanation. By February 1917, dissatisfaction in Russia over the war had reached a critical mass. Shortages of food, clothing, boots, and ammunition sparked protests, particularly in Petrograd (St. Petersburg). When army deserters joined in, the protests turned into riots. When soldiers stationed in Petrograd joined in, the riots turned into revolution. The tsar was forced to abdicate, and a provisional government led by Alexander Kerensky stepped in.

Though Kerensky's resume was impressive (vice chair of the Petrograd Soviet, minister of justice, minister of war, and then prime minister), the provisional government was as ineffective as it was unpopular. With Russia exhausted after three years of warfare, Vladimir Lenin and the Bolsheviks led a coup against the Kerensky government. With the Bolsheviks in power and the Russian army disintegrating, Lenin pulled Russia out of the war in the spring of 1918. This allowed Germany to concentrate its forces on the western front where they would meet General John Pershing and his American Expeditionary Force.

•••

In June 1917, Wilson signed the Espionage Act, which made it a crime—punishable by death—to possess or transmit classified documents or any kind of information related to national defense.[11] In early November, British

Foreign Secretary Arthur Balfour issued the "Balfour Declaration" which declared Britain's sympathy for Jewish Zionist aspirations and expressed the British government's official support for "the establishment in Palestine of a national home for the Jewish people." Furthermore, Balfour said the British government should do nothing to undermine the civil or religious rights of the non-Jewish communities in living Palestine.[12]

•••

In Wilson's 1917 annual message, he blamed Germany for the war, particularly Germany's lack of democracy. If only the Russian people knew what Wilson knew—that democracies do not make war on each other—they would have joined the allies. If they were less suspicious and distrusting, they could have built a government based on freedom and democracy. "The Russian people have been poisoned by the very same falsehoods that have kept the German people in the dark, and the poison has been administered by the very same hand. The only possible antidote is the truth," he said. Wilson dismissed critics who did not share his vision, but also knew he had to win the war before he administered the antidote. In Wilson's words:

> Let there be no misunderstanding. Our present and immediate task is to win the war and nothing shall turn us aside from it until it is accomplished. Every power and resource we possess, whether of men, of money, or of materials, is being devoted and will continue to be devoted to that purpose until it is achieved. Those who desire to bring peace about before that purpose is achieved I counsel to carry their advice elsewhere.[13]

Wilson said any peace would be premature "before autocracy has been taught its final and convincing lesson." He asked how the United States would know when it won the war, and then answered his own question. We will know "when the German people say to us, through properly accredited representatives, that they are ready to agree to a settlement based upon justice and reparation of the wrongs their rulers have done." Among the wrongs Germany's rulers committed was invading Belgium and France, and attempting to dominate people and land that did not belong to them. Although Austria-Hungary, as well as Turkey and Bulgaria were Germany's allies, Wilson considered them Germany's victims, but asked Congress to declare war on them anyway.

By then, American soldiers had been in Europe a few short months, but the transformation of Wilson's attitude was dramatic. His description of Germany's leaders as "ambitious and intriguing masters" is too similar to George Washington's warning against foreign intrigue or European ambition to be a coincidence. The change in Wilson's attitude, from less than a year earlier when he advocated "peace without victory" is evident.

Only when Wilson speculated on the postwar peace did he soften his tone, making the case that Germany should not be punished because of the irresponsible acts of its rulers. Wilson argued against a vindictive peace, which would result in Germany losing territory and paying punitive indemnities. Wilson's formula was for the victors to renounce all selfish claims, and to build the postwar peace on a foundation of "generosity and justice." Wilson said he had no ill will toward the German Empire, and no intention of interfering with Germany's internal affairs. No one was threatening Germany's existence or independence. From Wilson's perspective, this was a war of high principle, a war to emancipate the German people from their Prussian masters.

•••

On January 18, 1918, Woodrow Wilson addressed a joint session of Congress in which he proposed a fourteen-point program to establish "a new international order based upon broad and universal principles of right and justice." Of Wilson's fourteen points, the first five consisted of open diplomacy, free navigation, free trade, arms reduction, and ending colonialism—all of which are deeply rooted in the doctrine of practical idealism. Points six through thirteen specified the people and territories that would be beneficiaries of self-determination, or what Wilson described as "readjustment of frontiers…along clearly recognizable lines of nationality."[14] In particular, Wilson advocated restoration and recognition of all Belgian, French, Italian, Polish, and Russian territory. He said the territories of the former Austro-Hungarian Empire, such as Romania, Serbia, and Montenegro should have the opportunity to develop autonomously. He said the Turkish portion of the former Ottoman Empire should have sovereignty, and that other nationalities living under Turkish rule should be autonomous. In his fourteenth point, he proposed the League of Nations, which as we already know was not particularly radical; Theodore Roosevelt proposed creating an "organization of the civilized nations" in his 1905 annual message.

•••

In March 1918, representatives of the Wilson administration held peace talks with representatives of the Central Empires to ascertain the possibility of expanding the Brest-Litovsk negotiations into a larger peace conference. Named for the City of Brest, located approximately one hundred miles east of Warsaw in what is now Byelorussia, the Treaty of Brest-Litovsk would formalize Russia's withdrawal from the war. According to Article I, "Germany, Austria-Hungary, Bulgaria and Turkey on the one hand and Russia on the other declare that the condition of war between them has ceased. They have decided to live in peace and accord in the future."[15]

Also in March 1918, Germany launched its spring offensive and the Allies appointed French Field Marshal Ferdinand Foch to command allied forces in France. German forces broke through the British lines and threatened Paris. In June, the Americans would become a major force in the war, beginning with the Battle of Belleau Wood east of Paris. As the Germans broke through the line and forced French troops to retreat, American Army and Marine reinforcements arrived just in time. Facing machine gun and mortar fire, American troops repeatedly assaulted German positions, taking and inflicting heavy casualties. The victory at Belleau Wood was the Americans' most important contribution to the war up to that point, and marked the end Germany's spring offensive.

In July, French and American forces would go on to victory in the Battle of Chateau-Thierry. Beginning in August, a particularly deadly strain of influenza began to spread, creating a global epidemic that killed more than twenty-five million people during the next six months. Also in August, British forces attacked at Amiens. In September, the Americans took the offensive at Meuse-Argonne, and stayed on the offensive through the end of the war.

The allies presented their terms of surrender on November 10, 1918. One day later the Germans accepted the armistice, and the war was over. Among other things, the Germans agreed to withdraw from Belgium, France and Alsace-Lorraine, and pull their troops back to the left bank of the Rhine; surrender their artillery, planes and other small arms; surrender thousands of locomotives and railway coaches; surrender their East African colonies; and renounce the Treaty of Brest-Litovsk.

Wilson's 1918 annual message a month later was destined to be the last one he would deliver in person. In October 1919, he suffered a stroke from which he never recovered. But before the stroke, before the Senate refused to ratify the Versailles and League of Nations treaties, before the frustrations and disappointments of Paris—for a fleeting moment—Wilson was determined to realize his vision of a new world order. American forces arrived at the front lines at a moment when the outcome of the war was uncertain, and a few months later Germany was defeated.

Now that the war was over it was time for the world to turn its attention to the tasks of peace, he said, "a peace secure against the violence of irresponsible monarchs and ambitious military coteries and made ready for a new order, for new foundations of justice and fair dealing." One of Wilson's tasks was to join personally in the upcoming Paris peace conference. "I realize the great inconveniences that will attend my leaving the country, particularly at this time, but the conclusion that it was my paramount duty to go has been forced upon me by considerations which I hope will seem as conclusive to you as they have seemed to me," he said. Why? According to Wilson, his attendance was required because his fourteen points would serve as the foundation of the negotiations, and leaders from the allies and the axis powers "very reasonably desire my personal counsel in their interpretation and application."[16]

In 1919, after returning from Paris, Wilson toured the country campaigning for the Treaty of Versailles and the League of Nations. At a whistle-stop in Colorado a few days before the stroke, he gave his last speech as president. Standing on the rear platform of his railcar, he said the treaty was a covenant that would alter the political structure of Europe, revolutionize the international system, and eliminate the root causes of war. And without American support, the League of Nations would collapse like a house of cards. After the speech, he collapsed and was forced immediately to return to Washington. The stroke actually took place a week later, and would leave him disabled for the rest of his term. Wilson's seventh annual message was delivered to Congress two months later.

In his 1919 annual message, he apologized for not being present, and said members of his cabinet were keeping him informed. In fact, Wilson's wife was serving as de facto chief of staff, controlling access to the president, supervising White House staff and delegating tasks to cabinet members. By then, however, the Senate had already voted to reject the treaty. Massachusetts Republican Senator Henry Cabot Lodge (and chair of the Committee on Foreign Relations) led the opposition, arguing that membership in the league would infringe on the country's sovereignty. In particular, Lodge took exception to Article 10, which in his interpretation would require the United States to come to the aid of any member of the league under attack.

The entire Treaty of Versailles is far too unwieldy to reproduce, but the so-called War Guilt Clause (Article 231) is noteworthy. "The Allied and Associated Governments affirm and Germany accepts the responsibility of Germany and her allies *for causing all the loss and damage* to which the Allied and Associated Governments and their nationals have been subjected as a consequence of the war imposed upon them by the aggression of Germany and her allies."[17]

Something about the War Guilt Clause is inconsistent with the doctrine of practical idealism. After all, it was none other than George Washington who advised us to have no permanent allies and no permanent enemies. In the first few months after the war, the Germans saw Woodrow Wilson as their savior. As the harsh terms of the treaty were revealed—the war reparations, disarmament, loss of its colonies, loss of 13 percent of its territory and 10 percent of its population, exclusion from the League of Nations, and worst of all, the war guilt—the Germans saw him not as a savior but as a hypocrite.

It is worth remembering Wilson entertained grand visions of the postwar international system in December 1915, well before the 1919 Paris peace conference when he said the war in Europe presented a unique opportunity to reorganize and reconstruct "the whole face of international affairs."[18] Almost eighty-seven years later, George W. Bush (in his *2002 National Security Strategy*) made an equally idealistic declaration when he said we had the best chance since the seventeenth century "to build a world where great powers compete in peace instead of continually prepare for war." It is possible the Treaty of Versailles failed because the League of Nations failed. It is possible the League of Nations failed because the United States refused to join. It is also possible Wilson's vision of a new world order was nothing but misguided idealism, and any attempt to reorganize or rebuild the international system is hopelessly impractical.

Wilson's eighth and final annual message returned to the familiar "new world order" theme, comparing the United States' victory in the Great War to the Civil War. The birth of the nation, he said, came with the faith that a new world order would prevail. And only by this faith could the world be lifted out of confusion and despair. Because the Old World rejected the spirit of democracy, he said, "It is surely the manifest destiny of the United States to lead in the attempt to make this spirit prevail." Finally, Wilson's message reminded Congress the people of the Philippines had maintained a stable government and thus fulfilled the condition Congress set for them to gain their independence. It is our duty, he said, to keep our promise and grant their independence.[19]

4

Arms Control
Washington Naval Limitation Treaty; League of Nations; Kellogg-Briand Pact; Crash of 1929; Smoot-Hawley Tariff Act

Ohio senator Warren Harding won the 1920 presidential election, promising "a return to normalcy" to war-weary Americans. Harding contributed nothing new to the doctrine of practical idealism, but he would reinforce several dominant themes. In his 1921 inaugural address, Harding said, "In the beginning the Old World scoffed at our experiment," but "today our foundations of political and social belief stand unshaken." Then he gave a novel explanation for why the League of Nations was rejected, comparing it to a "world supergovernment."

The United States' refusal to join the League was based not on selfish motives or suspicion of others, he said, but on national security and "patriotic adherence to the things which made us what we are." Clearly, Harding believed one of those things was divine intervention, declaring the establishment of the United States showed the hand of God at work. Another of those things was "the inherited policy of noninvolvement in Old World affairs." Although Harding said he recognized and acknowledged a "new order in the world," calling his administration's foreign policy an "inheritance" demonstrates certain a lack of imagination. He referred to the "great truths" of the founding fathers, and parroted George Washington's 125-year-old farewell address: "Confident of our ability to work out our own destiny, and jealously guarding our right to do so, we seek no part in directing the destinies of the Old World. We do not mean to be entangled."

In his 1922 annual message, Harding reported completion of the Washington Naval Limitation Treaty of 1922, the purpose of which was to prevent an arms race between the United States, France, Italy, and Japan.[1] According to Harding the arms limitation treaty was a model for the world and would abolish "every probability of war on the Pacific." In addition, Harding restated his well-known opposition to the United States' membership in the League of Nations: "We have had expressed the hostility of the American people to a supergovernment or to any commitment where either a council or an assembly of leagued powers may chart our course." Beyond that, however, his foreign policy was devoid of coherence. When Harding attempts to describe the new world order, he refers to both an old order and a new order, but never exactly defines what those terms mean. For example, he said "There never again will be precisely the old order," and "There is no acceptance of pre-war conditions anywhere in the world." Did he mean a world war could never happen again because the new order would not permit it? Did he mean the death of the European monarchies or the end of secret diplomacy? Was he referring to the birth of Russian socialism? Unfortunately, we will never know. In August 1923, Warren Harding fell ill and died while traveling in San Francisco and Vice President Calvin Coolidge became president.

Calvin Coolidge began his 1923 annual message with the subject of foreign affairs. The foreign policy of his administration would have "one cardinal principle," he said, "It is an American principle. It must be an American policy." In his 1925 inaugural, Coolidge made a similar statement: "We believe that we can best serve our own country and most successfully discharge our obligations to humanity by continuing to be openly and candidly, intensely and scrupulously, American."

He provided additional explanation, arguing that if we wanted to continue to be distinctively American, it was our responsibility "to make that term comprehensive enough to embrace the legitimate desires of a civilized and enlightened people determined in all their relations to pursue a conscientious and religious life." It was our responsibility to live up to the American ideal, and not permit ourselves to be "dwarfed by slogans." Although Coolidge did not explicitly say so, one slogan must have been self-determination or perhaps another Wilsonian principle.

Like Theodore Roosevelt, Calvin Coolidge did not hesitate to compare human behavior with national behavior. In his 1924 annual message, he said, "Ultimately nations, like individuals, can not depend upon each other but must depend upon themselves." Although he pledged America would help other nations in times of crisis, he said every nation had to work out its own salvation. According to Coolidge, the world situation could be "improved only by hard work and self-denial." His advice to European countries recovering from the devastating effects of WWI was to reduce expenses, increase savings, and pay down debt.

Coolidge strongly supported the Hague Tribunal (which the United States had been a member of for twenty-five years), as well as the establishment of a permanent world court. One of the issues where he was unequivocal was in his opposition to American membership in the League of Nations. In his 1923 annual message, he said:

> Our country has definitely refused to adopt and ratify the covenant of the League of Nations. We have not felt warranted in assuming the responsibilities which its members have assumed. I am not proposing any change in this policy; neither is the Senate. The incident, so far as we are concerned, is closed. The League exists as a foreign agency. We hope it will be helpful. But the United States sees no reason to limit its own freedom and independence of action by joining it. We shall do well to recognize this basic fact in all national affairs and govern ourselves accordingly.[2]

Another issue where his position was unequivocal was his support for the hundred-year-old Monroe Doctrine. "It must be maintained. But in maintaining it we must not be forgetful that a great change has taken place," he said. What was the great change from 1823? According to Coolidge, the United States was now a great and powerful nation, no longer fearful of foreign domination. With the United States' new power, it had a new responsibility to help stabilize a turbulent world. Then, sure he opposed Wilson, but unable to articulate an alternative, Coolidge said, "We want idealism. We want that vision which lifts men and nations above themselves. These are virtues by reason of their own merit. But they must not be cloistered; they must not be impractical; they must not be ineffective."[3]

In his 1925 annual message, Coolidge restated his support for the Hague Tribunal and opposition to American membership in the League of Nations. He reported to Congress there was much interest and discussion in the country over the prospect of outlawing "aggressive" war. He was sympathetic to the idea because it was "in harmony with the traditional policy of our country," which opposed aggressive war and favored maintaining a permanent and honorable peace. In order to guard U.S. sovereignty, Coolidge's support for a permanent world court was deliberately ambiguous. He recommended establishing it—as long as the court was independent of the League of Nations—but he refused to be bound by judgments in cases where the American government had not submitted to it voluntarily. "This court would provide a practical and convenient tribunal before which we could go voluntarily, but to which we could not be summoned," he said. Although he expressed his support for the "codification of international law," he said the United States would be immune from all court judgments.

As usual, Coolidge devoted considerable time to foreign affairs in his 1925 message, and tried to express his version of practical idealism. He declared the United States was leading the "general readjustment" of the postwar world, and then made a profound insight: "If we wish to erect new structures, we must have a definite knowledge of the old foundations. We must realize that human nature is about the most constant thing in the universe and that the essentials of human relationship do not change." Perhaps he overstated the significance of human nature in the universe, though we really have no way of knowing. However, he did point toward the critical link between human nature and international politics. Objecting to the League of Nations because it encroaches on American national sovereignty is one thing, but objecting to the league because it is incompatible with human nature is quite another.

Coolidge was committed to arms limitations, but never to disarmament. He specifically stated his desire to avoid extremes in terms of isolation or entanglement, of pacifism or militarism. As if apologizing for the territorial conquests of his predecessors, Coolidge said, "We extended our domain over distant islands in order to safeguard our own interests and accepted the consequent obligation to bestow justice and liberty upon less favored peoples."

Along with arms limitations, Coolidge supported exploring new ways to resolve international conflicts peacefully. As stated, he was supportive (within limits) of the World Court, but knew sustainable world peace would not be found in any formula, treaty, or covenant. From his 1925 inaugural:

> Some of the best thought of mankind has long been seeking for a formula for permanent peace. Undoubtedly the clarification of the principles of international law would be helpful, and the efforts of scholars to prepare such a work for adoption by the various nations should have our sympathy and support. Much may be hoped for from the earnest studies of those who advocate the outlawing of aggressive war. *But all these plans and preparations, these treaties and covenants, will not of themselves be adequate.*[4]

He believed political rivalries, power struggles, and arms races were the leading causes of war. As long as this was the case, humans would always outsmart any *human-made* formula for peace. According to Coolidge, the only hope for permanent peace rested in the human heart. "Parchment will fail, the sword will fail," said Coolidge, "it is only the spiritual nature of man that can be triumphant."

In his 1925 annual message, Coolidge expressed his support for the Locarno agreements, signed in October that year between Germany, Belgium, France, Great Britain, and Italy.[5] It was an unremarkable collective security agreement, which essentially reinforced the Treaty of Versailles, and reaffirmed the demilitarized zone and international borders established by Versailles Treaty. It guaranteed Germany, Belgium, and France would not invade each other and provided a special commission for peaceful conflict resolution though arbitration.

The United States did not ratify the Treaty of Versailles, and would never join the League of Nations. According to Coolidge, the discussion was closed. In his 1924 annual message, Coolidge stated clearly—and correctly —that no treaty, formula, or covenant would bring permanent peace.

In 1925, however, Coolidge said of the Locarno Pact, "When these agreements are finally adopted, they will provide *guarantees of peace*." (Italics added). What accounts for the apparent contradiction is Coolidge's faith in arms limitations? The Washington Naval Limitation Treaty of 1922—the only significant foreign policy accomplishment of the Harding administration—set the precedent. In Coolidge's 1927 annual message, Coolidge argued that arms reductions in no way reduced or threatened the United States' national defense, and proudly said the Washington Treaty demonstrated the United States' "unprecedented attitude of generosity."

Although Coolidge said disarmament was the "general policy of our country," he was willing to reduce the size of the peacetime army, but not the navy. Reducing the size of the peacetime army was one of Coolidge's methods of "liquidating the war." In Coolidge's 1924 annual message, he said the United States' success was a direct result of its "constant refusal to maintain a military establishment that could be thought to menace the security of others." In this respect, Coolidge mythologized the past because by 1925, America's naval forces were as large as any in the world, and had been so for decades. As far as maintaining a small army was concerned, the reason was not to avoid threatening other countries, but because a large standing army was widely considered a threat to internal security.

In his sixth and final annual message (1928), Coolidge reported he had signed eleven new arbitration treaties, with twenty-two others under consideration. The most important was the Kellogg-Briand Pact between the United States and fourteen other countries, in which signatories renounced war as an instrument of national policy.[6] Coolidge called it a "most solemn declaration against war," and one of the most important treaties ever presented to the Senate. However, Coolidge reassured Congress—he knew his audience—the treaty would not "supersede our inalienable sovereign right and duty of national defense" or anything else Congress wanted to do for that matter.

Finally, with the Great Depression and Second World War still beyond the horizon, Coolidge blissfully reported in his 1928 message, "The country is in the midst of an era of prosperity more extensive and of peace more permanent than it has ever before experienced. But, having reached this position, we should not fail to comprehend that it can easily be lost."

•••

In 1928, Herbert Hoover, secretary of commerce to Presidents Harding and Coolidge, won the presidential election. In his 1929 inaugural address, Hoover gave no indication of any of the country's looming economic challenges. Any survey of the county's situation at home and abroad, he said would discover much good news and few causes for concern. Hoover repeated what had become a familiar refrain: America had no imperial ambition and no plans for territorial expansion, and those who disagreed were simply unable to see destiny at work. In Hoover's words, "Superficial observers seem to find no destiny for our abounding increase in population, in wealth and power except that of imperialism. They fail to see that the American people are engrossed in the building for themselves of a new economic system, a new social system, a new political system all of which are characterized by aspirations of freedom of opportunity and thereby are the negation of imperialism."[7]

Hoover shared Coolidge's enthusiasm for the Kellogg-Briand Pact, which Hoover carelessly believed would eliminate war as an instrument of national policy. He saw the treaty as a step toward "greater and greater perfection" of peaceful conflict resolution between nations. As if the issue were still a matter of debate, Hoover said the United States would not join the League of Nations. In fact, he considered it a mandate from the election to avoid any policy that would involve the country in "the controversies of foreign nations."

On October 29, 1929 the stock market crashed, losing about 12 percent of its value on sixteen million shares traded. Hoover began his first annual message by quoting Article II of the Constitution, which requires the president to report to Congress on the state of the union from time to time. The stock market crash occurred two months earlier, and Hoover had not yet grasped the significance of the event. "The problems with which we are confronted are the problems of growth and of progress," he said.

By then, fifty-four nations had signed on to the Kellogg-Briand Pact, which Hoover believed would eliminate the causes of international conflict. Once again, Hoover declared his opposition to the League of Nations, vowing not to take "the slightest step" toward membership. Regardless, it was foolish for Coolidge and Hoover to be so idealistic about the Kellogg-Briand Pact while holding the League of Nations in such contempt.

In a section of Hoover's 1929 annual message titled *General Economic Situation,* he reported on the stock market crash and a series of voluntary measures he instituted to encourage economic stability and minimize job losses. Although the tone of Hoover's analysis was calm and reassuring, at the end of the second paragraph he actually predicted the depression:

> The long upward trend of fundamental progress... gave rise to over-optimism as to profits, which translated itself into a wave of uncontrolled speculation in securities, resulting in the diversion of capital from business to the stock market and the inevitable crash. The natural consequences have been a reduction in the consumption of luxuries and semi-necessities by those who have met with losses, and a number of persons thrown temporarily out of employment. Prices of agricultural products dealt in upon the great markets have been affected in sympathy with the stock crash.
>
> The sudden threat of unemployment and especially the recollection of the economic consequences of previous crashes under a much less secured financial system created unwarranted pessimism and fear. It was recalled that past storms

of similar character had resulted in retrenchment of construction, reduction of wages, and laying off of workers. The natural result was the tendency of business agencies throughout the country to pause in their plans and proposals for continuation and extension of their businesses, and this hesitation unchecked could in itself intensify into a depression with widespread unemployment and suffering.[8]

In September 1930, events took place in Germany that would later prove to be meaningful. With unemployment high and inflation out of control, the National Socialist Party rose from obscurity to win more than a hundred seats in the Reichstag. In Hoover's 1930 annual message, his report on foreign affairs was brief. Following on the arms limitation policies of Harding and Coolidge, Hoover announced the London Naval Pact, which limited the size of the U.S. Navy to parity with the other strongest naval powers. Hoover reported there was "political unrest in the world," in Asia and South America, but made no mention of Germany.

At first, Hoover blamed speculators for causing the depression—investors who diverted capital into speculation rather than productive enterprise. If speculation had been the only factor, he said, the economy would have already corrected itself. Other factors, according to Hoover, included worldwide overproduction of basic commodities and raw materials—wheat, rubber, coffee, sugar, copper, silver, zinc, and cotton—which created a cumulative effect of falling prices, lower incomes, higher unemployment, political agitation, political unrest, and so on. As far as what action the Hoover administration proposed to take, he said, "Economic depression cannot be cured by legislative action or executive pronouncement. Economic wounds must be healed by the action of the cells of the economic body— the producers and consumers themselves." Whether it was good economic policy or not, Hoover gave responsibility for economic recovery to the voters, who would ultimately force him from office.

In an effort to protect domestic production, Congress enacted the Smoot-Hawley Tariff Act in June 1930. The protectionist measure increased tariffs and other nontariff barriers, which of course led to retaliation by America's trading partners and plunged the global economy deeper into depression. Hoover saw little urgency for government intervention in the economy for two reasons. One was based on his underestimation of the depth of the crisis, and the other was based on his faith the crisis would be self-correcting.

In his brief 1931 annual message, Hoover began his report of the country's foreign affairs with this statement: "The economic depression has continued and deepened in every part of the world during the past year." The economic crisis had created a climate of political instability, said Hoover, leading to revolutions in nineteen countries affecting more than half of the world's population. Hoover was just becoming concerned about the imminent disaster in Germany, which he feared would collapse if the United States did not intervene. In fact, the United States did intervene by convincing France and Britain to postpone Germany's war reparations payments for one year. Finally, he voiced concerns about increased tensions between China and Japan—mostly because the Kellogg-Briand Pact was being ignored.

•••

Franklin Roosevelt—former assistant secretary of the navy and governor of New York—won the 1932 presidential election. Roosevelt ran on the "Three R's: relief, recovery, and reform," and promised voters a "new deal." With unemployment in the United States at 25 percent and the economy in chaos, Roosevelt defeated Hoover in a landslide.

Hoover's 1932 annual message, delivered a few weeks following the election, contained a section titled *Economic Cooperation with Other Nations.* In that section, Hoover outlined his recommendations to Roosevelt, which he called the "three great fields of international action." Hoover's recommendations are interesting for what they reveal about his understanding of international politics. First, he recommended world disarmament because it would increase political stability and reduce the tax burden on the world's leading countries. Second, he recommended that the United States decrease its offensive military power and increase its defensive power because (somehow) it would "open new vistas of economic expansion." Third, he recommended economic cooperation with foreign nations in response to the worldwide depression caused by the Great War.

Finally, Hoover made an observation highlighting the significance of *American exceptionalism* within the doctrine of practical idealism. According to Hoover, "today as never before the welfare of mankind and the preservation of civilization depend upon our solution of these questions." As we will soon discover, neither Wilson nor Hoover would be the last American presidents to convinced themselves the United States was destined to play a unique role in international affairs.

5

World War II

Good Neighbor; Germany Annexes the Sudetenland, Three-Powers; Four Freedoms; Pearl Harbor; Europe First; Germany and Japan Surrender

Roosevelt did not have much to say about foreign policy in his 1933 inaugural address, which is understandable because he faced other compelling matters. Facing an unprecedented economic crisis, Roosevelt said, "Our greatest primary task is to put people to work." In fact, there would be little of substance in terms of foreign policy in any of Roosevelt's annual messages until 1936 when world events took a turn for the worse. He did mention the "good neighbor policy," the foundation of which was self-respect, keeping one's promises, and respecting the rights of others, themes that would reappear throughout his presidency.

In 1933, German president Paul von Hindenburg appointed Adolf Hitler chancellor of Germany. The U.S. Navy launched the USS *Ranger,* the United States' first ship designed and constructed as an aircraft carrier. The Reichstag building was set on fire. Roosevelt delivered his first fireside chat (on banking). The Nazis completed construction of their first concentration camp, in Dachau. And formal diplomatic relations were established for the first time between the United States and Soviet Union.

Meanwhile, Austrian chancellor Engelbert Dollfuss died in an assassination, and Adolf Hitler became Führer. In Roosevelt's 1935 annual message, he expressed doubts about keeping the peace and hoped for the day when international relations would be guided by "world welfare" rather than power and privilege. Old jealousies and old passions had awakened, and new ambitions for weapons and power had reared their ugly heads, he said, perhaps referring to Japan's recent renunciation of the Washington Naval Treaty and the London Naval Treaty.

In 1935, Italian premier Benito Mussolini and French foreign minister Pierre Laval negotiated an agreement not to oppose each other's colonial claims. There was a plebiscite in the Saarland (a small territory between France and Germany under the jurisdiction of the League of Nations since WWI), and 90 percent of the people voted for reunification with Germany. In China, the Kuomintang government surrendered control of northeastern China to the Japan, and Mao Zedong rose to become leader of the Communist Party. Hitler renounced the Treaty of Versailles and began to rearm, and Italy invaded Ethiopia. In August that year, Congress passed—and Roosevelt signed—the Neutrality Act, which prohibited shipments of war materiel in the event of a war in Europe.[1]

•••

Roosevelt began his 1936 annual message by recalling his first inaugural speech, in which he devoted most of his time to domestic issues, and the subject of foreign affairs consisted of one short paragraph. "You will remember that on that fourth of March, 1933, the world picture was an image of substantial peace." Roosevelt reminded his audience the only reference to international affairs he made in that speech was to declare his good neighbor policy. Roosevelt restated his commitment to that policy and reported the Western Hemisphere was one place where the good neighbor policy prevailed.

In 1936, Japanese military officers staged a coup and replaced antiwar prime minister Okada Keisuke with prowar foreign minister Hirota Koki. Germany reoccupied the Rhineland in violation of the Locarno Pact and the Treaty of Versailles. Italy annexed Ethiopia. The Spanish civil war began. Germany and Japan signed a pact agreeing to consult in case of an attack by the Soviet Union. Jesse Owens won four gold medals in the Summer Olympic Games in Berlin. And in November, Franklin Roosevelt easily defeated Alf Landon, the Republican governor of Kansas to win a second term.

In his 1937 inaugural address, Roosevelt gave a concise description of his political philosophy, which helps explain his approach to international politics. He said as the complexity of human relationships increased, the power to govern those relationships (the power to stop evil and the power to do good), must also increase. Roosevelt believed his administration was more than a good neighbor. By wiping out "the line that divides the practical from the ideal," the American people under his leadership were creating "an instrument of unimagined power for the establishment of a morally better world."

By the end of 1937, Franklin Roosevelt would try, and fail to pack the Supreme Court with justices more sympathetic to his New Deal programs.

In Spain, the German Luftwaffe bombed the northern Basque town of Guernica in the ongoing civil war. Japan invaded Manchuria. And in Germany, Adolf Hitler announced his intention to acquire more Lebensraum (living space) for the German people.

In his 1938 annual message, Roosevelt restated his general support for disarmament and nonviolent conflict resolution. He said the United States' traditional policy was "to live at peace with other nations," and noted the connection between nations who failed to fulfill their treaty obligations, and those that were nondemocratic, militaristic, and discontented with their territorial boundaries. Although the United States would make relatively few preparations for self-defense prior to December 1941, it was becoming clear that the aggressive policies of Italy, Japan, and Germany would have far-reaching effects. In 1938, Germany would invade Austria and then annex it. Leaders from Britain and France would appease Germany's demands for annexation of Czechoslovakia's Sudetenland. Nazi troops would arrest or murder thousands of German Jews, and loot and burn Jewish businesses and synagogues. And in Saudi Arabia, oil was discovered.

●●●

In his 1939 annual message, Roosevelt reported undeclared wars were raging practically everywhere, even though world war had been averted for the moment. The opponents of democracy had attacked freedom of religion and democracy, two principles Americans held most deeply. Where democracy and religious freedom disappeared, said Roosevelt, faith in world peace gave way to threats and brutality. Because Roosevelt could not tolerate—or even imagine—any government would degrade these American principles, the time had come, he said, for us to begin preparing to defend the principles on which we founded our government, our churches and our entire civilization. The world was so small and weapons so powerful the United States would never be safe, he said, and even if our enemies stayed in Europe and Asia and never invaded the Western Hemisphere, it would be unwise to allow them to surround us.

●●●

In 1939, Spanish forces loyal to Francisco Franco captured Madrid, bringing an end to the Spanish civil war. German troops occupied Bohemia and Moravia—and then Czechoslovakia would cease to exist. Italy invaded Albania. Germany and Italy signed the Pact of Steel. In Germany, the last Jewish-owned businesses were closed. The Soviet Union and Germany partitioned Eastern Europe with the Molotov-Ribbentrop Pact.[2] Germany invaded Poland. Then Australia, Britain, Canada, France, and South Africa declared war on Germany, which marked the beginning of WWII.

Following Germany's invasion of Poland, Roosevelt sat down for one of his fireside chats on September 3, 1939. Time had expired that a miracle would prevent the war. Though the crisis was caused by "the use of force and the threat of force," he said, America—on behalf of humanity—should strive for a permanent peace. Although most Americans wanted nothing more than to be left alone, they were being forced to realize that conflicts taking place thousands of miles from American shores affected them. For this reason, Roosevelt said, his aides were preparing a proclamation of American neutrality—in accord with international law and American tradition. The historic precedent, he said, "goes back to the days of the Administration of President George Washington." He hoped and believed the country could stay out of the war, and pledged to make every effort to make that happen. For now, while the country was still officially neutral, he urged the American people to keep an open mind, to be willing to consider new facts, and to listen to their conscience. Thus, he reserved the option of abandoning neutrality, if and when, the time was right.

Roosevelt began his 1940 annual message with a discussion of foreign affairs—practically apologizing for doing so because he did not want to imply he was overlooking domestic affairs. Roosevelt said he understood those who argued that all we needed to do to stay out of the war was to mind our own business. In response to this rhetorical devise, he said we were fooling ourselves if we thought staying out of the war was the same as saying it was none of our business. Like it or not, Americans could no longer afford to insulate themselves from world events. Roosevelt offered this not as a theory, but as a fact of modern life with a mountain of evidence to support it. We were deluding ourselves if we thought the United States could live as a self-contained unit inside a high wall of isolation, secure, happy, and prosperous, while the rest of the world fell apart.

Roosevelt sympathized with those who would never again consent to sending Americans to fight on European soil. Then—choosing his words carefully in order to keep his options open—he said: "But, as I remember, nobody has asked them to consent—for nobody expects such an undertaking." The great majority of Americans had not abandoned the hope or expectation that the country would not "become involved in *military participation* in these wars," he said. (Italics added). Roosevelt wanted to ensure his audience he would do everything in his power to maintain the good neighbor policy and promised to exhaust every instrument of diplomacy before resorting to war.

•••

In 1940, Germany committed mass executions of Poles. Adolf Hitler and Benito Mussolini formed an alliance against Britain and France. The Auschwitz concentration camp opened, and Germany invaded Denmark, Belgium, the Netherlands, Luxembourg, and France.

In late May 1940, shortly after the allies evacuated from the French town of Dunkirk, Roosevelt gave another of his fireside chats. Roosevelt said the eyewitness accounts of events in Europe were shocking. Millions of people were on the move, homeless refugees were running from Germany's army with no food, no medical attention, not knowing where the road would end. The way to prevent the destructive forces sweeping Europe from reaching American shores was to continue strengthening our military defenses. "We have spent large sums of money on the national defense" he said, "This money has been used to make our Army and Navy today the largest, the best equipped, and the best trained peace-time military establishment in the whole history of this country."[3]

Later in 1940, the Vichy government was created in France. The Soviet Union annexed Lithuania, Latvia, and Estonia. Germany began its nightly bombing of London. Britain halted Germany's invasion in the Battle of Britain. The German Luftwaffe bombed Coventry and the British Royal Air Force retaliated by bombing Hamburg. In late September, Germany, Italy, and Japan signed the Three-Power Pact and made a commitment to cooperate in Europe and East Asia. Their goal was "to establish and maintain a new order of things calculated to promote the mutual prosperity and welfare of the peoples concerned."[4]

In the 1940 presidential election, Roosevelt defeated Wendell Willkie of Indiana. A few days after Christmas 1940, Roosevelt sat down for another fireside chat with the people who recently elected him to an unprecedented third term. The topic, he said, was not war, but national security. He wanted to convey what the new crisis meant to their daily lives, and hoped the nation would respond to this new national security threat the same way they responded to the economic crisis. The recently signed Three-Power Pact, said Roosevelt, was "a program aimed at world control." Essentially, Germany, Italy, and Japan were threatening to unite against the United States if we dared to interfere with their plans. "The Nazi masters of Germany have made it clear that they intend not only to dominate all life and thought in their own country, but also to enslave the whole of Europe, and then to use the resources of Europe to dominate the rest of the world." In Roosevelt's words:

> One hundred and seventeen years ago the Monroe Doctrine was conceived by our Government as a measure of defense in the face of a threat against this hemisphere by an alliance in Continental Europe. Thereafter, we stood on guard in the Atlantic, with the British as neighbors. There was no treaty. There was no "unwritten agreement". And yet, there was the feeling, proven correct by history, that we as neighbors could settle any disputes in peaceful fashion. The fact is that during the whole of this time the Western Hemisphere has remained free from aggression from Europe or from Asia.[5]

For the time being, there was no immediate threat because the British and Greeks were keeping Italy and Germany at bay, and China was holding Japan in check. Concurring with Theodore Roosevelt's interpretation, Franklin Roosevelt said the geographic scope of the Monroe Doctrine extended far beyond the Western Hemisphere to include both approaches to the Panama Canal, the Caribbean (in the east) and the maritime highway between the Philippines and Hawaii (in the west). Now, Roosevelt said it was an issue of vital national security that the Three-Power Pact countries "not gain control of the oceans which lead to this hemisphere."

No matter how bad the Treaty of Versailles was, there was no comparison to the so-called pacification then spreading across Europe and Asia. "Every realist knows that the democratic way of life is at this moment being directly assailed in every part of the world," he said. The defenders of democracy were fighting back on four continents, and if their defense failed, Germany and Japan would gain control over the combined resources of Europe, Asia, Africa, and Australia. Because "the vast resources and wealth of this American Hemisphere constitute the most tempting loot" in the world, said Roosevelt prophetically, we would have no choice but to put the country on a permanent war footing in order to survive.

Roosevelt then listed the three elements of his continuously evolving foreign policy. First, he pledged an "all-inclusive national defense" free of partisan differences. Second, he pledged his full support for the "resolute peoples" everywhere who through their resistance were helping keep the United States strong and secure. Third, he promised never to agree to any peace agreement "dictated by aggressors and sponsored by appeasers." Taken together, the policy was clear and coherent, acceptable to Roosevelt's broad constituency, and operational militarily if need be. The next step would be to mobilize the national economy. "Therefore" said Roosevelt, "the immediate need is a swift and driving increase in our armament production."

Converting the American economy from a peacetime to a wartime footing was no small task. The greatest challenge came at the beginning, said Roosevelt, when new factories, tools, and assembly lines had to be built before the urgently needed war materiel could be produced. Roosevelt also asked Congress to appropriate funds to manufacture weapons, ammunition, and supplies for America's allies already fighting the war (though Roosevelt was deliberately not calling them "allies" yet). "They do not need man power" he said, "but they do need billions of dollars worth of the weapons of defense." For the time being, the greatest contribution Roosevelt could make was to convince the country to serve as the arsenal of democracy.

Roosevelt was well aware he could never let Britain or anyone else resisting Germany and Japan surrender. He warned Congress time was approaching when the countries the United States was supplying would no longer be able to pay cash. Roosevelt flatly rejected lending them money to pay for the weapons. Instead, he touted the Lend-Lease program and argued the need to mobilize the economy and develop the country's armed forces. Then, Roosevelt spoke directly to Britain, and our other allies fighting overseas:

Let us say to the democracies: "We Americans are vitally concerned in your defense of freedom. We are putting forth our energies, our resources and our organizing powers to give you the strength to regain and maintain a free world. We shall send you, in ever-increasing numbers, ships, planes, tanks, guns. This is our purpose and our pledge". In fulfillment of this purpose we will not be intimidated by the threats of dictators that they will regard as a breach of international law or as an act of war our aid to the democracies which dare to resist their aggression.[6]

By the end of his 1941 annual message—also known as the Four Freedoms Speech—Roosevelt transformed the conflict from a proxy fight for democracy in Britain into to a Lincolnesque struggle *not altogether for today, but for a vast future also.* According to Roosevelt, the United States and its allies were fighting for four essential freedoms: freedom of speech; freedom of worship; freedom from want; and freedom from fear. One difference between Roosevelt's four freedoms and Woodrow Wilson's fourteen points is Roosevelt's emphasis on human rights, as opposed to Wilson's emphasis on the rights of groups within the international system.

•••

In 1941, British troops attacked the Italians in Eritrea (northeast Africa). Australian and British forces captured Tobruk (a Mediterranean port town in eastern Libya) from the Germans. In occupied France, Germany installed Pierre Laval to the Vichy government. The Soviet Union and Japan signed a neutrality agreement. The British Royal Navy took possession of an *enigma* cryptography machine after capturing a German submarine. In the North Atlantic, the British Royal Navy sank the German battleship *Bismarck*. Germany attacked the Soviet Union. Roosevelt proclaimed a national emergency and ordered all Japanese assets in the United States seized. In Germany, the Nazis began planning genocide of all Jews in Nazi-occupied territories. In the Soviet Union, German forces put Leningrad under siege, and launched an offensive against Moscow.

In early September 1941, a German U-boat launched a torpedo at an American destroyer, the USS *Greer* in the North Atlantic. Although the *Greer* was undamaged and managed to fire back, the incident helped escalate the undeclared war between German U-boats and American escort ships on "neutrality patrol." In Roosevelt's fireside chat shortly afterward, he said the Nazi's effort to control the Atlantic was part of Hitler's master plan. As soon as the Nazis got control of the shipping channels between Europe and North America, they would start establishing footholds and bridgeheads in the Western Hemisphere. In Roosevelt's words:

To be ultimately successful in world mastery, Hitler knows that he must get control of the seas. He must first destroy the bridge of ships which we are building across the Atlantic and over which we shall continue to roll the implements of war to help destroy him, to destroy all his works in the end. He must wipe out our patrol on sea and in the air if he is to do it. He must silence the British Navy.[7]

Roosevelt defended the British Navy because free navigation of the seas was fundamental to the doctrine of practical idealism. As he said in his 1941 annual message, if Britain were to fall, the Axis powers would control every major ocean, and every continent except for North and South America. This was why the United States had to furnish material support to the British, and why it would have to furnish much more in the future. If Britain were to fall, the only resistance to the Axis powers would come from the United States. If Britain were to fall, the world would enter "a new and terrible era" dominated by threats and brutality. "Obviously, as long as the British Navy retains its power" he said "no such danger exists."

•••

On December 7, 1941, the Japanese navy launched a surprise attack on the U.S. fleet at Pearl Harbor. One day after the attack, Roosevelt asked Congress to declare war on Japan in his famous "Day of Infamy" speech. Given the distance from Japan to the Hawaiian Islands—and the simultaneous coordinated attacks on Malaya, Hong Kong, Guam, the Philippines, Wake Island, and Midway Island—it was obvious the Japanese had planned the attacks well in advance. Although thousands of lives had been lost, and the United States' Pacific fleet had suffered a serious blow, Roosevelt rightly predicted that no matter how long it took to recover, the United States would emerge victorious. Before the close of business on December 8, Congress declared war on Japan.

•••

On December 9, one day after the war declaration and two days after Pearl Harbor, Roosevelt had another fireside chat with his constituents. Japan's attack on Pearl Harbor, he said was "the climax of a decade of international immorality." Japan's course in Asia since 1931 paralleled Germany's in Europe and Italy's in Africa. "Today, it has become far more than a parallel. It is actual collaboration so well calculated that all the continents of the world, and all the oceans, are now considered by the Axis strategists as one gigantic battlefield," he said. As such, America was now in the war. We were in it all the way and "Every single man, woman, and child is a partner in the most tremendous undertaking of our American history."

Roosevelt told the country to be prepared for the capture of Guam, Midway, and the Wake Islands, all strategically located islands that the Japanese attacked during the same operation as Pearl Harbor. He said he shared the anxiety of all the families who had men in uniform, and all the families who had relatives in cities bombed by the Japanese. He then turned his attention to two new policies his administration was implementing. The first was to accelerate production by implementing a seven-day workweek in all war-related industries. The second was to increase production capacity by launching a program to build new plants and additions to existing plants.

Finally, reminding his listeners of the consequences of repeating the failure of the Treaty of Versailles, Roosevelt said, "We are going to win the war and we are going to win the peace that follows."

In his 1942 annual message, Roosevelt reminded Congress a year ago when he said the dictators would not wait for us, but would choose the time and place for their attack. Now, everybody knew their choice for time and place: a quiet Sunday morning in early December in the Hawaiian Islands. And we knew method. It was, said Roosevelt, "the method of Hitler himself." In Hitler's grand plans for global domination, Japan's first task was to cut off the supply lines through which the United States furnished weapons, ammunition, and war materiel to Britain, Russia, and China. The intention of Japan's Pearl Harbor attack was to stun and confuse the United States in the hope the American people would panic and divert resources away from Europe to protect the Pacific. Roosevelt reported, however, Hitler's trick was unsuccessful: "We have not been stunned. We have not been terrified or confused." The quiet resolve of Congress that day, said Roosevelt, was proof that Hitler had failed.

Once again, Roosevelt carefully laid out his policies. "Plans have been laid here and in the other capitals for *coordinated and cooperative action by all the United Nations* —military action and economic action," he said. (Italics added). The name he gave the alliance was newsworthy, as was his call for "coordinated and cooperative action." Later in the speech, he said consultations among the allies would produce a general strategy, that superior forces were assembling, and the defenders of democracy would no longer have to fight alone. Gone were the days, he said, "when the aggressors could attack and destroy their victims one by one without unity of resistance."

Roosevelt's objectives were clear: to establish the four freedoms everywhere in the world. Again, Roosevelt wanted to emphasized he was no Woodrow Wilson; the United States would not only win the war, it would win the peace, too. "We [were] not making all this sacrifice of human effort and human lives to return to the kind of world we had after the last world war," he said. Then, lapsing slipping into the kind of rhetoric Wilson probably would have admired, Roosevelt said that we were fighting "to cleanse the world of ancient evils."

Roosevelt closed his 1942 annual message by acknowledging British prime minister Winston Churchill, who had been visiting the United States since December. "Mr. Churchill and I understand each other, our motives and our purposes," he said, "All in our Nation have been cheered by Mr. Churchill's visit. We have been deeply stirred by his great message to us. He is welcome in our midst." Early in 1942, the Japanese would capture Manila, and put Bataan under siege. Japan would declare war on the Netherlands and invade the Dutch East Indies, Burma, and Singapore. In Northern Ireland, the first American troops would begin landing in Europe.

•••

In February 1942, Franklin Roosevelt signed Executive Order 9066, which led to the internment of more than a hundred thousand Japanese Americans in prison camps such as the one located in Manzanar, California. The United States and United Kingdom signed the Master Lend-Lease Agreement declaring that defending the United Kingdom was in the United States' vital interest. The agreement authorized the president to supply the United Kingdom with "defense articles, defense services, and defense information" at the president's discretion. The agreement deferred indefinitely—until the end of the emergency—the terms and conditions on which the United Kingdom would receive the aid. In return, the United Kingdom agreed to contribute to the defense of the United States any way it could.[8]

On February 23, Roosevelt held another fireside chat with his constituents. In an inspired use of the medium of radio, Roosevelt asked his listeners to open up their world maps, and to spread them out so they could follow along with him. (The image of the family gathered around the radio in the front room, atlas opened to a map of the world, listening as Roosevelt describes Japanese movements near the Philippines—is both vivid and powerful.) Two things that made this war different from previous wars, he said, were technology and geography. The two great oceans that separate us from Europe and Asia would no longer protect us as they used to, he said, and great battles would be fought on every continent, every island, every ocean, and every flight path in the world. America's allies were fighting battles in such faraway places because we had to protect our supply and communication lines against an enemy determined to cut them. The Axis policy was to "divide and conquer," to separate us from our British, Chinese, and Russian allies. In Roosevelt's words:

> Look at your map. Look at the vast area of China, with its millions of fighting men. Look at the vast area of Russia, with its powerful armies and proven military might. Look at the British Isles, Australia, New Zealand, the Dutch Indies, India, the Near East, and the continent of Africa, with their resources of raw materials, and of peoples determined to resist Axis domination. Look too at North America, Central America, and South America. It is obvious what would happen if all of these great reservoirs of power were cut off from each other either by enemy action or by self-imposed isolation.[9]

If Japan cut the lines to China—which had been fighting Japan for five years—we would no longer be able to send aid to China for its self-defense. If we lost communication to the South Pacific, Australia and New Zealand would fall under Japanese domination. If we were unable to supply Britain and the Soviet Union with weapons and supplies, the Nazis would overrun the Middle East and North Africa, which would put them within striking distance of the Western Hemisphere.

Roosevelt asked the listening audience to look at their maps again, particularly the vast Pacific Ocean west of the Hawaiian Islands. Roosevelt reported the Japanese had surrounded the Philippines on three sides before the war started, making it difficult for reinforcements or supplies to get through. It was a long-standing U.S. military policy if the Japanese attacked the Philippines, and threatened to surround the islands, American and Filipino troops would fight a delaying action, retreating slowly into the Bataan Peninsula and Corregidor. "Nothing that has occurred in the past two months has caused us to revise this basic strategy," he said.

That is precisely what happened. When Japanese troops attacked the Philippines and began to surround the islands, Allied forces retreated into the Bataan Peninsula and Corregidor, forcing General Douglas MacArthur to evacuate to Australia. Japanese forces attacked the American and Filipino forces left behind on the Bataan Peninsula, and captured more than seventy thousand troops. They led their prisoners to the town of Tarlac on a 250-mile forced march—the Bataan death march. On Corregidor, however, the last American forces in the Philippines stubbornly refused to surrender, at least for the time being.

In late April 1942, Roosevelt addressed the nation again. The most important development of the year so far, he said, was on the eastern front. (In Eastern Ukraine, the Soviet Union counterattacked and defeated German troops in and around the City of Kharkov.) In addition, Roosevelt reported the Japanese had taken control of large sections of the Philippines, as well as the Malayan Peninsula, Singapore, and the Dutch East Indies. He paid tribute to "the Filipino and American officers and men who held out so long on Bataan Peninsula, to those grim and gallant fighters who still hold Corregidor." Then he made an obvious reference to the top-secret Doolittle Raid, which took place ten days earlier: "It is even reported from Japan that somebody has dropped bombs on Tokyo, and on other principal centers of Japanese war industries. If this [is] true, it is the first time in history that Japan has suffered such indignities."

The event Roosevelt took obvious delight in reporting was the bombing raid on Tokyo led by Lieutenant Colonel Jimmy Doolittle. The plan called for sixteen B-25 bombers (modified for extra fuel capacity) to take off from the deck of the USS *Hornet,* bomb targets in Japan, and then land in China. All of the planes reached Japan and hit various targets, but fuel ran low because the planes had to takeoff farther out to sea than originally planned. Several of the planes never reached China, and several crewmembers were taken as prisoner. The raid was not a significant military victory, but was a major public relations victory. Attacking the Japanese mainland—less than six months after Pearl Harbor—boosted morale in America, and shocked Japanese who thought their defenses were impenetrable.

•••

Throughout most of 1942, great battles took place in Africa and the Pacific: the Battle of Coral Sea, the Battle of Midway, the Battle of

Guadalcanal, and the Second Battle of El Alamein. In France, the Vichy government arrested thousands of Jews. In Poland, Jews were forced from the Warsaw ghetto. And allied forces (Canadian mostly) launched an unsuccessful raid on the German occupied port of Dieppe, France.

Following Doolittle's raid on Tokyo, the Japanese hoped to retake the offensive and destroy the U.S. Pacific Fleet. By early May 1942, Japan had conquered most of Southeast Asia, and planned to occupy the Allied base at Port Moresby in New Guinea. Naval Intelligence discovered Japanese forces, under the command of Vice Admiral Shigeyoshi Inoue, were on the move. Rear Admiral Frank Jack Fletcher, commanding the USS *Yorktown*, would meet him in the Battle of Coral Sea, the first major aircraft carrier engagement of the war. The battle was a modest tactical victory for Japan. They lost a small carrier and one destroyer, and sustained damage to one large carrier. Japanese aircraft crippled the USS *Neosho* and sank the USS *Sims*. In addition, the Americans lost one large carrier (the *Lexington* had to be abandoned and destroyed). The *Yorktown* was damaged, but would be repaired in time for Midway. Although the Japanese occupied Tulagi, which was where Britain's prewar government center in the Solomon Islands was located, the allies disrupted Japan's plans for an amphibious assault on Port Moresby.

The Battle of Midway took place in early June 1942. The battle began with Japanese aircraft bombing the tiny American base at Midway atoll in the middle of the Pacific Ocean. Again under the command of Admiral Isoroku Yamamoto, the Japanese planned to knock out Midway's defenses, invade the islands, and establish a Japanese air base. U.S. Naval Intelligence deduced Yamamoto's intentions, however, and U.S. Pacific Fleet commander Admiral Chester Nimitz and his staff developed their own plan to ambush the Japanese. By the time the battle was over, Japan would lose four aircraft carriers, and the United States only one. The base at Midway was damaged, but operational, and Midway would eventually prove to be the most important battle for the U.S. Pacific Fleet in WWII.

In early August, the first American offensive of the Pacific Campaign began with sixteen thousand American troops landing on the northern beaches of Guadalcanal in the Solomon Islands. The primary objective was an unfinished airfield (later renamed Henderson Field), which the Japanese were building near Lunga Point. The mountains on Guadalcanal are eight thousand feet high, even though the island is only ninety miles long and twenty-five miles wide. Heat, humidity, water shortages, and malaria knocked thousands of troops out of action. The grueling fight for Guadalcanal lasted for six months before American troops overcame Japanese resistance. It was a costly victory for the Allies (six thousand American casualties vs. twenty-four thousand for the Japanese), but it halted the Japanese drive toward Australia, and enabled the Allies to launch a series of attacks closer and closer to Japan.

By the summer of 1942, the Germans had already suffered huge losses since they began their invasion of the Soviet Union. Hitler believed the Red Army was equally weak, and ordered German forces under the command of General Frederick Paulus to advance toward Stalingrad. The Russian Steppes around Stalingrad served as an excellent terrain for tank warfare, and by November, the Germans had Stalingrad mostly surrounded, but not completely subdued. While fighting continued around the city—in homes, cellars, and underground sewers—the Soviets concentrated their forces outside the city. When the Soviets counterattacked, they trapped the German, Romanian, and Italian troops. The Germans were cut off, and as the cold Russian winter set in, the Germans were forced to rely on the Luftwaffe to airlift supplies. As heating oil, medicine, and food ran low, thousands died from frostbite, disease, and starvation. Without adequate clothing to withstand freezing temperatures, with his army running low on ammunition, Field Marshal Paulus surrendered his army in early February 1943.

•••

Roosevelt began his 1943 annual message by declaring it was "one of the great moments in the history of the nation," and that "The past year was perhaps the most crucial for modern civilization; the coming year will be filled with violent conflicts—yet with high promise of better things."[10] The most significant developments in the entire war "by far," said Roosevelt, took place on the Russian front with the defense of Stalingrad and the Russian counterattack. (He called the defense of Stalingrad "implacable," which seemed to be an odd choice of words, until the author consulted a dictionary. It means "not to be appeased.")

Roosevelt described the other major events of 1942, particularly Japan's advances in the Philippines, the East Indies, Malaya, and Burma; the Allies' resistance in the Pacific and Indian Oceans; the British victory in North Africa; and the landing of American and British troops in North Africa. "The Axis powers knew that they must win the war in 1942—or eventually lose everything. I do not need to tell you that our enemies did not win the war in 1942," he said. Roosevelt called the Battle of Midway "our most important victory" in the war thus far. In saying so, he did not want to diminish the significance of our other victories in the Pacific, but Midway was unique because it was the first engagement against the Japanese that was essentially offensive in nature. "Last year, we stopped them," he said, "This year, we intend to advance."

When Roosevelt turned his attention to the European theater, he explained the Allied strategy to relieve pressure on the Russian front by opening a second front. The first part of this strategy was El Alamein—the first major victory in WWII by a British-led force, and thus a pivotal battle for the Allies in North Africa. The second part was the massive amphibious assault in French North Africa. Roosevelt was confident the Allies would drive the Axis powers completely out of North Africa when the final Allied assault took place. Roosevelt praised the Free French who had just joined the fight in North Africa and acknowledged America's other allies. "We pay tribute to the fighting leaders of our allies, to Winston Churchill, to Joseph Stalin, and to the Generalissimo Chiang Kai-shek. Yes, there is a very great unanimity between the leaders of the United Nations."

Roosevelt—and others—had been using the phrase "United Nations" for several months by then, but this instance is significant because Roosevelt listed the countries which would eventually comprise the permanent membership of the UN Security Council. To remind Americans what they were fighting for, Roosevelt raised the subject of the postwar world. "Victory in this war is the first and greatest goal before us," he said, and "Victory in the peace is the next." The peace following WWI was neither decent nor durable, so what we—the United Nations—were fighting for was a decent and durable peace with economic stability for the entire world. A durable peace would mean permanent disarmament of Germany, Italy, and Japan. In a thinly veiled criticism of Woodrow Wilson, Roosevelt said, "After the first World war we tried to achieve a formula for permanent peace, based on a *magnificent idealism*. We failed. But, by our failure, we have learned that we cannot maintain peace at this stage of human development by good intentions alone." (Italics added.)

During the first months of 1943, Roosevelt and Prime Minister Churchill met in Casablanca. In Tunisia, Americans met the Germans in battle in the Atlas Mountains at Kasserine Pass. In Poland, Nazis purged the Jewish ghetto in Krakow. In July, south of Moscow, the Battle of Kursk began, the largest tank battle in history. In the Solomon Islands, the American and Japanese navies met in battle. On the island of Sicily, Allied forces began their invasion of Europe. Allied forces began bombing Hamburg, causing a firestorm in the city. And in Italy, Benito Mussolini resigned.

In Roosevelt's July 1943 fireside chat, he reported the Axis powers were beginning to crack, and the corrupt Italian fascist regime was falling apart. Roosevelt called Mussolini a criminal, and said his resignation was a token gesture that would have no effect on the United States' demand for Italy's unconditional surrender. In Roosevelt's eyes, the Italian people were victims of fascist tyranny, so demanding unconditional surrender was not conquest but liberation. "It is our determination to restore these conquered peoples to the dignity of human beings, masters of their own fate, entitled to freedom of speech, freedom of religion, freedom from want, and freedom from fear." Surrender was the necessary first step on the path toward rebuilding the country—and establishing the four freedoms.

Once again, Roosevelt praised the success of the Soviets fighting on the eastern front, and called their efforts the "most decisive fighting" in the war. Perhaps a little too generous with his praise, Roosevelt said, "I am glad that the British and we have been able to *contribute somewhat* to the great striking power of the Russian armies."[11] As if he believed he could hold the alliance together with his charm, Roosevelt added, "The world has never seen greater devotion, determination, and self-sacrifice than have been displayed by the Russian people and their armies, under the leadership of Marshal Joseph Stalin." While it is true the Russian people demonstrated great devotion, determination, and self-sacrifice, it was under Stalin's threat to execute any soldier or officer who retreated.

•••

In August 1943, Allied forces arrived in Messina on the island of Sicily. In September, Allied forces under Montgomery invaded the Italian mainland, and General Dwight Eisenhower announced the Allies had reached an armistice with Italy. American and Japanese forces clashed repeatedly in the South Pacific. (Fighting was particularly fierce around the Gilbert and Solomon Islands.) Britain's Royal Air Force bombed the cities of Kassel and Berlin. In the United States, Roosevelt closed down the Works Progress Administration—one of the programs that epitomized the New Deal—because unemployment was no longer a problem. In Europe, General Dwight Eisenhower became supreme commander of all Allied forces.

In his 1943 Christmas Eve fireside chat, Roosevelt reported on his recent travels in the Middle East, recalling less than a month ago, he was "in a big Army transport plane over the little town of Bethlehem, in Palestine." Roosevelt was referring to his meetings in Cairo with Churchill and Chinese leader Chiang Kai-Shek, and then with Churchill and Stalin in Tehran. He reported the Cairo and Teheran conferences were devoted not merely to consideration of military strategy, but to postwar planning as well. Roosevelt and Churchill had met many times before and knew each other very well, but the conferences gave Roosevelt an opportunity to meet Chiang Kai-shek and Joseph Stalin for the first time.

At the Teheran conference, Roosevelt, Churchill, and Stalin agreed unanimously that Germany would have to be disarmed. The German people would not be "enslaved," said Roosevelt, but the country must be purged of Nazism, Prussian militarism, and any idea that Germans were a master race. Roosevelt mocked American isolationists (who he called "cheerful idiots"), who believed we could prevent war if we all stayed home and locked our front doors. Taking another jibe at Woodrow Wilson, he said, "The well-intentioned but ill-fated experiments of former years did not work." And just how could we make sure we did not repeat those tragic mistakes? "We must be prepared to keep the peace by force," he said.

Roosevelt praised Stalin for his relentless determination and stalwart good humor, and characterized his discussions with Stalin as "intense and consistently amicable." One issue over which Stalin was more intense than amicable was Operation Overlord—the proposed invasion of Nazi-occupied

France. Although the Red Army was steadily advancing toward Berlin, Stalin wanted to relieve pressure on the eastern front, and strongly urged Roosevelt and Churchill to launch the invasion of France sooner rather than later. Roosevelt then gave his prediction of what Germany could expect in 1944: "The Russian Army will continue its stern offensives on Germany's eastern front, the Allied armies in Italy and Africa will bring relentless pressure on Germany from the south, and now the encirclement will be complete as great American and British forces attack from other points of the compass."[12]

To begin his 1944 annual message, Roosevelt said the United States had become "an active partner" in the war against human slavery. Yet again, Roosevelt raised the issue of postwar planning, and reminded his audience of his Cairo and Teheran conferences, and Secretary of State Cordell Hull's Moscow conference. In addition to discussing management of the war, Roosevelt said the conferences also addressed the future peace. According to Roosevelt, "In the last war such discussions, such meetings, did not even begin until the shooting had stopped and the delegates began to assemble at the peace table. There had been no previous opportunities for man-to-man discussions which lead to meetings of minds. The result was a peace which was not a peace. That was a mistake which we are not repeating in this war."[13]

We know Woodrow Wilson shared his postwar vision of "peace without victory" in January 1917, months before he asked the Senate to declare war, and two years before the Paris peace conference. As if the ghosts of Woodrow Wilson and Henry Cabot Lodge were both standing behind Roosevelt whispering their warnings, Roosevelt reassured his audience he had negotiated no secret deals. "Of course we made some commitments," military commitments he said, but "no secret treaties or political or financial commitments." He said it was in the nation's and the world's best interest to "join together in a just and durable system of peace." Finally, Roosevelt said his "supreme objective" was national security.

•••

On June 5, 1944, Allied forces captured Rome, a symbolic victory because the strategic objective in the region had always been to control the Mediterranean, the shipping channels, the islands, and the ports in order to secure Allied supply lines. However, the capture of Rome came at an auspicious time because Allied forces were getting ready for another attack. The following day, Allied forces would land in Normandy, France.

At the 1943 Teheran conference, Roosevelt and Churchill had committed themselves to opening up a second front in Western Europe to relieve pressure on the Soviets on the eastern front. The second front opened in the wee hours of June 6, 1944, when Allied paratroopers landed in Normandy and gunships opened a massive artillery barrage on the shore area. Thousands of vessels, aircraft, landing craft, and men crossed the English Channel and assaulted German defensive positions, part of the Atlantic Wall.

Although casualties were high, the Allies secured the beach within a few days. They towed two artificial "Mulberry" harbors across the channel in order to expedite delivering supplies. The invasion was stalled temporarily in the countryside behind the beaches, which were covered with tall hedgerows growing on banks one to two hundred yards apart. The hedgerow country worked to the Germans' advantage on the defensive and made maneuvering tanks difficult. German forces put up strong resistance as British forces tried to capture the key city of Caen. When the Germans committed their reserves against British forces in late July, American forces broke out and advanced east, toward Paris and Berlin. French forces entered Paris later that summer.

On June 12, 1944, less than a week after the Allied invasion, Roosevelt again spoke to the nation in a fireside chat. Roosevelt wanted to respond to his critics—and remind his audience—how different the world looked just two years earlier. The Germans were in control of almost all of Europe and they were on the offensive in Russia; they were in control of most of North Africa and threatening the Suez Canal. The Japanese were in control of most of the Central Pacific, and driving toward Australia and New Zealand. "But today we are on the offensive all over the world," he said, "bringing the attack to our enemies." Allied submarine, naval, and air attacks inflicted so much damage on the Japanese they no longer had the power to stop the Allies' forward momentum.

Because Roosevelt and his military advisors decided to defeat Germany first, the fall of Tokyo was still a long way away. As soon as the Allies captured Berlin, Roosevelt said he would shift resources to the Pacific and force the Japanese to surrender unconditionally. Meanwhile, Soviet forces were inflicting severe punishment on the Germans in the eastern front. Allied ground forces were advancing up the Italian peninsula, and Allied air forces were destroying German war industries from the sky.

●●●

In July 1944, the world's major industrialized economies signed the Bretton Woods agreement. British and Canadian forces captured Caen. Hideki Tojo resigned as prime minister of Japan. American forces invaded the island of Guam. In August, delegates from Britain, China, Russia, and the United States gathered in Washington, DC (the Dumbarton Oaks Conference) to discuss creation of the United Nations. Allied forces liberated Paris in August and Brussels in September. In October, Churchill and Stalin met in Moscow to discuss the future of Europe.

In the fall of 1944, American naval forces engaged the Japanese navy in the Battle of Leyte Gulf. Although Allied forces suffered substantial losses, they sank a Japanese destroyer and several carriers (including the *Zuikaku*, the last remaining Japanese carrier that attacked Pearl Harbor), and effectively eliminated Japan's ability to project power in the Pacific. Later, American forces would begin bombing Tokyo. In November, Franklin Roosevelt defeated Thomas Dewey and won reelection to a fourth term with Missouri senator Harry Truman as his running mate.

In mid-December 1944, Germany launched a ferocious surprise counterattack through the Ardennes Forest against Allied forces in eastern Belgium. The Ardennes offensive—known as the Battle of the Bulge—would be Germany's last major offensive on the western front. Germany's objective was to cut the Allied line in the center, slow the Allied advance toward Berlin, and then recapture the Belgian port city of Antwerp. Aided by winter weather (low visibility limited the effectiveness of Allied air power), the surprise attack was successful and thousands of Allied troops were wounded, killed, or captured. When the Germans surrounded the American 101st Airborne Division in Bastogne and demanded their surrender, General Anthony McAuliffe politely refused. Running low on fuel and ammunition, the German advance stalled west of Bastogne near the Meuse River.

In his 1945 annual message, Roosevelt reported on the recent events in Ardennes Forest and Belgium, suggesting the German offensive had already reached high tide. Since Christmas, Allied forces resumed the offensive and relieved the troops at Bastogne, while Germans forces were in full retreat. Then Roosevelt gave a fascinating review of the strategy he used to manage the war for the previous three years, and which would eventually lead the country to victory. Roosevelt knew the country's natural resources and superior production capacity would eventually prove decisive, but early in the conflict, what the United States needed most was time to mobilize the economy and develop its armed forces. The early battles in both theaters—Europe and the Pacific—were defensive, fought as delaying actions in order to buy time to build the overwhelming force needed to destroy Japan's and Germany's will and capacity to make war.

He explained his decision to defeat Germany first and then Japan as follows: the Europe-first strategy was militarily and morally right "from the very day we were attacked," he said, because we could not "throw Britain and Russia to the Nazi wolves." In addition, attacking the numerous Japanese garrisons with coordinated air, ground, and naval forces throughout the Pacific required extensive preliminary operations to establish and secure our supply lines. In contrast, because the bases we needed to assault Germany directly were already available—on the unsinkable aircraft carrier known as Great Britain (which is the largest island of the British Isles)—we could begin operations as soon as we put troops in the field.

It was hard to argue with the results: the Allies liberated Belgium, France, and Greece, plus parts of Czechoslovakia, Holland, Norway, Poland, and Yugoslavia. Romania and Bulgaria had surrendered. And now, Allied forces were invading Germany. In the Pacific, Allied forces liberated many Pacific Islands, and were beginning to bomb the Japanese home islands from the air. The greatest victory so far was of course the Allied invasion of Normandy, followed by the steady advance across France, Belgium, and Luxembourg almost to the banks of the Rhine River. Roosevelt said Operation Overlord was "the greatest amphibious operation in the history of the world." (The Allied invasion of Leyte was the largest amphibious operation in the Pacific.) The thing that made Operation Overlord so great, said Roosevelt was the ability of two nations—Britain and America—to plan, work, and fight together in close cooperation.

Victory in the protracted Battle of the Atlantic was another huge factor that made the Allies' other victories possible. "Without this success over German submarines" said Roosevelt, "we could not have built up our invasion forces or air forces in Great Britain, nor could we have kept a steady stream of supplies flowing to them after they had landed in France." The Germans had been harassing ships sailing between North America and Britain since 1939, and had sunk hundreds of thousands of tons. However, in 1941 the British Royal Navy captured an *enigma* cryptography machine from a German submarine, which enabled the allies to decode German communications and track U-boat locations. Eventually the Allies sailed exclusively in convoys, which proved to be one of a series of defensive tactics against Germany's "wolfpack" approach. Technological advances in sonar and radar enabled the Allies' new long-range planes to patrol shipping channels and provide air cover for convoys, but the Battle of the Atlantic would continue until Germany surrendered.

In his 1945 annual message, Roosevelt also reported on the Italian campaign, which he believed some members of the press and public might have underrated because of the well-publicized Normandy invasion. Even though the Italian campaign was no longer the only front in Western Europe, it was still an important part of the overall strategy to defeat the Germans. Allied forces from the United States, Britain, Brazil, and other countries were fighting across the mountainous Italian terrain to keep the pressure on twenty German divisions, which might otherwise be fighting elsewhere.

In the Pacific, said Roosevelt, U.S. forces have driven Japanese forces back more than three thousand miles. After recapturing the Philippines and numerous other islands, the United States began to bomb the Japanese from a base in the Mariana Islands. He was particularly proud of the joint army and navy operations between Admiral Halsey and General MacArthur during the Battle of Leyte Gulf. Making sure not to overlook any theater of operation, Roosevelt said he was "rendering all possible aid to China." At that time, all aid into China was arriving by air. Allied air forces, which included many Chinese pilots, had flown over thirty-five thousand sorties against the Japanese in 1944. They sank thousands of tons of ships and helped halt Japan's advances in Burma.

Once again, Roosevelt turned his attention to the postwar peace: "In the field of foreign policy, we propose to stand together with the United Nations not for the war alone but for the victory for which the war is fought." As in many of Roosevelt's previous speeches, his rhetoric was a balance of pragmatism and idealism. He said the Allies were an association of people, not governments, and the hope of all people—in England, Russia, China, France, and throughout the world—was for a secure and durable peace. Reminiscent of George Washington's advice to make no permanent alliances or permanent enemies, Roosevelt said the closer the Allies came to victory, the more conscious we would become of our differences, and he warned his listeners not let our differences blind us to our common interests. Then Roosevelt provided a one-paragraph summary of the doctrine of practical idealism in nonpolicy wonk terms:

> In the future world the misuse of power, as implied in the term "power politics," must not be a controlling factor in international relations. That is the heart of the principles to which we have subscribed. We cannot deny that power is a factor in world politics any more than we can deny its existence as a factor in national politics. But in a democratic world, as in a democratic Nation, power must be linked with responsibility, and obliged to defend and justify itself within the framework of the general good.[14]

In his 1945 inaugural address two weeks later, Roosevelt spoke very briefly—just 450 words. He repeated familiar themes, particularly his vision of an international order capable of sustaining peace—but only after the United States achieved *total victory in war*.

•••

In February 1945, American troops assaulted Iwo Jima on their way north to Japan. Iwo Jima, an island 750 miles south of Japan, served as a forward communications post to warn the Japanese home islands of incoming Allied bombers. The battle began with a massive naval and air bombardment followed by an amphibious assault. When the marines hit the beeches, Japanese troops fired on them from an extensive network of caves, concrete bunkers, and pillboxes. The marines fought their way up Suribachi Mountain and planted the American flag on February 23, but because of the stubborn, determined resistance of the Japanese, it would take another month to secure the island. There were more than twenty thousand Japanese troops stationed on the island, and fewer than eleven hundred survived. The Americans lost more than twenty-six thousand killed and wounded.

Elsewhere early in 1945, the Red Army entered Warsaw, and then arrived at the Auschwitz Concentration Camp. Allied aircraft bombed Dresden, causing a firestorm in which thousands of civilians died. American aircraft bombed Tokyo, causing a similar firestorm in which tens of thousands of civilians died. The Red Army occupied Hungary, and Allied troops returned to Bataan and Manila. Roosevelt, Churchill, and Stalin met at Yalta, on the north shore of the Black Sea. With the end of the war in sight and Roosevelt's health beginning to fail, the big three agreed to disarm and demilitarize Germany and created the Allied Control Council, which divided Germany into four occupation zones. They also agreed to allow elections in the liberated countries, begin negotiations to establish the United Nations, and assess war reparations payments against Germany.

On March 1, Roosevelt addressed Congress to report the results of the Yalta conference. His two main goals for the conference were to ensure Germany's unconditional surrender and "to build the foundation for an international accord that would bring order and security after the chaos of the war." Roosevelt, Churchill, and Stalin also discussed the political control and reconstruction of countries freed from the Nazis. "Days were spent in discussing these momentous matters and we argued freely and frankly across the table," he said, "But at the end, on every point, unanimous agreement was reached." The British, Soviets, and Americans remained united in their common goal to defeat Germany, but Roosevelt's report that the allies shared a common vision of the postwar peace was overly optimistic.

Unconditional surrender means Great Britain, Russia, France, and the United States each control an occupation zone in Germany. The Allies would abolish the Nazi Party, put Nazi war criminals on trial, dismantle Germany's armed forces, and destroy Germany's capacity to produce armaments. Roosevelt explicitly stated he wanted to avoid the mistakes made after WWI when we demanded Germany make monetary war reparations payments. "We do not want the German people to starve, or to become a burden on the rest of the world," he said, "Our objective in handling Germany is simple—it is to secure the peace of the rest of the world now and in the future."[15]

Roosevelt predicted (erroneously) Yalta would signal the "end of the system of unilateral action, the exclusive alliances, the spheres of influence, the balances of power, and all the other expedients that have been tried for centuries—and have always failed." The negotiations regarding Poland proved otherwise. At Yalta, Poland would lose approximately 20 percent of its territory (almost thirty thousand square miles) and receive a large tract of eastern Germany, though no representatives from Poland attended. (As a reminder, Germany invaded Poland in 1939, approximately one week after Germany and the Soviet Union signed the Molotov-RibbentropPact, which assigned spheres of influence in Eastern Europe.) Roosevelt feebly called the new agreement on Poland an "outstanding example of joint action."

•••

That spring, the Red Army entered Berlin and Vienna. American troops landed on the island of Okinawa. Allied forces arrived at the Buchenwald

Concentration Camp. On April 12, in Warm Springs, Georgia, Franklin Roosevelt died of a cerebral hemorrhage. Vice President Harry Truman, the modest former senator from Missouri, took the oath of office later that day. In late April, Benito Mussolini was captured, beaten, and killed, and Adolf Hitler committed suicide.

In early May 1945, Truman announced Germany's formal surrender. In July, Truman, Stalin, and Churchill (along with Clement Atlee) met at Potsdam near Berlin. On August 6 and again on August 9, American forces attacked Hiroshima and Nagasaki with nuclear weapons, killing more than a hundred thousand civilians. On September 1, Truman announced Japan's formal surrender.[16] On October 24, 1945, representatives from fifty countries met in San Francisco at the United Nations (UN) Conference on International Organization, and drafted the UN Charter. The United Nations was officially born.

PART III

Cold War and Limited War, 1946–1988

6

Limited War I: Korea
Truman Doctrine; Marshall Plan; National Security Act; Desegregating the Military; North Atlantic Treaty Organization; Korean War

In Truman's 1946 annual message, he recalled Roosevelt's words from his last annual message, in which he predicted the watershed events of 1945, the demise of fascism in Europe, the defeat of Nazi Germany and Imperial Japan, and the birth of the United Nations. "It was the greatest year of achievement in human history," said Truman. In the lengthy foreign policy section of his message, Truman envisioned a sustainable peace built on the foundation of the Allied victory. The first task was to deprive our enemies of the will and ability to start another war. (Truman called it "clinching" our victory.) The second task was to make sure our allies did not become enemies.

Truman reported on the conferences at Yalta and Potsdam, plus the meeting in London of the Council of Foreign Ministers from the previous September. He reported on the Inter-American Conference on Problems of War and Peace held in Mexico City. The most significant accomplishment of the Mexico conference was a collective security agreement, in which an attack on any member would be considered an act of aggression against every member. According to Truman, the long list of international conferences and meetings was proof of the United States' commitment to prevent war.

Topping the list was the first meeting of the UN General Assembly. Truman called it "the real beginning of our bold adventure toward the preservation of world peace." Truman said it was important for the United Nations to succeed because small and large countries alike would all have a voice. He pledged, however, never to sacrifice American ideals, our vital interests or the interests of our friends just to keep the peace. Here is an example of Truman's clear thinking on practical idealism: "The power which the United States demonstrated during the war is the fact that underlies every phase of our relations with other countries. We cannot escape the responsibility which it thrusts upon us. What we think, plan, say, and do is of profound significance to the future of every corner of the world."

This was not a reminder he was the only chief executive in history to order a nuclear attack—no reminder was necessary. It was a report on the state of the union, in the world as he saw it. Relations between the United States and other nations were fundamentally political: based on power. Truman acknowledged the United States was in a very strong position with a huge advantage in power relative to the rest of the world. Because of this power differential, the burden of responsibility (balancing pragmatism and idealism) rested squarely on the United States.

Truman then outlined the fundamental principles of his foreign policy, paraphrased and condensed below:

1. We have no plans for territorial expansion or aggression against any other state.
2. All people have the right to sovereignty and self-government.
3. All people have the right to self-government without foreign interference.
4. We will not approve of any territorial changes unless the people concerned agree.
5. We pledge to help our defeated enemies establish peaceful democratic governments.
6. We refuse to recognize any government forced on any nation by a foreign power.
7. All nations have equal rights to navigate the seas, rivers, and waterways.
8. All states should have equal access to the world's raw materials.
9. Countries in the Western Hemisphere will work together without outside interference.
10. We will promote economic collaboration to improve standards of living for everyone.
11. We will promote freedom of expression and freedom of religion.
12. We will work with the United Nations to promote peace, but if necessary, we will use force.[1]

•••

In mid-March 1947, Truman addressed a joint session of Congress. In this speech, Truman requested four hundred million dollars in economic aid and relief assistance for Greece and Turkey. Although the purpose of the aid was to counter the communist threat in Europe, Truman did not specifically use the word "containment" in the speech. George Kennan's famous "X" article in which he coined containment as a long-term strategy to counter Soviet expansion would not appear in the journal *Foreign Affairs* until July 1947.

Because Great Britain could no longer afford to help the Greek government fight their civil war against communist insurgents, Truman announced the United States would provide support to Greece and Turkey to check communist influence in the Mediterranean. Truman said communist "terrorists" (many of whom were former members of the resistance movement fighting Nazi occupation) were threatening the existence of the Greek state. Acknowledging Greece's problems with corruption and election fraud, he said with some understatement, "The Government of Greece is not perfect." Even so, we had an obligation to help.

One of the reasons we fought WWII, he said, was for a way of life free from coercion. One of the reasons we took the lead in creating the United Nations was to make freedom and independence possible for all members. This became the premise of the Truman Doctrine: totalitarian regimes were inherently aggressive and therefore a threat to international peace and U.S. national security. Once you accept the premise and consider the specter of appeasement, then appeasing communists is just as bad as appeasing fascists. Once you accept the premise that only the United States is in a position to help people maintain their freedom against totalitarian regimes, then containment of communism is the only choice Truman could have made.

Truman said something else in this speech, which years later would prove prescient: "It is necessary only to glance at a map to realize that the survival and integrity of the Greek nation are of grave importance in a much wider situation. If Greece should fall under the control of an armed minority, the effect upon its neighbor, Turkey, would be immediate and serious. Confusion and disorder might well spread throughout the entire Middle East."[2] Of course, this is the domino theory—years before Eisenhower used the phrase—which asserts communist takeover of one country threatens other countries in the region. On this basis, the United States would provide support to countries resisting communist takeover, "primarily through economic and financial assistance." Note the word primarily, which does not exclude military assistance. The origin of this is, of course, Roosevelt's Four Freedoms Speech, which pledged support for people who resisted aggression everywhere, not only those resisting communism.

On June 5, 1947, less than ninety days following the announcement of the Truman Doctrine, Secretary of State George Marshall gave a speech at Harvard University, where he announced the European Recovery Program. The Marshall Plan, as it would be called, provided aid and loans over a four-year period to rebuild the social, political, and economic structure of postwar Europe. Like Truman, Marshall believed the United States had a responsibility to rebuild Europe's economy. Like Truman, Marshall also shared the popular assumption that hunger and poverty exacerbate political instability—and facilitate the spread of communism.

In July 1947, the U.S. National Security Act created the Central Intelligence Agency, Department of Defense, Joint Chiefs of Staff, and the National Security Council. In November, the UN General Assembly voted to partition Palestine between the Arabs and Jews.

In Truman's 1948 annual message, he said his highest foreign policy priority was to support the global economic system disrupted by the war. The centerpiece was of course the Marshall Plan, which he called the "decisive contribution to world peace." He urged Congress to fund the European Recovery Program through mid-1952. For Truman, practical idealism was more than a theory. It was "a sound, constructive, and practical course in carrying out our determination to achieve peace."

•••

In June 1948, the Soviet Union blockaded West Berlin, and the United States launched the Berlin airlift in response. In May, Israel became a sovereign state, and was then attacked by Egypt, Transjordan, Lebanon, Syria, Iraq, and Saudi Arabia. In the United States, the first peacetime draft was established.

•••

One recurring criticism of American foreign policy is hypocrisy, because at home anyway, we do not always practice what we preach. In particular, African-Americans fighting overseas during WWII were denied basic human rights when they returned home. In July 1948, Truman issued Executive Order 9981, which led to the desegregation of the American military. As Truman declared, "there shall be equality of treatment and opportunity for all persons in the armed services without regard to race, color, religion or national origin."[3] Rather than deny our obvious shortcomings or allow our imperfections to become an excuse for inaction, Truman based his action on the one redeeming feature of all democracies: the defects are always visible.

Truman deserved credit for taking action to solve an ugly problem, but he had to campaign vigorously during the 1948 presidential election to avoid being voted out of office. Although Truman's supporters would shout, "Give 'em hell, Harry," his cold war and civil rights policies were not universally popular. However, in November 1948, Truman narrowly won reelection over Thomas Dewey, the Republican governor of New York.

Truman used the occasion of his one and only inaugural address to fill in a few of the blanks of the Truman Doctrine. His "essential principles" were freedom and equality. Applied to foreign policy, all nations therefore had the right to self-determination and self-government. Although this might appear identical to Woodrow Wilson, it is not. For Wilson, self-determination was the antidote to war, but for Truman self-determination was the antidote to communism. Wilson's ambition was to end war for all time, while Truman's ambition was to defeat a rival political and economic system. Regardless of the recognition that Ronald Reagan receives for winning the cold war, the United States won because it relentlessly enforced the Truman Doctrine.[4]

In April 1949, Truman announced creation of the NATO (North Atlantic Treaty Organization). The original members were Belgium, Canada, Denmark, France, Iceland, Italy, Luxembourg, the Netherlands, Norway, Portugal, the United Kingdom, and the United States. Greece and Turkey would become members in 1952 and West Germany in 1955. The stated purpose of NATO was to promote peace, stability, and security in the North Atlantic area. The treaty's preamble reaffirmed, and gave teeth to the general principles of the United Nations. The heart of the treaty was—and still is— the collective security agreement in Article 5, which states an attack against any member is an attack against all members.[5]

Truman considered NATO the first step toward creating sustainable peace and prosperity among the members. As we have already learned, however, it was not the first step or even the second, but one of several practical applications of the Truman Doctrine. Although several of Truman's successors placed a great deal of emphasis on their anticommunist credentials, the Truman Doctrine (like the man himself) was more prodemocracy and proconsultation than anticommunist. The NATO treaty was "a simple document" he said, "but if it had existed in 1914 and in 1939, supported by the nations who are represented here today, I believe it would have prevented the acts of aggression which led to two world wars." It is impossible to say for certain, but he was probably right.

•••

Throughout 1949, Mao Zedong consolidated his power in China. By October, the People's Republic was formally established, and by December Kuomintang forces under Chiang Kai-shek withdrew to the island of Formosa (Taiwan). In Israel, elections were held for the first time and David Ben-Gurion became prime minister. In May 1949, Israel became a member of the United Nations. The Soviet Union lifted the Berlin blockade. In August, they tested their first nuclear weapon.

In late October 1949, Truman delivered a speech in New York City to dedicate the new UN headquarters, which Truman called "the center of man's hope for peace" and "the most important buildings in the world." October 24 was UN Day—the fourth anniversary of the day the UN Charter went into effect. Truman said the United Nations embodied the principles expressed in its charter: the commitment to peace and a better life for people the world over. It was because of this commitment the United Nations was greater than any one of its members, and thus could never be ignored, infringed, or dissolved. In this respect, said Truman, the United Nations was like the U.S. Constitution, an expression of the will of the people for peace and unity.

Truman was particularly pleased with the United Nations' Universal Declaration of Human Rights and the Convention on Genocide. In the past, disrespect for human rights was how tyranny and war began, but now respect for human rights had become "a matter of international concern." He was adamant that men and women everywhere—without regard to race, language, or religion—all had equal rights. Once again, Truman used the occasion to expand on another element of the Truman Doctrine: technical assistance to underdeveloped countries. There could be no permanent peace while hundreds of millions of men, women, and children lacked adequate food, clothing, and shelter. The challenges of the twentieth century were not natural forces, he said, but human relations—a penetrating insight spoken in Truman's typical midwestern way.

In his 1950 annual message, Truman's comments on foreign policy were brief. He said the United States' bipartisan foreign policy goal was peace. Our bipartisan principles—meaning American principles—stood for peace and freedom, and against tyranny and oppression. As if the antidote to isolationism was the more entanglements the better, Truman expressed his "wholehearted support" not just for the United Nations, but also for a host of international organizations. Truman strongly recommended the United States join the International Trade Organization and was particularly hopeful about the role the United Nations and the International Atomic Energy Commission could play in limiting and controlling "weapons of mass destruction."[6]

•••

In January 1950, the United Kingdom and Israel gave diplomatic recognition to the PRC (People's Republic of China). In February, the Soviet Union and PRC signed a mutual defense treaty. In March, the Soviet Union announced development of a nuclear weapon. And on June 25, 1950, the Korean War began.

On July 19, Truman addressed the nation about events on the Korean Peninsula. "Korea is a small country, thousands of miles away" he said, "but what is happening there is important to every American." The attack was a clear violation of the UN Charter and showed the contempt North Korea's communist leaders had for the United Nations' basic principles. The attack made the territorial ambition of the communist movement apparent to everyone. Following WWII, said Truman, Japanese forces in Korea surrendered to American forces south of the thirty-eighth parallel and to Soviet forces north of the thirty-eighth parallel. The United Nations tried to establish Korea as an independent sovereign nation, and a UN commission was sent to supervise an election. The Soviets refused to participate in the UN-sponsored election, and installed a communist government in

North Korea under Kim Il-Sung. In 1948, the Republic of Korea was established south of the thirty-eighth parallel, and Syngman Rhee became president.

On June 25, North Korean troops launched an attack across the thirty-eighth parallel. "It was an act of raw aggression, without a shadow of justification," he said. Truman, who was in his hometown of Independence, Missouri when he received word of the attack from Secretary of State Dean Acheson, authorized Acheson to request an emergency meeting of the UN Security Council—which took place less than twenty-four hours later. In a subsequent meeting, the Security Council recommended members of the United Nations help defend South Korea and restore peace. When fifty-two of fifty-nine members agreed to support South Korea's defense, Truman was pleased to report the United Nations learned the lesson of Munich: "Appeasement leads only to further aggression and ultimately to war."[7]

After the UN vote, Australia, Britain, Canada, France, the Netherlands, and New Zealand joined U.S. forces under the UN flag, all under the command of General Douglas MacArthur. American and Australian air force and navy aircraft supported a delaying action, which prevented the North from completely overrunning the Korean Peninsula. With support from naval and air forces, U.S. ground troops forced North Korea to make costly frontal attacks, which slowed their advance and allowed MacArthur to bring in more reinforcements. South Korean and American forces established a secure base in the southern part of the peninsula near Pusan, approximately two hundred miles southeast of Seoul.

So far, this was the first major test of the United States' willingness to enforce the Truman Doctrine, and a sign of things to come. In his July 19 address, Truman said it was time to increase the United States' military strength, and listed three requirements. First, send more men, equipment, and supplies to Korea. Second, build up our armed forces over and above the needs in Korea. And third, expedite our work developing common defenses with other countries. Truman said he would ask Congress to increase defense spending and announced his intention "to make substantial increases in taxes" to help finance national defense requirements.

In September 1950, UN troops landed behind the North Korean troops at Inchon, approximately twenty miles west of Seoul. The UN troops gained a foothold on the beach, captured Seoul, and cut North Korea's supply lines. As the North retreated up the peninsula, UN forces followed in hot pursuit and linked up with the troops at Inchon. The UN forces drove the North back across the thirty-eighth parallel—ignoring warnings from the Chinese government. In mid-October, Chinese forces (massed along the Yalu River) crossed the river and attacked. Some of the toughest fighting took place in late November, in the mountains of North Korea during the Battle of Chosin Reservoir. With aircraft borrowed from the Soviet Union, the Chinese forces pushed the UN troops back over the thirty-eighth parallel toward Hungnam, on the east coast. Shortly after New Year's Day, Chinese and North Korean forces recaptured Seoul.

In Truman's 1951 annual message, he said American troops in Korea were resisting the attempt of the communist dictatorship of the Soviet Union to take over the world one country at a time. When the Soviets' subversive methods did not work, he said, they induced their "puppet states" to provoke a proxy war. Seeing no difference between Soviet imperialism and the czar's, Truman accused them of being "more ambitious, more crafty, and more menacing" than ever. Interestingly, Truman mentioned China only twice in his 1951 message, once when describing the United States' history of friendly relations in Asia, and again when he conveniently blamed "Soviet imperialists" for the 1949 communist revolution in China.

Fortunately, said Truman, the free world had the power, resources, and principles to counter the Soviet threat. Our principles gave us the kind of power communism would never have. Our principles united us with our friends and allies in a way the Soviet Empire never could. Then Truman shifted his war rationale from American principles toward American interests, almost identical to the argument Franklin Roosevelt made in 1942 regarding the consequences if crucial resources or shipping channels fell into enemy German or Japanese hands. "If Western Europe were to fall to Soviet Russia," said Truman, "it would double the Soviet supply of coal and triple the Soviet supply of steel. If Western Europe were to fall or if our access to raw materials disrupted, the communists could impose their will on the world without ever having to attack the US directly. If the free countries of Asia and Africa should fall to Soviet Russia, we would lose the sources of many of our most vital raw materials, including uranium, which is the basis of our atomic power."

Not surprisingly, Truman had "a practical, realistic program of action" to meet the challenge. First, he pledged to provide economic assistance to stop the spread of communism and promote economic development. People with jobs, homes, and a future would be our strongest allies against the Kremlin, and the "electrifying result" of the Marshall Plan gave us all the proof we needed. Truman also advocated increasing economic assistance to "our good neighbors" in Central and South America and other parts of the world. He urged Congress to increase defense spending and enact a "major increase in taxes to meet the cost of the defense effort." Finally, he promised to help friendly countries defend themselves by providing military assistance to Europe and Asia, particularly Japan and Korea. To preempt his critics, he reminded them of the disastrous consequences of appeasement in Manchuria in 1931, Ethiopia in 1935, and Austria in 1938. If we had stood up then as we are doing now, he said, the history of the twentieth century would have been very different.[8]

•••

In February 1951, the twenty-second amendment to the U.S. Constitution was ratified, which established presidential term limits. In March, UN forces attacked Chinese and North Korean forces and recaptured Seoul. In Western Europe, six countries (including Belgium, France, Holland, Italy, Luxembourg, and West Germany) established the European Coal and Steel Community. Based on French foreign minister Robert Schuman's proposal to integrate West Europe's coal and steel industries, Jean Monnet became the first president of this predecessor to the European Union. In July, negotiations to end the Korean War began. In September, the United States, Australia, and New Zealand signed the ANZUS (Australia, New Zealand, United States security) Treaty.

In the spring of 1951, Truman relieved General MacArthur from command, and replaced him with General Matthew Ridgeway. On April 11, Truman spoke to the nation about his policies in Korea and the Far East. "In the simplest terms" he said, "what we are doing in Korea is this: We are trying to prevent a third world war. I think most people in this country recognized that fact last June."[9] Truman wanted to remind the country the Soviet Union would not stop trying to spread communism everywhere it could. The United States had no choice but to prevent it, he said, although if we did have choices with respect to the timing and the means. Truman asked, "What is the best time to meet the threat and how is the best way to meet it?" Paving the way for George W. Bush's rationale for the Iraq War fifty years later, Truman said, "The best time to meet the threat is in the beginning. It is easier to put out a fire in the beginning when it is small than after it has become a roaring blaze."

As he did before, Truman drew an analogy to the late 1930s, before the shooting started and Hitler could still have been stopped, when the fire could have been extinguished while it was small. The cold war looked very different in 1951 than it did in the late 1980s when the corrupt and corroded Soviet Union was on the verge of collapse. In 1951, communists were probing for weakness everywhere they could, in Greece, Berlin, and Korea—the "boldest and most dangerous move" they had made thus far. The lesson Truman wanted to teach the Soviets was aggression would always have a price and never come easy.

Truman said he deliberately chose to fight a limited war in Korea to *prevent* a third world war, not start one. In addition, he was proud the conflict had not spread beyond Korea, a clear repudiation of Douglas MacArthur's unwise recommendation to bomb mainland China or Manchuria—perhaps with nuclear weapons. If we did that, said Truman, we could start a general war, entangle ourselves in Asia, and produce the exact opposite of what we are trying to accomplish. Because MacArthur disagreed with that policy, Truman felt compelled to relieve him to avoid any misunderstanding about what the policy was—or who the commander in chief was.

In his 1952 annual message, Truman said his first priority was to stabilize the situation in Korea and resist the Chinese "invasion." That meant more fighting until we could negotiate a settlement without resorting to appeasement. Truman also reported the Soviet Union recently tested two nuclear bombs and continued to increase its already excessive armed forces. Failing to improve our civil defense system would be "an open invitation" to a surprise nuclear attack. He spoke directly to those who thought he was exaggerating the severity of the threat, reminding them of three fundamental elements of practical idealism. First, one Pearl Harbor is enough and we should do everything in our power never to let anything like it happen again. Second, we need our allies and they need us. Third, our values and principles are in constant danger, and every generation has the responsibility to defend them.[10]

•••

With Truman's popularity among voters plummeting, he chose not to run for reelection. Many Republicans and Democrats admired former commander Dwight Eisenhower, and both parties courted him over the years. Eventually, Eisenhower chose to run as a Republican, and easily won the 1952 presidential election. In late November, president-elect Eisenhower would fulfill a campaign promise to travel to Korea.

Truman delivered his 1953 annual message two weeks before Eisenhower took the oath of office. He chose the occasion to summarize his nearly eight-year presidency. Truman took the oath of office on April 12, 1945. The following month the Nazis surrendered. "Then, in July" he said, "that great white flash of light, man-made at Alamogordo, heralded swift and final victory in World War II—and opened the doorway to the atomic age."

Among his successes, Truman counted creating the Department of Defense and the National Security Council. The major work in progress was the development of a durable structure of security and world peace. "That is still the overriding question of our time" he said, "We cannot know the answer yet; perhaps we will not know it finally for a long time to come." WWII radically altered the distribution of power in the world, and the United States and Soviet Union, with their vast human and natural resources, emerged as the two strongest nations. What a tragedy it was for the postwar world these two nations believed in principles diametrically opposed to one another. Regardless, Americans still had a duty to share the inheritance of the American Revolution, and help nations devastated from war rebuild their political and economic institutions, not as satellites but as full partners.

Unfortunately, said Truman, the Soviet Union's goal was exactly the opposite. Whereas we believe God created people with inalienable rights, the Soviets believe people had no rights and lived at the whim of the state. When the Kremlin looked at the postwar world, they saw it as an opportunity for exploitation, not reconstruction. All one had to do was look at the map of Europe. To the west, Europe was thriving. To the east, Europe suffered under the cold, gray uniformity of Soviet dictatorship. Nothing could illustrate more clearly the difference between our values and theirs. Nothing else was necessary to explain why we had to fight and win the cold war.

Truman lamented it was not that long ago when the Americans and Russians were allies fighting the Nazis. We hoped our wartime collaboration would continue into peacetime, but it was not meant to be. The world was divided because every agreement the United States made with the Soviets in wartime, they violated in peacetime. "They, not we, began the Cold War," he said.

According to Truman, this is what we faced:

> The Soviet Union occupies a territory of 8 million square miles. Beyond its borders, East and West, are the nearly five million square miles of the satellite states—virtually incorporated into the Soviet Union—and of China, now its close partner. This vast land mass contains an enormous store of natural resources sufficient to support an economic development comparable to our own. That is the Stalinist world. It is a world of great natural diversity in geography and climate, in distribution of resources, in population, language, and living standards, in economic and cultural development. It is a world whose people are not all convinced communists by any means. It is a world where history and national traditions, particularly in its borderlands, tend more toward separation than unification, and run counter to the enforced combination that has been made of these areas today.[11]

Their secret police were everywhere and had unlimited authority. They used terror and slavery as instruments of official policy. Although the Communist Party had a monopoly on power, their one great weakness, said Truman, was they bled their people white to maintain their huge military establishment. Given their geographic location in Europe and Asia, their vast human and natural resources and ruthless system of government, what could they possibly be trying to accomplish? They are trying to extend the boundaries of communism whenever, wherever, and however they can. They used whatever means available to them: their own armed forces, armed insurrection, and labor revolts. Of course, they also used propaganda. Their Marxist interpretation of history was the distorted lens through which they saw the world. Although "They seem really to believe that history is on their side," Truman predicted the Soviet Union would "eventually have to change its ways or fall."

Truman spoke at length about nuclear weapons. When the United States was the world's only nuclear power (1945–1949), it was enough to deter a nuclear attack. When the Soviets announced they possessed nuclear weapons—nine months before North Korea invaded the south—the United

States' new challenge was to maintain its technological leadership in the field. The new challenge was also to develop a new strategic doctrine. Truman believed his administration successfully met the challenge through a combination of military buildup, scientific advances, and economic development. Truman emphasized we could never have national security without economic development. Because of scientific breakthroughs during his term, the United States' nuclear weapons were far more powerful than earlier models, which Truman said were "capable of creating explosions of a new order of magnitude, dwarfing the mushroom clouds of Hiroshima and Nagasaki." In Truman's words: "The war of the future would be one in which man could extinguish millions of lives at one blow, demolish the great cities of the world, wipe out the cultural achievements of the past—and destroy the very structure of a civilization that has been slowly and painfully built up through hundreds of generations. Such a war is not a possible policy for rational men."[12]

One week before Dwight Eisenhower took the oath of office, Truman delivered his farewell address. He offered no revelations, and had no political statements or policy announcements to make. He wondered what historians would write about his presidency and hoped people would remember the course he set toward winning the cold war. He said communism was "the overriding issue of our time," and recalled his numerous confrontations with the Soviets, particularly confrontations over Greece and Turkey, and the Berlin airlift. Of course, there was the Korean War. Although it was not an easy decision for him to send troops into battle, he was sure his decision was right.[13]

Truman knew many Americans wondered if the cold war would ever end. Repeating some remarks he made in his 1953 annual message, he predicted the United States would eventually prevail because the Soviet Union was fatally flawed. He did not know if there would be a coup, a revolution, if the satellites would defect, or if the Kremlin would simply give up, but said with absolute certainty the Soviet Union would "ultimately lose its competition with our free society." Thirty-five years later—just as Truman predicted—the Kremlin simply gave up.

7

Strategic Defense
Armistice in South Korea; Domino Theory; Public Diplomacy; Eisenhower Doctrine; Suez Crisis; Troops in Lebanon

Dwight Eisenhower was a true believer in American exceptionalism. In his 1953 inaugural address, he outlined the foreign policy principles that would guide him. First, he considered it his primary task to maintain the United States' armed forces strong enough to deter aggression. Second, he pledged never to resort to appeasement. Third, he pledged the United States would honor and respect each nation's heritage by never attempting to *force* other nations to adopt America's political and economic institutions. Fourth, he promised America's full cooperation in providing for common defense, but expected America's allies to provide for their own security. Fifth, because a strong economy was as important as a strong military, he pledged to pursue economic policies that would increase productivity and trade. Sixth, Eisenhower vowed to support regional security alliances consistent with the principles of the United Nations, and pledged to enforce the Monroe Doctrine. Seventh, Eisenhower would "hold all continents and peoples in equal regard and honor." Eighth, he expressed his hope the United Nations would one day be "an effective force."

In Eisenhower's 1953 annual message the following month, he said, "Our country has come through a painful period of trial and disillusionment since the victory of 1945." Communist aggression crushed our hopes for the postwar peace. It was a costly lesson, he said—insinuating preemptive action without making any explicit threat—that taught us not to wait for our adversary to make the first move. To remedy what he believed were the defects in Truman's foreign policy Eisenhower proposed to be more principled and more proactive. According to Eisenhower's version of practical idealism, U.S. foreign policy would be bipartisan and multilateral, involve the executive and legislative branches, give equal recognition to Asia and Europe, rule out secret diplomacy, support European integration, and promote free trade.

Then Eisenhower turned his attention to the war in Korea, which he called "the most painful phase of Communist aggression" in the world. Because it was part of the same plan targeting Indochina, Malaya, and Taiwan, he said any resolution of the crisis in Korea would also affect these areas. Eisenhower wanted to increase the number of South Korean forces and provide training and equipment so Koreans could play a larger role in their own self-defense.

• • •

In early March 1953, Joseph Stalin suffered a stroke and died a few days later. The following month, Eisenhower delivered a speech to the American Society of Newspaper Editors, and called Stalin's death "the end of an era."[1] After enduring more than a quarter century of brutal dictatorship, he said, the Soviet Union's new leaders had a new chance for peace. During WWII, the Allies fulfilled their common purpose when the American and Russian soldiers triumphantly met in Central Europe. Their common purpose lasted a brief moment, however, and the wartime allies took separate paths.

America's path was marked by basic principles, which governed its conduct in world affairs. What were these basic principles? Following in the footsteps of George Washington, Ulysses Grant, Theodore Roosevelt, Woodrow Wilson, Franklin Roosevelt, and Harry Truman among and others, Eisenhower described his version of practical idealism. First, we have no permanent enemies. Second, our national security is best achieved by cooperating with other nations, not by isolating ourselves. Third, all people have an inalienable right to choose their own political and economic institutions. Fourth, no nation has the right to dictate another nation's form of government. Fifth, sustainable peace can never be achieved through an arms race.

• • •

In July 1953, the United States, the PRC, North Korea, and South Korea signed an armistice agreement to establish a complete cessation of hostilities until a final peaceful settlement could be negotiated. Under the terms of the agreement, the parties agreed to establish a demilitarized zone between opposing forces on the thirty-eighth parallel, set limits on maximum troop levels and numbers of combat aircraft, armored vehicles, weapons, and ammunition. The agreement also provided for a military commission to implement other terms of the armistice, such as exchange of prisoners of war and demilitarization of the Han River Estuary.[2]

• • •

On December 8, 1953, Eisenhower delivered his "Atoms for Peace" speech in New York to the UN General Assembly. He reported the United States conducted forty-two nuclear tests since it set off the first atomic explosion in July 1945. The United States' stockpile of atomic weapons, increased on a daily basis, was many times more powerful than all the explosives used by all the combatants during all the years of WWII. Atomic weapons came in a wide variety of sizes and every branch of the U.S. armed services was capable of using them.

The trouble was, said Eisenhower, the technology to develop atomic weapons was no longer a secret, and the United States no longer had a monopoly. British, Canadian, and Russian scientists all devoted significant resources and developed their own capabilities. Other countries—perhaps all others—would eventually develop their own. Even the United States' huge numerical superiority would not necessarily deter an irrational surprise attack. Aware of the situation, American policy-makers developed an extensive array of warning and defensive systems. If anyone attacked the United States, Eisenhower promised the reaction would be swift and terrible, inflicting damage and laying waste to the aggressor's homeland. Eisenhower did not stop there because he refused to accept the inevitability civilization would destroy itself. Neither did he want to confirm peoples' worst fears the United States and the Soviet Union were forever doomed to stare at each other across the abyss. Any solution would require allies and adversaries alike to work together over a period of months and years.

In his 1954 annual message, Eisenhower said there was much to be thankful for this year. American soldiers were no longer fighting and dying in Korea—though many were still based there. Ominously, he remarked French forces were putting up a vigorous resistance in Indochina, assisted with "timely aid" from the United States. According to Eisenhower, the best way to minimize the communist threat without resorting to war was strong alliances. Naturally, the United States had the greatest responsibility for maintaining that unity. One practical example of the United States' leadership was a new mutual security pact recently negotiated with South Korea.[3] Another example was Eisenhower's pledge to base substantial American military forces in Okinawa, Japan in case South Korea came under attack again. In addition to the bases in Okinawa, Eisenhower asked Congress to provide military and economic aid to Taiwan and Indochina—though he did not specifically mention the possibility of United States intervention in Vietnam.

In April 1954, Eisenhower held a press conference and responded to a question about the strategic importance of Indochina. According to Eisenhower, "You have, of course, both the specific and the general when you talk about such things. First of all, you have the specific value of a locality in its production of materials that the world needs. Then you have the possibility that many human beings pass under a dictatorship that is inimical to the free world. Finally, you have broader considerations that might follow what you would call the "falling domino" principle."[4]

This marked the first occasion any American president would specifically express what would later become known as the domino theory. We already know Harry Truman expressed the same theory without calling it by name in his 1946 annual message. Truman was talking about Greece and Turkey rather than Indochina, but the principle was identical: communist takeover of one country threatens other countries in the region. This was the assumption beneath the Truman Doctrine, the Marshall Plan, the policy of containment, and ultimately the entire cold war. This is also the assumption beneath George W. Bush's invasion of Iraq, except in reverse. In Bush's highly speculative version, if one country becomes democratic, then other countries in the region will follow.

•••

In his 1955 annual message, Eisenhower presented a list of recent political developments in various regions of the world. Recent treaties with Turkey and Pakistan had laid the foundation for increased strength in the Middle East. An alliance with Greece, Turkey, and Yugoslavia enhanced political stability in the Mediterranean. A free and democratic West Germany would participate as an equal in the NATO alliance.

Eisenhower reported the Southeast Asia Collective Defense Treaty, otherwise known as the Manila Pact, was signed in September 1954. The treaty recognized "the sovereign equality" of all signatories and reiterated the Wilsonian principles of self-determination and self-government. The parties agreed to settle international disputes by peaceful means, to maintain their respective defensive capabilities, to promote economic development, and undertake measures for common defense should any member be attacked. The treaty included a clause, which stated the United States' military responsibilities were limited "only to communist aggression."[5]

A companion to the Manila Pact was the Pacific Charter, also signed the previous September. Modeled after the Atlantic Charter, the Pacific Charter's members included Australia, France, New Zealand, Pakistan, the Philippines, Thailand, the United Kingdom, and the United States. The charter's distinctly Wilsonian principles included equal rights, self-determination, and self-government. The charter's section on collective security said any attempt to subvert the freedom of any member, or threaten the sovereignty or territorial integrity of any member would meet with an appropriate response.[6]

For the first time, Eisenhower raised the issue of *public diplomacy*. He urged Congress to consider the advantages of a worldwide public relations program, which would "keep the peoples of the world truthfully advised of our actions and purposes." Eisenhower said even though the transition to a peacetime economy was largely complete, national security still consumed two-thirds of the federal government's budget. Cost-effectiveness was always important to Eisenhower and he wanted to make sure the government was protecting the American people effectively and efficiently. Toward that end, he continued to urge negotiating arms limitations. Until we had a realistic arms limitation agreement, however, there was no choice but to continue pushing nuclear weapons development. As usual, Eisenhower's defense budget would emphasize mobility, airpower, and other weapons that gave the United States "rapid and destructive striking power."

•••

In Eisenhower's 1956 annual message, he noted the Korean War had been over more than two years, and our collective security and defense systems were stronger. In the foreign policy section of his speech, titled *The Discharge of Our World Responsibility,* he renewed his commitment to bipartisanship. He said the cold war had entered a new phase because the Soviet Union's tactics had shifted from violence to "division, enticement, and duplicity." Though the threat was less obvious, he said their new tactics were just as dangerous. According to Eisenhower, the best way to counter the communist military threat was still collective security. That meant warning the Soviets and Chinese that aggression on their part would meet with a strong response on our part. And we should use "the awesome power of the atom," as a deterrent to make sure the warning got through.

Eisenhower said the sum total of the United States' foreign policy should be to wage peace with as much resourcefulness, dedication, and urgency as if we were at war. Adding his voice to the doctrine of practical idealism, he said, "Our weapons are the principles and ideas embodied in our historic traditions." In practice, this means maintaining a powerful military deterrent, helping Asian countries maintain their independence from communist coercion, and helping European countries work toward political and economic integration. In the Middle East, it means helping solve the Arab–Israeli conflict, and in Latin America, it means increasing economic trade and economic cooperation.

Eisenhower called on Congress to help him strengthen our program for collective security. Sounding very similar to Harry Truman and George Marshall, he said people living in poverty were particularly susceptible to communist subversion, and our most effective response should be a comprehensive economic development program. Referring again to public diplomacy, he recommended increasing the budget for the United States Information Agency (USIA) and said fighting poverty would help influence world public opinion.[7]

•••

In July 1956, Egyptian president Gamal Abdel Nasser nationalized the Suez Canal, ownership of which was shared between Britain and France.

In October, Israeli troops invaded Egypt across the Sinai Peninsula. France and the United Kingdom—Israel's allies—bombed Egypt, trying to coerce it to reopen the Suez. In October, there was a revolt against Soviet domination in Hungary. In early November, Soviet troops and tanks brutally and effectively suppressed the popular uprising, killing thousands of Hungarian insurgents and forcing many others to flee the country.

Also in November, Dwight Eisenhower would win the 1956 presidential election. Eisenhower had suffered a heart attack in the fall of 1955, and even though he was more popular than ever, there was widespread speculation that his health might not permit him to run, let alone govern the country. Eisenhower's health recovered, and his margin of victory over Democrat Adlai Stevenson was wider than it was four years earlier.

•••

On January 5, 1957, Eisenhower addressed a joint session of Congress on events in the Middle East, announcing what would later would become known later as the Eisenhower Doctrine. He was due to give his annual message in a few days, but events in the Middle East could not wait. Before he laid out the facts as he saw them, he wanted to remind Congress that world peace and justice for all remained the foundation of U.S. foreign policy. Eisenhower repeated his willingness to negotiate with any nation large or small, if it meant reaching a better understanding.

With the Suez Crisis, the situation in the Middle East reached a new chapter. "In past decades many of the countries in that area were not fully self-governing. Other nations exercised considerable authority in the area and the security of the region was largely built around their power," he said—which was somewhat of an understatement. According to Eisenhower, official U.S. policy supported independence and full sovereignty for every nation in the region. Eisenhower's use of the words self-government, sovereignty, and independence—but not democracy—is noteworthy. Britain and France signed the Sykes-Picot Agreement in May 1916 while they were still fighting WWI. The terms of the confidential agreement defined their respective spheres of influence in the postwar Middle East, which was then nominally under the control of the crumbling Ottoman Empire. By 1957, the only democracy in the region was Israel, which won its sovereignty, independence, and right to self-government by fighting for it less than a decade before.

"The evolution to independence has in the main been a peaceful process," he said. What concerned him most, however, was communist influence in the region. "Russia's rulers have long sought to dominate the Middle East. That was true of the Czars and it is true of the Bolsheviks," he said. He wondered aloud why the Soviets would even be interested in the region because they were not dependent on the Suez Canal or Middle Eastern oil reserves. In contrast, European nations were particularly dependent on Middle

Eastern oil for transportation and production. If the Soviets became too influential in the region, Eisenhower predicted disastrous consequences for the region's three great religions and Europe's economy. Eisenhower said, "If the nations of that area should lose their independence, if they were dominated by alien forces hostile to freedom, that would be both a tragedy for the area and for many other free nations whose economic life would be subject to near strangulation. Western Europe would be endangered just as though there had been no Marshall Plan, no North Atlantic Treaty Organization."[8]

Facing the possibility the Soviet Union would intervene on Egypt's side, Eisenhower persuaded the British and French to cease fire and withdraw their forces. Because of the Middle East's oil reserves, Eisenhower said it was important for the United States to support the "independence of the freedom-loving nations of the area" against the communist menace. Without stating exactly who those "freedom-loving nations" were, Eisenhower proposed a kind of Marshal Plan with some muscle behind it, including economic development assistance and military assistance—including U.S. troops—for any nation facing communist aggression. The juxtaposition of American economic interests, oil in this case, and American principles is characteristic of practical idealism. If we delete "international communism" and insert "international terrorism," the current incumbent could deliver the same speech practically verbatim.

In his 1957 annual message one week later, Eisenhower reported American national security was threatened by the Soviet Union's "strongly armed imperialistic dictatorship." Because of this, he wanted Americans always to remember two truths about national security. First, because the United States could not even guarantee its own security in isolation, we must have allies. (Eisenhower's definition of security had a specific meaning: having powerful friends capable of defending themselves.) Second, our survival required maintaining the most powerful, modern, and mobile peacetime force in the world.

Eisenhower also knew a comprehensive national security program required more than military power alone, and more military power than the United States could supply on its own. "The finest military establishment we can produce must work closely in cooperation with the forces of our friends," he said. Eisenhower knew from personal experience working with allies was often difficult, but despite the difficulties, our network of alliances and collective security agreements enhanced our security and the security of our allies. Eisenhower also knew a large peacetime defense budget was bad *economic* policy, which partly explains his standing offer to the Soviets to negotiate a nuclear arms limitation agreement. It is always in America's *economic* interest to keep defense spending under control.

•••

In January 1957, British prime minister Anthony Eden resigned, and Israeli forces (along with the British and French) withdrew from the Sinai Peninsula. In March, the Suez Canal reopened. The Treaty of Rome formally established the European Economic Community. In July, the International Atomic Energy Agency was established. That fall, the Soviet Union launched Sputnik I, the first artificial satellite to orbit planet Earth, and Sputnik II with the first mammal (a dog) to travel in outer space.

In his 1958 annual message, Eisenhower said if we based our foreign policy exclusively on military power, we would invite an "Age of Terror."[9] If we neglect areas such as economic development, trade, diplomacy, and education, there would be no real peace in the world—a useful reminder in the post-9/11 era. Confronting the Soviet Union's all-inclusive military, industrial, scientific, educational, and propaganda machine required responding with American power and American principles. In short, because the Soviet Union was waging *total cold war,* the United States should respond with practical idealism.

What assets could we bring to bear? For one, America's military power made aggression prohibitively expensive. According to Eisenhower, our military power served as a shield "behind which the patient constructive work of peace can go on." His reference is reminiscent of George Washington's policy of neutrality to buy time so the United States' fledgling democratic institutions could develop. In the late eighteenth century, the shield was neutrality. Now that neutrality is long obsolete, the United States' shield consists of a global network of alliances and "a vast complex of ground, sea, and air units, superbly equipped and strategically deployed around the world."

•••

On New Year's Day 1958, the Treaty of Rome took effect, formally launching the EU (European Union). In February, Egypt and Syria formed the United Arab Republic; Gamal Abdel Nasser became its first president. In March, Prince Faisal became King of Saudi Arabia and Nikita Khrushchev became premier of the Soviet Union. In July, Arab nationalists overthrew the Iraqi monarchy; Abdul Karim Qassim became its new leader.

In May 1958, Lebanese president Camille Chamoun requested military assistance from the United States. In July, five thousand U.S. Marines landed in Lebanon to suppress what Eisenhower believed was communist-led civil unrest. Worried about the recent Iraqi revolution creating more instability in the region, Eisenhower wanted a show of force. From the Suez crisis, we know Eisenhower was particularly concerned that political instability anywhere in the Middle East would have adverse economic consequences in the United States and Western Europe. The marines were in Lebanon less than four months; Eisenhower withdrew them in late October that year.

In January 1959, Fidel Castro overthrew Cuban president Fulgencio Batista. The United States recognized the new Cuban government soon afterwards. In March, the PRC invaded Tibet. In June, the first submarine to carry ballistic missiles, the USS *George Washington,* was launched. In December, the United States, Soviet Union, Argentina, Australia, Belgium, Britain, Chile, France, Japan, New Zealand, Norway, and South Africa signed the Antarctic Treaty, which set aside Antarctica as a preserve to facilitate scientific research and international scientific cooperation. The treaty banned all military activities including bases and fortifications, military maneuvers, and weapons testing. Other sections of the treaty forbid all territorial claims and disposal of radioactive waste.[10]

•••

In Eisenhower's 1960 annual message, he recalled he began his presidency "with one long-held resolve overriding all others," that the United States would be a potent force for peace in the world. We lived in a "divided world of uneasy equilibrium" he said, because both sides possessed not only weapons of mass destruction, but weapons with the potential for mutual destruction. "No other fact of today's world equals this in importance" he said, "it colors everything we say, plan, and do."

Although he cautioned against permitting the Soviet Union's *apparent* expressions of interest in reducing tensions to mislead us, he was optimistic about the ongoing nuclear test ban negotiations. He said there was another potential opportunity in disarmament talks, but the Soviets had not clarified their intentions to allow inspections and verification, which Eisenhower considered essential for real disarmament. The one unequivocal bright spot was the Antarctica Treaty, which Eisenhower called "a significant contribution toward peace, international cooperation, and the advancement of science."

While the United States negotiated arms reductions with the Soviet Union, Eisenhower promised to maintain a large peacetime military force until he obtained a concrete and verifiable agreement—an approach Ronald Reagan would take decades later. He repeated his pledge never to use nuclear weapons except in self-defense—and warned any nation that attacked the United States would "promptly suffer a terrible destruction." For the time being, America's military power made aggression prohibitively expensive. Our long-range bombers and nuclear-powered Polaris submarines (which would enter service that year) were capable of firing on targets anywhere in the world.

•••

In November 1960, former navy lieutenant, WWII hero, and senator from Massachusetts, John Kennedy, won the 1960 presidential election, narrowly defeating Eisenhower's vice president, Richard Nixon.

In Dwight Eisenhower's 1961 annual message, his eighth and final, he recalled since he became president in 1953, his comprehensive foreign policy reinforced America's leadership in the world.[11] He noted the armistice ending the Korean War was signed within a few months after he took office. During the Suez crisis, his administration helped end the hostilities. In 1958, he took action to preserve peace in the Middle East by intervening in Lebanon. Soviet troops no longer occupied Austria, and West Berlin was free. Although communist regimes in Guatemala and Iran had been deposed, he warned that communist penetration in Cuba continued to be a serious threat.

Other foreign policy successes for which Eisenhower took credit included establishing the SEATO (Southeast Asia Treaty Organization), strengthening NATO, ANZUS, and the Organization of American States, and finalizing a mutual security treaty with Japan. Eisenhower considered these alliances the foundation of peace and security for the entire world. Creating the International Atomic Energy Agency and signing the Treaty of Antarctica were both important milestones. Eisenhower's unequivocal support for the United Nations and his equally unequivocal condemnation "of the wholesale murder of the people of Tibet by the Chinese Communists and the brutal Soviet repression of the people of Hungary" was admirable. His dedication to public diplomacy, specifically his support for the U.S. Information Agency's mission to explain our policies, respond to the propaganda of our enemies, and project a clear image of American culture, showed wisdom.

In mid-January 1961, a few days before Eisenhower stepped down as president, he delivered his farewell address. America, he said was "the strongest, the most influential and most productive nation in the world." We should always be proud of this fact and always remember our leadership depends on how we use our power to keep the peace, promote human development, and safeguard freedom. Anything less would be unworthy.

He predicted that international communism—he called it a ruthless, hostile ideology—would persistently challenge our leadership. Meeting the challenge would require perseverance and good judgment to balance our desire for immediate action with our long-term national interests. In order to meet the challenge, the country created a large and permanent military establishment. Because we could not risk improvising our national security in an emergency, we had to keep our military strong, mobile, and ready for action. While we must recognize the necessity of maintaining a large military establishment and arms industry, we must also recognize the implications. We must never permit this combination to jeopardize our democratic processes or our freedom. "In the councils of government, we must guard against the acquisition of unwarranted influence, whether sought or unsought, by the military-industrial complex," Eisenhower said, "The potential for the disastrous rise of misplaced power exists and will persist."[12]

In a belated rebuttal, Ronald Reagan said, "You know, we only have a military-industrial complex until a time of danger, and then it becomes the arsenal of democracy. Spending for defense is investing in things that are priceless—peace and freedom."[13] Of course, Reagan aimed his retort not at Eisenhower, but at conspiracy theorists who quote Eisenhower for their own purpose. Nonetheless, the fact Reagan felt compelled to respond to Eisenhower twenty-four years later merits our attention. After all, it was none other than George Washington who said the best way to secure peace is to be "at all times ready for war."[14]

8

Monroe Doctrine III and Limited War II: Vietnam
Alliance for Progress; Berlin Wall; Cuban Missile Crisis; Gulf of Tonkin; War Escalation; Tet Offensive

John Kennedy began his presidency with one of the most memorable speeches in American history. More idealistic than practical, Kennedy risked creating false expectations by committing the country to the defense of human rights around the world, and thus overextending the United States' armed forces. Although the rhetoric is inspiring, the speech demonstrates the need to find the right balance between pragmatism and idealism. In Kennedy's words:

> Let the word go forth from this time and place, to friend and foe alike, that the torch has been passed to a new generation of Americans—born in this century, tempered by war, disciplined by a hard and bitter peace, proud of our ancient heritage—and unwilling to witness or permit the slow undoing of those human rights to which this nation has always been committed, and to which we are committed today at home and around the world. Let every nation know, whether it wishes us well or ill, that we shall pay any price, bear any burden, meet any hardship, support any friend, oppose any foe to assure the survival and the success of liberty.[1]

The speech also included brief descriptions of what friends, foes, and others could expect. To America's allies, Kennedy pledged loyalty. To newly independent nations, he pledged tyrants would not replace their former their colonial masters. To people who were still striving for their independence,

Kennedy pledged "our best efforts to help them help themselves." To the nations of Latin America, Kennedy offered a special pledge (the new Alliance for Progress) and renewed commitment to the Monroe Doctrine. Finally, he envisioned a long struggle and rightly predicted the work would not be finished during his lifetime.

In Kennedy's 1961 annual message ten days later, he said all the other problems the country faced paled in comparison to foreign policy. Like his inaugural address, this speech included snapshots of various regional issues. In Asia, China was threatening regional security. In Africa, Kennedy reported on the bloody civil war in the Congo, and pledged his faith in the United Nations' ability to restore peace. In Europe, he reported NATO remained America's most powerful ally.

Kennedy reported communist agents had established "a base on Cuba" only ninety miles from Florida. He pledged support for social and economic reform in Cuba and even offered to enter into trade negotiations, but could not permit such a flagrant violation of the Monroe Doctrine. He repeated his commitment to keep the Western Hemisphere free of foreign domination, and said it would be a serious mistake if we allowed ourselves to believe either the Soviet Union or China had lost their ambitions for world domination.

To meet the challenge, Kennedy proposed strengthening our military because in the past we lacked "a consistent, coherent military strategy." What was he thinking? It is doubtful he was criticizing Roosevelt or Truman, so he must have been talking about his immediate predecessor. Dwight Eisenhower had the same weakness, and was unable to disguise his disdain for the Truman administration when he promised his policy would be principled and proactive, and not just react to world events. In Eisenhower's first annual message, he pledged his foreign policy would be consistent and coherent, exactly the same vocabulary Kennedy would appropriate—eight years later—to criticize Eisenhower. However, any suggestion Eisenhower's defense policy lacked consistency or coherence is simply ridiculous.

In March 1961, Kennedy delivered a speech to the Latin American diplomatic corps on the Alliance for Progress. Kennedy proposed a ten-year "plan for the Americas" and praised the benefits of economic integration. He advocated creating a common market, free trade area for Central and South America, and called for a meeting of the Inter-American Economic and Social Council to begin the "massive planning effort" required for the Alliance for Progress. He offered American assistance to solve problems with commodity markets, and repeated his support for increased funding for the Food-for-Peace program. Most importantly, Kennedy reaffirmed the United States' commitment to collective security (and by implication, the 138-year-old Monroe Doctrine), pledging to "come to the defense of any American nation whose independence is endangered." Although there would be no need for that, there would be a need to limit foreign influence in the hemisphere, later on in Cuba.

•••

In 1960, Fidel Castro nationalized all American and foreign-owned property. In January 1961, (shortly before Eisenhower left office) the United States broke off diplomatic relations with Cuba. In mid-April 1961 approximately fifteen hundred Cuban exiles, trained and armed by the United States landed at Cuba's Bay of Pigs, located on the Cuba's southern coast approximately one hundred miles southeast of Havana. Their goal was to overthrow Fidel Castro, who overthrew Fulgencio Batista's government in 1959. The Cuban exile/invaders believed they would be greeted as liberators and win the support of the local population. Within two days of the invasion, however, the exiles were surrounded. Almost a hundred were killed and the rest were captured.

In the summer of 1961, Kennedy had recently returned from Europe, and was concerned about Nikita Khrushchev's warnings and threats, and the Soviet Union's recent increases in military spending. Khrushchev's shoe pounding tantrum at a UN meeting the previous October was also cause for concern. In late July 1961, Kennedy delivered an address on the developing crisis in West Berlin. The problem there was not the only thing on his mind; there was another situation developing in Southeast Asia.

In his national address, Kennedy described West Berlin as "a showcase of liberty," "an island of freedom," "a beacon of hope," and "an escape hatch for refugees." Of those four images, certainly the last one stuck in the Soviet craw, and that was why it had become the focal point of cold war confrontation. (Since WWII, millions of refugees voted with their feet by fleeing East Germany.) Although Berlin was more than a hundred miles behind the iron curtain and surrounded by Soviet troops it was not part of East Germany, but a separate territory under the control of the allied occupation forces. We had every right to be there, and the Soviet Union had no right to restrict our access. Furthermore, West Germany was a member of NATO, having joined in 1955. "The NATO shield was long ago extended to cover West Berlin" said Kennedy, "and we have given our word that an attack upon that city will be regarded as an attack upon us all."

Kennedy warned the Soviets not to make the mistake of assuming we were too soft. He said we would fulfill our commitment to Berlin and we would not permit the communists to force us out. As long as the communists unilaterally threatened to terminate the United States' rights in West Berlin, we must be ready to defend those rights. As long as the Soviets threatened to use military force, we must be ready to fight. The actions Kennedy outlined were part of a long-term military buildup designed to counter the international communist threat. The military buildup would increase the range of options available to him, giving him "a wider choice than humiliation or all-out nuclear action."

Shifting his attention from principles to practical matters, Kennedy outlined the steps he intended to take. First, ask Congress for a major new appropriation for every branch of the armed services. Second, ask Congress for the authority to activate certain reserve units and individual reservists, extend tours of duty, and activate several Air National Guard squadrons. Third, delay deactivation of several B-47 bombers and other aircraft to expand our airlift and sealift capability. Fourth, he would step-up procurement of nonnuclear weapons, ammunition, equipment, and other items.[2]

Shifting back to matters of principle, Kennedy said he was willing to negotiate some issues, but totally rejected the idea he would ever negotiate West Berlin's freedom. He acknowledged the Soviet Union's legitimate security concerns in Central and Eastern Europe, and held out the hope freedom and security could exist simultaneously. The source of the trouble is not Berlin he said, but Moscow because they were stirring up trouble, denying free elections, and opposing German unification. In sum, Kennedy was ready to negotiate and ready to defend American interests, but could not believe the Soviets would risk starting a third world war.

•••

In August 1961, the East German government began building the Berlin Wall. Since WWII, approximately two and a half million East Germans had crossed into the west, and the East German government was determined to prevent any more of their skilled workers from fleeing. When it was finished, the ninety-six mile long wall would surround West Berlin. The East Germans would later add a fence running parallel to the wall and other security features including trenches, barbed wire, bunkers, and numerous watchtowers.

In September that year, Kennedy spoke to the UN General Assembly about two emerging crises.[3] The first was Southeast Asia. He said there had been several border violations in Burma, Cambodia, and India, and that South Vietnam was under attack. Kennedy was concerned Laotian territory was being used to infiltrate South Vietnam, so the only question for him was whether the world community—meaning the United Nations—could protect small and weak nations from these persistent border violations. If these tactics were successful in Laos and South Vietnam, the floodgates would be wide open, using a new metaphor to describe the domino theory. The other crisis was Berlin. Kennedy placed the blame squarely on the Soviet Union's violation of the "solemn agreements" made regarding the occupation of Germany. There was a crisis in Berlin, said Kennedy, because the Soviets were threatening the United States' vital interests by forcing us to surrender the freedom of the people living in West Berlin. This is something we could not do.

•••

In his 1962 annual message, Kennedy said since the end of WWII there was "a global civil war" dividing and tormenting the human race in a clash of ideas and wills. Through it all, the basic goal of U.S. foreign policy was to maintain a peaceful world community of free and independent states. According to Kennedy, there were five pillars supporting this goal: military strength; UN peacekeeping forces; good relations with Latin America; assistance to new and developing nations; and the NATO alliance.

Kennedy also said something that may be the most profound lesson of the cold war. He said governments who received U.S. aid might have different opinions than ours, "but events in Africa, the Middle East, and Eastern Europe teach us never to write off any nation as lost to the Communists." Kennedy said we should support the independence of those nonaligned nations who preferred to refrain from entangling alliances, which of course, was an obvious reference to George Washington's 1794 Farewell Address. The comment before that, about not writing off any nation, follows another of Washington's timeless principles, to avoid making permanent alliances as well as permanent enemies.

●●●

In January 1962, the Soviet Union negotiated a trade agreement with Cuba. In February, the United States imposed an embargo on Cuban goods. In September, the Soviet Union began shipping arms to Cuba. The following month, American reconnaissance planes flying over Cuba photographed the installation of nuclear weapons on the island, which would give the Soviets a substantial increase in their first strike capability.

On October 22, 1962, Kennedy addressed the nation. "This Government, as promised, has maintained the closest surveillance of the Soviet Military buildup on the island of Cuba," he said, "Within the past week, unmistakable evidence has established the fact that a series of offensive missile sites is now in preparation on that imprisoned island. The purpose of these bases can be none other than to provide a nuclear strike capability against the Western Hemisphere.[4]

Kennedy reported two types of missiles, both of which were capable of carrying nuclear warheads and were clearly offensive weapons of mass destruction. One had a range of approximately one thousand miles and the other type—which he said appeared not to be completed—had a range of two thousand miles. In addition, surveillance reports indicated airbases were under construction in Cuba, and aircraft capable of carrying nuclear weapons were being uncrated and assembled. The Soviet Union's extraordinary buildup of missiles in Cuba was a clear and present danger, and a violation of American policy in the hemisphere. There was no way Kennedy could accept the Soviet Union's deliberately provocative decision to deploy offensive nuclear weapons in such close proximity to American territory. His only option was "to secure their withdrawal or elimination from the Western Hemisphere." Anything less would have been appeasement.

Kennedy reported taking a series of steps. First, he ordered a quarantine of all military equipment shipped to Cuba. Any ships bound for Cuba found to have offensive weapons would be turned away. Second, he directed surveillance to be increased and ordered U.S. armed forces "to prepare for any eventualities." Third, "It shall be the policy of this Nation to regard any nuclear missile launched from Cuba against any nation in the Western Hemisphere as an attack by the Soviet Union on the United States, requiring a full retaliatory response upon the Soviet Union." Fourth, he ordered the base at Guantánamo to be reinforced and put on standby alert. Fifth, he called for consultations with the Organization of American States. Sixth, he requested an emergency meeting of the UN Security Council. Kennedy then spoke directly to the Cuban people: "These new weapons are not in your interest. They contribute nothing to your peace and well-being. They can only undermine it." Finally, he called on Chairman Khrushchev to withdraw the weapons and refrain from doing anything that might make matters worse.

At first, the Soviets denied everything. Then Ambassador Adlai Stevenson went before an emergency session of the United Nations offering proof in the form of aerial reconnaissance photographs of the missile installations. A few days into the crisis, the Soviets offered to withdraw the missiles if the United States promised not to invade Cuba. Meanwhile, negotiators looked for ways to save face and prevent nuclear war. They negotiated a separate unpublicized deal in which the United States agreed to withdraw its missiles from Turkey if the Soviets reciprocated in Cuba. Thirteen days into the incredibly tense confrontation, Moscow ordered the missiles removed from Cuba. In November, Kennedy quietly ordered the NATO missiles removed from Turkey.

•••

After the embarrassing Bay of Pigs fiasco, the Cuban missile crisis was a triumph for the Kennedy administration. In his 1963 annual message, Kennedy said not long ago communism appeared to be "a unified, confident, and expanding empire," but no one could say that now. America had undertaken "the most far-reaching defense improvements in the peacetime history of this country" and was making steady progress building a new world order. Although a deadly threat had been removed from Cuba, now was not the time for complacency. The situation in Southeast Asia was precarious and getting worse.

In terms of foreign policy, Kennedy's four highest priorities were the Atlantic Alliance, developing nations, Chinese–Soviet relations, and world peace. Kennedy reported the Atlantic Alliance was as strong as ever. With the era of continental rivalry, imperialism and colonialism over, a new era day of political and economic interdependence was dawning. Since WWII, the United States enthusiastically supported European integration and shared the burden of common defense.

The first task of the Atlantic Alliance being common defense, Kennedy announced plans for the United States and the United Kingdom to begin cooperating on nuclear weapons. Kennedy mentioned France would soon be a nuclear power, and it was time to begin planning for a "truly multilateral nuclear force within an increasingly intimate NATO." Because nuclear deterrence was only part of NATO's common defense strategy, a review of conventional force levels was underway to ensure we had a full range of military options. The other significant issue with the Atlantic Alliance was trade and economic growth. Kennedy was still concerned about the huge balance of payments deficit and intended to use his new authority under the Trade Expansion Act to nudge the Europeans toward economic cooperation and away from protectionism.

Still recovering from the shock over the Soviet Union's attempt to transform Cuba into a first-strike nuclear base, Kennedy turned his attention to the subject of nonaligned and developing nations. As the colonial era receded into the past and the ambitions of the neocolonial communists became more evident, the world was learning the cold war was not just a struggle between capitalism and communism but between freedom and oppression. The world was learning that the desire for freedom was the same in Berlin—or Vietnam—as it was anywhere else.

While the United States was spending billions of dollars a year to contain communism, it made no sense to begrudge spending a small fraction of that amount on foreign aid. Despite the relatively small budget, the United States' mutual defense and assistance program provided food, clothing (and weapons) to millions of people. It was because of this program, according to Kennedy, that not one nation who won its independence since WWII had fallen to communism.

Feeling pressure not to appear soft on communism, Kennedy was cautiously optimistic about "the increasing strains and tensions within the Communist bloc." According to Kennedy, communism had two fatal flaws that carried the seeds of its own destruction. One was the force of nationalism and the other was the inefficiency of their economies. In Kennedy's words:

New Nations asked to choose between two competing systems need only compare conditions in East and West Germany, Eastern and Western Europe, North and South Viet-Nam [*sic*]. They need only compare the disillusionment of Communist Cuba with the promise of the Alliance for Progress. And all the world knows that no successful system builds a wall to keep its people in and freedom out—and the wall of shame dividing Berlin is a symbol of Communist failure.[5]

His observation was certainly accurate, though he and several of his advisors had a huge blind spot when it came to the forces of nationalism. Clearly, American policy-makers supported self-determination and nationalism, at least when the communist influence was negligible. The quotation above foreshadows the United States' future failures in Vietnam, when Kennedy implied nations would be "asked to choose between two competing systems." Furthermore, Kennedy said he would "let our adversaries choose" whether we would have peaceful competition, wars of liberation, subversion, or disarmament. He was not just talking about the Berlin Crisis, but Southeast Asia as well.

Kennedy gave the commencement address at American University that June. World peace was the topic, specifically negotiating a nuclear test ban treaty and perhaps ending the arms race with the Soviet Union. Total war no longer made any sense because the two strongest powers would be the two primary targets, and thus suffer the worst destruction in any nuclear exchange. Kennedy hoped for "complete disarmament," but would have to settle for less. In his words:

> The United States, as the world knows, will never start a war. We do not want a war. We do not now expect a war. This generation of Americans has already had enough—more than enough—of war and hate and oppression. We shall be prepared if others wish it. We shall be alert to try to stop it. But we shall also do our part to build a world of peace where the weak are safe and the strong are just. We are not helpless before that task or hopeless of its success. Confident and unafraid, we labor on—not toward a strategy of annihilation but toward a strategy of peace.[6]

While traveling through Europe in the summer of 1963, Kennedy visited several cities in West Germany. In West Berlin, he delivered another memorable speech.[7] Speaking before a cheering crowd, Kennedy repeated his assertion that the Berlin Wall—not even two years old by then—symbolized communism's most obvious failure. There were some people in the world, he said, who did not understand the great issue between the communists and us, and some who still believed communism was the wave of the future. Others admitted even though communism was an evil system, maybe we could still find a way to work with them. In response Kennedy would simply say, "Let them come to Berlin." Kennedy asked the huge crowd assembled in the Rudolph-Wilde Square (later renamed John F. Kennedy Square) in Berlin's American sector, not to lose sight of the day when Berlin and all of Europe would be reunified. Until that day, Berlin would be an island of freedom. "All free men, wherever they may live, are citizens of Berlin, and, therefore, as a free man, I take pride in the words *Ich bin ein Berliner*."

Back in the White House on July 26, Kennedy delivered an address to announce American, British, and Soviet negotiators had reached agreement on a major nuclear test ban treaty. The new treaty, which would take effect in October 1963—barely a year after the Cuban missile crisis—banned all nuclear testing in the atmosphere, under water and in outer space. The preamble of the treaty stated its principal aim was to end the arms race and eliminate incentives to produce and test nuclear and other types of weapons.[8]

In his address, Kennedy assured his audience the treaty would never compromise our national defense, and that we could withdraw at any time if our interests were ever jeopardized in any way. The treaty was not a unilateral moratorium, and secret violations were possible because the treaty did not require on-site inspection, nor did it ban underground testing. Although it would substantially reduce nuclear testing and pollution, it would not eliminate the possibility of nuclear war. The treaty was not perfect, but perhaps could reduce some of the tension between Washington and Moscow, and thus was an important step toward peace.

•••

In November 1963, Kennedy traveled to Texas in advance of his upcoming reelection campaign. On November 22, Kennedy died in an assassination, and Vice President Lyndon Johnson succeeded him as president.

Five days later, Johnson addressed a joint session of Congress. "All I have I would have given gladly not to be standing here today," he said. Johnson pledged his support for Kennedy's domestic policy agenda, and said no memorial would be more fitting than to pass the civil rights bill. The framework of Johnson's foreign policy would rest on familiar themes: strong support for the United Nations, strong commitment to America's allies, military strength second to none, a strong and stable dollar, expansion of foreign trade, and a continuation of development aid to Asia, Africa, and Latin America. Johnson also pledged to continue Kennedy's foreign policy agenda, particularly the United States' commitments to West Berlin—and ominously—South Vietnam.[9]

In his 1964 annual message, Johnson said his ultimate goal was "a world without war, *a world made safe for diversity*" in which people, goods, and ideas could move freely across borders. (Italics added). Reading this, one cannot help but think it does not have the same ring as Woodrow Wilson's goal to make the world safe for democracy. Johnson then introduced a comprehensive foreign and defense policy framework, which consisted of ten points.

First, even though Johnson's defense budget would be smaller, he pledged to maintain the military superiority achieved by Kennedy's three-year buildup. Johnson said we would be "better prepared than ever before to defend the cause of freedom" whether we were threatened with outright aggression or by the infiltration and insurrection practiced by those in Havana and Hanoi. Second, he would continue to pursue arms control agreements. With or without arms control agreements, he pledged not to seek military power in excess of our needs because it is wasteful and provocative. Third, Johnson wanted to use food as "an instrument of peace" for needy people in developing nations by sale, trade, loan, or donation. Fourth, he pledged to pursue the peaceful exploration of space. Fifth, he called for expanded international trade as long as it was fair; our trading partners would have access to our market if they reciprocated. Sixth, Johnson pledged to preserve the value of the dollar and shrink the balance of payments deficit. Seventh, he pledged to strengthen the Alliance for Progress so we could be "better neighbors with the free states of the Americas." Eighth, Johnson pledged "a more rigorous administration of our development assistance." Ninth, he pledged to strengthen our alliances in the Atlantic and Pacific, and to help make the United Nations a more effective instrument for international order. Tenth, Johnson said—somewhat vaguely—he wanted work with our allies to develop new ways to close "the gap between the East and the West." Finally, he told Congress they should be prepared for the worst and act for the best. "We must be strong enough to win any war," he said and "wise enough to prevent one."

•••

In January 1964, American troops clashed with Panamanian insurgents in the Canal Zone. General Nguyen Khanh overthrew the South Vietnamese government. In April, Johnson and Khrushchev announced plans to reduce production of nuclear weapons. In July, the United States sent five thousand military advisers to South Vietnam, bringing the total number of uniformed Americans to twenty-one thousand.

In August 1964, North Vietnamese forces allegedly attacked two U.S. vessels in the Gulf of Tonkin, southeast of Hanoi, at the mouth of the Red River near the South China Sea. On August 5, Johnson delivered a message to Congress on the Tonkin Gulf incident.[10] According to Johnson, the North Vietnamese deliberately attacked U.S. naval vessels in international waters. In retaliation, Johnson ordered air strikes against North Vietnamese gunboats and facilities. Following this incident, Johnson asked Congress to draft a resolution to express "the unity and determination of the United States in supporting freedom and in protecting peace in Southeast Asia."

The United States had made a well-known commitment to the region since the Eisenhower administration, which was formalized by the Southeast Asia Collective Defense Treaty. Ratified by the Senate in 1955, Johnson said the treaty obligated the United States to counter communist aggression in the region, particularly North Vietnam's systematic "campaign of subversion" and guerilla warfare in South Vietnam and Laos. "Our purpose is peace" he said, "We have no military, political, or territorial ambitions in the area." North Vietnam was threatening regional stability, which according to Johnson, was a threat to American national security. This was no "jungle war," he said but part of the United States' effort to help South Vietnam and Laos defend themselves against communism and strengthen their independence.

Johnson urged Congress to affirm the United States' basic policy of assisting free nations in Southeast Asia in defense of their freedom.

On August 7, Congress passed the Gulf of Tonkin Resolution, explicitly authorizing Johnson, as commander in chief, to take all necessary steps—including the use of armed force—to maintain peace and security in Southeast Asia, and "repel any armed attack against the forces of the United States."[11]

•••

The 1964 presidential election took place less than a year after the Kennedy assassination, and a few months after Lyndon Johnson signed the historic Civil Rights Act of 1964 into law. The bill strengthened the Constitution's equal protection clause, and prohibited discrimination in areas such as education, housing, and employment. Johnson won his party's nomination by acclamation and campaigned on a platform of continued social programs—his Great Society agenda would begin in his second term—and limited war in Vietnam. Capitalizing on the Kennedy legacy, Johnson won the election by a huge majority over his Republican challenger, senator Barry Goldwater of Arizona.

In his 1965 annual message, Johnson said the state of the union depended in part on the state of the world, and thus we could not fulfill our goals in isolation. Even though the United States could not possibly settle all the conflicts or solve all the problems in the world, we should always demonstrate our concern, interest, compassion, and vigilance. Echoing Franklin Roosevelt, Johnson said we should always be good neighbors—as long as it never compromised our own safety and security. Then Johnson said something that every American should read and pause to consider. In three short sentences, Johnson summarized American exceptionalism—the grand mission of U.S. foreign policy—and articulated the second half of the doctrine of practical idealism: "Our own freedom and growth have never been the final goal of the American dream. We were never meant to be an oasis of liberty and abundance in a worldwide desert of disappointed dreams. Our Nation was created to help strike away the chains of ignorance and misery and tyranny wherever they keep man less than God means him to be."[12]

Johnson's 1965 annual message was really a report of the Kennedy–Johnson ticket. Once again, Johnson boasted the United States had the world's most powerful armed forces—the result of Kennedy's three-year military buildup. He reported the communist empire was beginning to crumble, as evidenced by the fact that no new nation had fallen to communism, and that we had a new treaty banning nuclear tests. He broke down the elements of his foreign policy into two broad categories: the communist and noncommunist world. In the section on communist countries, Johnson said we lived in a troubled and dangerous world, filled with different kinds of threats. Johnson sought "peaceful understandings" with the

Soviet Union, which he thought could be achieved by getting to know one another better. He invited the Soviet leaders to visit the United States, and perhaps to speak on American television. He reported that Eastern European nations were beginning to assert themselves, and said he would try to increase trade with countries in the region.

In contrast, he said communism in Asia wore "a more aggressive face." American troops were there because a friendly nation asked for our help, three successive presidents offered it, and Johnson refused to be the one to deviate from the course. The reason we have fought two wars in Asia in a generation, said Johnson, was because American national security depended on it. Our goal was peace, just as it had always been, but if we ignored North Vietnam's aggression, we would risk a larger war in the future. (This is almost identical to Truman's justification in April 1951 for confronting North Korea's aggression. Truman chose limited war in Korea to avoid a general war.)

In the section on noncommunist countries, Johnson said communism was not the only cause of trouble in the world. There were older and deeper causes found both in the misery of nations and the desire for freedom of people everywhere. Johnson—native son of Texas—always had a special affection for Latin America, and it would be his policy to strengthen those ties through Kennedy's Alliance for Progress. He also pledged to continue the same twenty-year-old policy toward the Atlantic community as his predecessors. His goal was a united Europe with close ties to the United States, particularly in foreign trade and common defense. "A great unfinished task" he said "is the reunification of Germany through self-determination."

•••

In his 1965 inaugural address, Johnson devoted little attention to foreign policy. His two major themes were the Great Society—and change: rapid, incredible change that would shake old values and uproot old ways, and place weapons of mass destruction in uncertain hands. Because of this, and because the dangers and troubles we once considered *foreign* now lived among us, Americans could no longer afford to isolate themselves. In a reprise of his recent annual message, Johnson said America's mission was to help show the way in this dynamic and unpredictable world. If American soldiers had to die and American treasure spent in countries we could barely find on the map, then that was the price we paid to fulfill our mission.

In April 1965, Johnson delivered a speech on the war in Vietnam at Johns Hopkins University. Americans and Southeast Asians, he said, were fighting and dying in the jungles of Vietnam for freedom, the same principle our ancestors fought for during the American Revolution. He said we had no territorial ambitions in Vietnam—affirming his anti-imperialist, anticolonialist policy, which Kennedy most recently restated. Why, he asked, was it necessary to fight this "dirty and brutal and difficult" war? We were fighting so every country would have the right to shape its own destiny. We were fighting because "force must often precede reason." And although many South Vietnamese were taking part in attacks on their own government, we were fighting because North Vietnam was determined to conquer the South.

Johnson spoke of unparalleled brutalities taking place, farmers murdered or kidnapped, families of men loyal to the government murdered, villages and towns raided and ravaged. Nothing in the "confused nature of this conflict" could hide the fact the North Vietnamese government was receiving support from communist China. In addition to their invasions of Tibet and India, and their aggression in Korea, Johnson charged China with fomenting violence on "almost every continent," and Vietnam was just part of the pattern.

Every American president since 1954 supported and helped defend Vietnam, said Johnson. We were fighting because we had a promise to keep, a "national pledge" to uphold, and to abandon this small, brave nation would dishonor that pledge. We were there, too for the sake of world order. Countries all over the world counted on us. Their well-being depended in part on the belief we would help defend them if they came under attack. If we abandoned Vietnam now, our allies would lose confidence in us and add to the unrest and instability in the world. Although Johnson did not invoke the domino theory, he did quote the Bible: *Hitherto shalt thou come, but no farther* (Job 38:11) and said if we backed away from Vietnam now we would just have to fight again someplace else. We were fighting, he said, for the same reason we fought WWII, because "The central lesson of our time is that the appetite of aggression is never satisfied."[13]

Johnson said again we wanted nothing for ourselves, and our only objective was the independence of South Vietnam. Johnson pledged to do everything necessary, *and only what was necessary,* to attain the objective—which is a textbook definition of limited war. Later in the speech he said, "We will use our power with restraint." Unfortunately, Johnson said it was necessary to increase our air attacks in order to check the North's aggression. He hoped this would boost the South's confidence and convince the North the United States was not going to withdraw. Johnson acknowledged air attacks alone would not attain the United States' objectives in Vietnam, but thought it would force the North Vietnamese to negotiate—a tactic which Richard Nixon would use a few years later.

He asked his audience to be patient and prepare for a long conflict—just as George W. Bush would do decades later. Johnson hoped the United States would ultimately prevail because we were fighting not for territorial conquest, but for principles. It is evident he considered communist expansion rather than homegrown nationalism the driving force in Vietnam. "Because we fight for values and we fight for principles, rather than territory or colonies," he said, "our patience and our determination are unending." In this case, however, it was the patience and determination of the Vietnamese that would eventually prove to be the decisive factor.

•••

In March 1965, more U.S. troops arrived in Vietnam. In April, fighting broke out in the Dominican Republic and Johnson sent U.S. troops ostensibly to protect American lives and property. In June, North Vietnamese and Viet Cong forces attacked and killed almost a thousand South Vietnamese troops in Dong Sai, approximately sixty miles northeast of Saigon. In late July, Johnson increased the number of U.S. troops in Vietnam from seventy-five to one hundred twenty-five thousand.

In mid-August, U.S. Marine and Naval forces launched a preemptive attack on a North Vietnamese stronghold near Quang Ngai approximately eighty miles east of Da Nang on the Vietnamese coast. In mid-November, the Battle of Ya Drang Valley took place in the Central Highlands of Vietnam near the Cambodian border. During several days of intense fighting, U.S. forces were surrounded and nearly overrun, but they prevented the North Vietnamese from taking control of the strategic Central Highlands, which would have cut Vietnam in two.

In his 1966 annual message, Johnson reported the nation was "engaged in a brutal and bitter conflict in Vietnam." The war was not an isolated incident, he said, but a continuation of the same policy the U.S. government consistently pursued since the end of WWII, the same policy that defended Korea under Truman and Cuba under Kennedy. It was the same policy that helped rebuild Western Europe, prevented Greece and Turkey from falling to communism, defended West Berlin's independence, maintained democracy and social justice in the Western Hemisphere, established the Peace Corps, and implemented the world's largest program of economic assistance.

Johnson then presented his historical analysis of events leading up to the war. He said the fundamental cause was there were some South Vietnamese "who wished to force Communist rule on their own people." When their progress slowed and their chances of success declined, North Vietnam decided to conquer the South. More soldiers and supplies moved from north to south, and that forced us to make a decision: either we abandon South Vietnam or we stand and fight. We chose to fight because we made a solemn pledge, "a pledge which has grown through the commitments of three American Presidents." Last year the war changed when large numbers of North Vietnamese infiltrated and joined forces with fighters in the South. Though he intended to fight a limited war, Johnson said recent developments forced him to increase our troop strength to one hundred ninety thousand.

Returning to the same rationale he used in his 1965 Johns Hopkins University speech, Johnson said the United States would stay in Asia and around the world because people were counting on us. People needed to have confidence we would help defend them if they were attacked. Yielding to North Vietnam's aggression would undermine that confidence. Then Johnson made an observation that indicated he was unaware how and why the United States would ultimately lose the war. He reported the Viet Cong had lost eight men for every one of ours. "The enemy is no longer close to victory" he said, "*Time is no longer on his side.*" (Italics added).

Johnson reported the United States was still actively engaged in peace talks—with more than three hundred private meetings last year alone. Johnson offered to meet at any conference table, discuss any proposal, and consider the views of any group. Johnson repeated his anti-imperialist, anticolonialist position that the United States sought no territory, no permanent military bases, nor economic domination of Vietnam.

•••

In Johnson's 1967 annual message, he said our greatest foreign policy challenge was whether we had the persistence to fight a costly war when the objective was limited, and the danger seemed remote. Was Johnson beginning to have doubts about the war? "No part of our foreign policy is so sacred that it ever remains beyond review," he said. He indicated conditions were changing and our response would need to be flexible, particularly as our foreign policy made the transition away from the "narrow nationalism" of the cold war.

Johnson reported our relations with the Soviet Union and Eastern Europe were in transition. His objective was *not* to continue the cold war but to end it, and the way to do that was to refrain from provocation and harsh rhetoric, and to work out our differences through negotiation and diplomacy. Johnson reported there were newly established direct flights between the United States and the Soviet Union, as well as a new cultural exchange agreement. The Export-Import Bank allowed commercial credit to several East European nations, and American embassies in Bulgaria and Hungary had been recently upgraded. He reported the Soviet Union had increased their capabilities in long-range missiles and began to build an antimissile defense system near Moscow. These were just a few examples why the Americans and Soviets had a duty to consider arms control and disarmament seriously—including nuclear and conventional weapons.

Johnson finally turned his attention to Southeast Asia and Vietnam. He said we were there because we were committed to the SEATO (Southeast Asia Treaty Organization), particularly our promise to come to the defense of any member under attack. We were there because the aggression of North Vietnam threatened "the peace of the entire region and perhaps the world." We were there because the people of South Vietnam had a right to choose their political and economic system. We were there because Congress authorized him—through the nefarious Gulf of Tonkin Resolution—to counter communist aggression in the region. Once again, he asserted we were fighting a limited war in order to prevent a larger war.

Johnson reminded his listeners how different Europe and Korea would be today if we failed to say *this far and no farther*. He wished he could report the conflict was almost over, but the North Vietnamese were proving to be a "stubborn adversary." The war would not be over in 1967 or even the following year. There would be "more cost, more loss, and more agony," because the North Vietnamese believed they could go on fighting longer than we could. There were almost five hundred thousand U.S. troops in Vietnam by then. Johnson received reports from General William Westmoreland who said the enemy could no longer succeed on the battlefield. Our task was to keep up the pressure until the North Vietnamese realized the war was costing them more than they could gain.

•••

In June 1967, the Six-Day War took place between Israel and the Arab nations of Egypt, Jordan, and Syria. The previous month, Egyptian president Gamal Abdel Nasser closed the Straits of Tiran to Israeli shipping and block-aded the Israeli port of Eilat at the northern tip of the Gulf of Aqaba, which the Israelis interpreted as an act of war. The Israeli air force attacked and virtually destroyed Egypt's air force and airfields, and then captured the Sinai. By the time the antagonists declared a cease-fire, Israel would also occupy the Gaza Strip, the West Bank of the Jordan River (including East Jerusalem) and the Golan Heights.

In November 1967, the UN Security Council adopted Resolution 242 and established principles to guide the Arab–Israeli peace settlement. The resolution declared the acquisition of territory by war inadmissible, and demanded that Israel withdraw its forces from all occupied territories. In addition, it acknowledged the sovereignty ("the territorial inviolability and political independence") of all states in the region.

•••

In his 1968 annual message, Johnson took pleasure reporting South Viet-nam recently held three elections, electing a president, vice president, and two houses of the legislature. His assessment about the effects of the United States' bombing campaign—which was supposed to destroy the North's air defenses and industrial capacity, interrupt the flow of men and materiel down the Ho Chi Minh Trail and undermine the North's will to fight—was less encouraging. Despite the ongoing bombing campaign, men and munitions continued to pour into the South. Despite defeating North Vietnam "in battle after battle," the North's stubborn refusal to admit defeat mystified Johnson, though it should have been clear his policy of limited war was failing.

Elsewhere in his 1968 message, Johnson reported on a breakthrough in trade negotiations, which resulted in lower tariffs and a new trade agreement among Latin American nations. He mentioned the economies of Korea, Japan, and Singapore were stronger than ever, and regional cooperation in Africa was taking hold. He recalled using the new hotline between Washington and Moscow for the first time during the Six-Day War. He gave a brief report of his successful two-day meeting with Soviet leader Alexei Kosygin the previous spring. Johnson hoped to present a new treaty on arms control for Senate ratification that year—similar to the treaty banning weapons in outer space. Despite these positive developments, Johnson said we would still need to maintain a military force capable of deterring any kind of threat.

Apparently oblivious the Tet Offensive would begin in less than a month, Johnson turned his attention to domestic matters, commenting that he wished "with all of my heart" the United States did not have to spend so much on defense.

•••

The Tet Offensive, which began in January 1968, was a cluster of battles and smaller engagements. The fighting was particularly brutal around Khe Sanh, near the Ho Chi Minh Trail, not far from the border between North and South Vietnam. The attack on Khe Sanh began several days before Tet (Vietnamese New Year), as a way to draw U.S. troops away from the urban centers in order to reinforce the United States' base at Khe Sanh, located in the hills near the Laotian border approximately sixty miles northwest of Hué.

Under the audacious leadership of Vo Nguyen Giap, North Vietnamese and Viet Cong forces launched numerous coordinated attacks in almost every major city, provincial or district capital in South Vietnam. In Hué, North Vietnamese forces attacked and executed thousands of civilians. In Saigon, they launched several raids, including one on the American embassy. The North hoped to provoke a popular uprising, but American forces defeated them almost everywhere (except in Hué, but American and South Vietnamese forces would retake Hué by the end of February). North Vietnam suffered yet another defeat, losing perhaps a hundred thousand killed, wounded, or captured, but delivered a powerful psychological blow. The scope and coordination of the Tet Offensive came as a surprise to many Americans who did not realize the North had the determination or the capacity. Convinced that resistance in the North was *not* diminishing and the United States was *not* winning, American public opinion—including a growing number of legislators—turned against the war.

•••

In March 1968, in a village in the Quang Ngai Province called My Lai, American troops murdered hundreds of civilians—mostly women and children—suspected of being Viet Cong guerrillas. And Congress enacted legislation repealing the requirement for a gold reserve to back the dollar.

•••

In late March 1968, Johnson addressed the nation on what he was doing to limit the war (as opposed to what he was doing to win it), and to announce his decision not to run for reelection.[14] He began by asserting peace in Vietnam was the issue that most preoccupied the American people and his administration. For years, he tried to negotiate a peace settlement, but Hanoi denounced his offer to halt the bombing of North Vietnam if they agreed to peace talks. Even as we tried to bring them to the bargaining table, they launched "a savage assault on the people, the government, and the allies of South Vietnam" over the Tet holiday season. Although the Tet Offensive caused "widespread disruption and suffering," the North took heavy casualties and failed to control any of the cities, towns, and villages they attacked. They failed, said Johnson because the South Vietnamese army was not destroyed, their government did not collapse, and it did not provoke the popular uprising the communists expected.

Johnson speculated the North was trying to make 1968 the decisive year in the war, but refused to believe they could destroy the South's will to fight. This is ironic to say the least because by the end of the speech Johnson would announce he was not running for reelection. His rationale was he should devote all his time and energy to serving as chief executive rather than campaigning for office. Johnson was clearly eager for serious, substantial peace talks and renewed his offer to halt the bombing, and as usual said he hoped North Vietnam would not take advantage of the cease-fire. Rather than wait for word from Hanoi he made an immediate, unilateral decision to de-escalate the conflict and substantially reduce the level of hostilities.

He ordered U.S. aircraft and naval vessels not to attack North Vietnam except in the area north of the demilitarized zone where the North was building up their forces and thus threatening the United States' forward positions. The area affected by the cease-fire would include most of North Vietnam's territory and population, and all the agricultural areas. Johnson refused to end all the bombing because it would endanger our troops, and once again said he hoped his counterpart in Hanoi would match his restraint. Johnson pledged to send his envoy anywhere and anytime "to discuss the means of bringing this ugly war to an end," and called on President Ho Chi Minh to respond in kind.

Johnson hoped against hope Hanoi would eventually understand the United States' strength was "invincible" and its resolve "unshakable." Our troops were not there for conquest, but to help the South Vietnamese secure their own freedom. According to Johnson, the South Vietnamese already knew what they needed to do to achieve independence: expand their armed forces, get out of the urban areas and into the countryside, increase taxes, get their best men to serve in government and the military, root out corruption and incompetence, and build a unified political coalition with the will to win.

Johnson offered to withdraw U.S. forces from South Vietnam if the North withdrew its forces and put an end to infiltration. He promised his listeners there would be peace in Southeast Asia some day. But it would only come when the people wanted it and were willing to work for it. He could not promise the results of his peace proposal would be any different from others he had proposed over the years, but he remained hopeful. After years of fighting the French and then the Americans without achieving a decisive military victory, Johnson believed North Vietnam was close to agreeing to a negotiated settlement (though North Vietnam's victory in May 1954 against the French in the Battle of Dien Bien Phu was rather decisive). Again, he warned Hanoi against misinterpreting his resolve just because it was an election year.

Johnson then eased into the announcement that would dramatically alter the upcoming election. He began by recalling how united the country was—if only for a brief moment—in November 1963 after John Kennedy died. But the war had caused such division he could not permit the presidency to contribute to the partisanship already dividing the country during an election year. "Accordingly, I shall not seek, and I will not accept, the nomination of my party for another term as your President" he said.

•••

In April 1968, the civil rights activist Reverend Martin Luther King Jr. died in an assassination in Memphis, Tennessee. In June, former U.S. Attorney General and senator from New York, Robert Kennedy died in an assassination in Los Angeles, California. In August, Soviet and Warsaw Pact forces invaded Czechoslovakia.

In late October, Johnson announced his decision to halt the bombing campaign in Vietnam. Johnson reported peace talks with the North Vietnamese had been going on since May, which Johnson implied were the direct result of his announcement to halt the bombing last March. For several weeks, the negotiations made no progress but recently there was a breakthrough of sorts—though Johnson did not say exactly what concessions, if any the North Vietnamese made. Nonetheless, because of new developments in the peace talks then taking place in Paris, Johnson ordered all bombing of North Vietnam to cease. He came to the decision he said "in the belief that this action can lead to progress toward a peaceful settlement of the Vietnamese war."

Johnson was optimistic negotiations would be productive because there was now an atmosphere conducive to progress, as long as the North respected the demilitarized zone and did not use the cease-fire to mount a new offensive. "The overriding consideration that governs us at this hour is the chance and the opportunity that we might have to save human lives... on both sides of the conflict," he said. It was possible we were being misled of course, but this was the only way Johnson could determine if the

North would act in good faith. He predicted there would be some very hard negotiating—and maybe some very hard fighting—still to come.

There was another issue at stake, which was Johnson's insistence South Vietnamese representatives participate in the peace talks. From the American perspective, this is reasonable, given the United States' fundamental objective in the war. "The very principle for which we are engaged in South Vietnam—the principle of self-determination—requires that the South Vietnamese people themselves be permitted to freely speak for themselves at the Paris talks" he said. Then Johnson permitted himself some observations about the war that were overly optimistic or mildly delusional. The government of South Vietnam and its armed forces were getting stronger and more effective, and the "brilliant leadership" of General Westmoreland was producing "truly remarkable results."

With the presidential election a few days away, Johnson reminded his audience of his announcement in March not to seek reelection. Since then he devoted "every resource of the Presidency" to his search for peace. All the presidential candidates were briefed regularly on the situation in Vietnam and the peace talks. Johnson said, "I do not know who will be inaugurated as the 37th President of the United States next January. But I do know that I shall do all that I can in the next few months to try to lighten his burdens as the contributions of the Presidents who preceded me have greatly lightened mine."[15]

Johnson found out less than a week later. His vice president, Hubert Humphrey, the former mayor of Minneapolis and senator from Minnesota won his party's nomination at the riotous Democratic National Convention in Chicago. The Republicans nominated former congressman, senator from California, and vice president Richard Nixon. George Wallace, former governor of Alabama ran as an independent and received almost ten million votes. Despite Humphrey's personal loyalty to Johnson, Humphrey tried to distance himself from Johnson's unpopular war policies during the campaign. The popular vote was close, but Richard Nixon convincingly won the Electoral College and the presidency.

●●●

Johnson's 1969 annual message was also his farewell address. Among the unresolved challenges facing the country he listed urban unrest, poverty, welfare, education, law and order, the crisis in the Middle East, difficulties with the communists, the threat of nuclear war, and the war in Vietnam. He made a few general remarks in support of free trade, the need for a stronger international monetary system and economic assistance to developing countries. He said Western Europe occupied "a very special place" in America's affairs and expressed his support for European unity. He said instability in the Middle East and lack of a peace settlement was a threat to Israel, the Arab States, and the entire world. He expressed his hopes

American and Soviet long-range missiles would be limited—and speculated more progress could have been made except for "the brutal invasion of Czechoslovakia." He looked forward to the day when relations with the Soviet Union would be better, and Russia would be "less afraid of diversity and individual freedom."

Johnson regretted his inability to restore peace to South Vietnam, and anticipated the possibility of much more fighting before a settlement would be reached. He believed, rightly so, Americans were united in the hope the war in Vietnam could be brought to an early and peaceful end. He said peace talks were underway in Paris, and the prospects for peace were better than they were four years ago. Finally, he said aggression would neither help the North Vietnamese achieve their goals nor bring victory to the "Communist cause." This statement appears to dismiss the possibility that Vietnamese nationalism rather than international communism was the driving force in Hanoi, and thus indicates Johnson's understanding of the situation in 1969 was no better than it was when he took office in 1963.

9

Arms Control II and Limited War III: Vietnam
Nixon Doctrine; Rapprochement with China; Peace Talks; OPEC Oil Embargo; War Powers Resolution

Peace was the recurring theme of Richard Nixon's 1969 inaugural address. For the first time in history, he said, "the leaders of the world are afraid of war" because "the people of the world want peace." He said Americans wanted peace but were "caught in war." He called on Americans to be peacemakers and lead the world onto the "high ground of peace" so history could say we "helped make the world safe for mankind." Not to be outdone by Woodrow Wilson, Nixon said we should make peace welcome where it is unknown, strong where it is weak, and permanent where it is temporary. A world in which people exchanged goods freely and competed peacefully was preferable to a world in which people lived "in angry isolation."

•••

In February 1969, Yasser Arafat became chairman of the Palestinian Liberation Organization. In March, Golda Meir became prime minister of Israel. On May 14, Nixon spoke to the nation on Vietnam, what he called "our most difficult and urgent problem." In his first few months as president, nothing preoccupied him as much as the war in Vietnam. He acknowledged he could have already ended the war by ordering our forces home. Although that would have been the popular thing to do, he said it would have been irresponsible.

In fact, Nixon concluded, there was no easy way to end the war. He was eager to explore new initiatives because, he said, "Repeating the old formulas and the tired rhetoric of the past is not enough." What were the new initiatives Nixon hoped would bring "true peace"? Before his inauguration, he ordered a comprehensive review of the United States' policies on Vietnam, which would explore a wide range of alternatives and take into consideration the opinions of critics and supporters of past policies. The review brought to light a number of operational problems: there was deep distrust between Washington and Saigon, the Paris peace talks were going nowhere, and North Vietnam was planning another offensive.

In response to these operational problems, Nixon took action on several fronts simultaneously. First, he "restored" the relationships between Washington and Saigon. Second, he strengthened South Vietnam's armed forces. (This was important because if there were any developments in the Paris peace talks, South Vietnamese troops would be able to do "some of the fighting" being done by American troops.) Third, he said we "frustrated" North Vietnam's recent offensive and the enemy failed to achieve their military objectives. His use of the term frustrated—instead of any number of alternatives he could have chosen—is noteworthy. Although the North did fail to achieve its military objectives, it achieved all of its political objectives. As of May 1969—a brief four months into his presidency—Nixon seems to have developed the same blind spot as Johnson.

Nixon said the status of the war at that moment was very different from two or four years ago. There were more than five hundred thousand American troops in Vietnam, with more than thirty-six thousand killed. Therefore, the choice *not* to intervene was no longer available. One could debate the way the war was being managed or if we should have gotten involved in the first place. Neither of those debates would solve the urgent question of the day. Bearing in mind it was Nixon who said we should reject old formulas and tired rhetoric—he decided not to attempt "to impose a purely military solution on the battlefield." In addition, he ruled out withdrawing from Vietnam unilaterally or accepting any peace settlement that resembled a defeat for the United States.

If we abandon Vietnam now, he predicted, the Viet Cong and the North Vietnamese might massacre millions of South Vietnamese men, women, and children. We might also jeopardize the long-term peace and stability of the world. In a stunning display of illogic, Nixon said if we abandoned Vietnam, other nations might question our reliability (but not our judgment) and "the *cause of peace* might not survive the damage." (Italics added.) In his words: "If Hanoi were to succeed in taking over South Vietnam by force—even after the power of the United States had been engaged—it would greatly strengthen those leaders who scorn negotiation, who advocate aggression, who minimize the risks of confrontation with the United States. It would bring peace now but it would enormously increase the danger of a bigger war later."[1]

Thus, we had to demonstrate to North Vietnam, and therefore to the world that confronting the United States was both costly and unrewarding. Nixon echoed what Johnson said in 1964 following the fraudulent Gulf of Tonkin incident: we had no military, political, or territorial ambitions in Vietnam. Like Johnson, Nixon said our objectives were *limited*. He wanted the South to be able to exert its political rights without force or intimidation. Any form of government was acceptable to Nixon—he had no objection to reunification—as long as it was the free choice of the people.

This brings us to the Paris peace talks. Because Nixon rejected either a unilateral withdrawal or any peace settlement resembling an American defeat, there would be no peace in Vietnam for the time being. What were the terms Nixon would accept? Nixon revealed only two. First, all Viet Cong, North Vietnamese, and American forces had to withdraw from the South. Second, there needed to be procedures to ensure power sharing among South Vietnam's various groups. Nixon offered to withdraw American troops if the North agreed to withdraw theirs from the South Vietnam, and from Cambodia and Laos, according to a mutually agreed timetable.

Nixon qualified the terms by adding the United States would begin withdrawing troops as soon as an agreement was reached. (He anticipated the complete withdraw would take twelve months.) An international supervisory body would be established to verify troop withdrawals and monitor elections. Also, both sides would release prisoners of war once arrangements could be made. Though he was willing to consider other proposals, he warned the North not to mistake his generosity or flexibility for weakness. Nixon reminded people of his campaign promise to end the war, and said his terms were generous. Finally, he said, "I have tried to present the facts about Vietnam with complete honesty, and I shall continue to do so in my reports to the American people."

•••

In July 1969, American astronaut Neil Armstrong became the first man to land on the moon. During a press conference while Nixon was traveling through Guam, he announced the United States' allies in Asia would need to provide a greater share of their self-defense in the future, except when a major power using nuclear weapons was involved.[2] This marked the debut of the Nixon Doctrine and the beginning of the process of "Vietnamization." Nixon then went on to visit South Vietnam and meet with President Nguyen Van Thieu.

In September 1969, Nixon addressed the UN General Assembly, expanding on his vision of the United States' role in world affairs and the United States' contribution to "the structure of peace."[3] With power comes responsibility he said, and since the end of WWII the United States assumed "the major responsibility for world peace." Because the world had recovered (mostly) from the turmoil caused by the war, the United States' allies could no longer be dependent on American assistance. Instead, the world was "maturing together into a new pattern of interdependence." Because of this, the United States would begin urging its allies to assume greater responsibility for their own security, individually and collectively. Actually, it was Eisenhower, not Nixon, who began urging the United States' allies to assume greater responsibility for their own security in his 1953 state of the union message.

Again, Nixon said nothing occupied as much of his time since he became president as searching for a way to end the war. He knew Americans wanted to end the war and pledged to take "every reasonable step" to do so. One unreasonable step would be to accept a peace settlement that would arbitrarily deny the self-determination of South Vietnam. As far as Nixon was concerned, this was "our one limited but fundamental objective." Nixon said it was almost a year since the bombing of North Vietnam stopped and three months since the troop withdrawals began. In other words, Vietnamization was moving forward—and Nixon was frustrated because the North was not reciprocating.

Expanding the scope of his remarks beyond Vietnam, Nixon turned his attention to broader foreign policy issues. Relations between the Americans and the Soviets were beginning to thaw, and for the first time since WWII, there was a spirit of trust and recognition of our mutual interests. The era of confrontation was over and the era of negotiation was beginning. Another issue under consideration included the Middle East peace settlement. Nixon was concerned (rightly) that the seeds of the next Arab–Israeli war had already been planted. But there would be no peace until each nation recognized its neighbor's right to exist, and its right to secure boundaries without substantial alterations in the map. Nixon lamented he was unsuccessful in his effort to negotiate with the Soviets to halt arms shipments to the Middle East or limit strategic arms. Perhaps hinting at his historic overture to China (which would take place in February 1972), Nixon said, "Whenever the leaders of Communist China choose to abandon their self-imposed isolation, we are ready to talk with them in the same frank and serious spirit."

●●●

In early November 1969, Nixon gave an update on the situation in Vietnam. The war had caused millions of Americans to lose confidence in the government. "The American people cannot and should not be asked to support a policy which involves the overriding issues of war and peace unless they know the truth about that policy," he said. Nixon then described his understanding of the situation when he came into office ten months earlier. In his words:

> The war had been going on for 4 years. 31,000 Americans had been killed in action. The training program for the South Vietnamese was behind schedule.

540,000 Americans were in Vietnam with no plans to reduce the number. No progress had been made at the negotiations in Paris and the United States had not put forth a comprehensive peace proposal. The war was causing deep division at home and criticism from many of our friends as well as our enemies abroad.[4]

Because of these circumstances, Nixon said some people urged him to order a unilateral and immediate withdrawal from Vietnam. As he said before, this course of action would have been both "popular and easy" with no political downside because he could just blame the defeat on Lyndon Johnson. However, he did not do this because he wanted to consider the consequences of his decision on future generations. The question was not whether Johnson's war would become Nixon's war, but how could America win the peace.

According to Nixon, the winding road that got us caught up in Vietnam began during the Eisenhower administration, when North Vietnam attempted to instigate a revolution in South Vietnam. Eisenhower's decision to supply the South with military and economic aid was his response to a concerted effort by the Soviet Union, the PRC, and North Vietnam to impose a communist government on the South. Then Kennedy sent sixteen thousand troops to Vietnam to serve as military advisors. Then Johnson sent combat troops. Nixon said he disagreed both with Johnson's decision to send combat troops and with Johnson's management of the war.

After ten months in office, Nixon continued to insist the reason he could not unilaterally withdraw U.S. forces from Vietnam was that it would have been a disaster for the South, for the United States and for "the cause of peace." If we withdrew our forces, the North Vietnamese communists would massacre the South. Then hinting at the real reason, Nixon said if we withdrew, it would be the first military defeat in the nation's history and would cause the world community to lose confidence in the United States' leadership. Our withdrawal would be "a disaster of immense magnitude" because it would appear we were betraying our allies. "Our defeat and humiliation in South Vietnam without question would promote recklessness in the councils of those great powers who have not yet abandoned their goals of world conquest," he said.

He repeated his proposal from the previous May: he would withdraw U.S. troops completely from Vietnam in one year; and there would be a cease-fire followed by free elections in the South. Anything was negotiable except the South's right to self-determination. Then Nixon revealed his "quest for peace" actually began before the date of inauguration. Soon after the November 1968 election (acting through an intermediary), Nixon said he made two private offers to Hanoi's leaders in the hope of a "rapid, comprehensive settlement." According to Nixon, Hanoi's response to his extraordinary overture was to demand the United States' surrender.

In addition, Nixon reported a number of his advisors were negotiating with the Soviets to induce them to stop supplying military equipment to the North—or at least to put a little pressure on Hanoi. Nixon also revealed he sent a letter directly to Ho Chi Minh, outside the usual diplomatic channels in the hope the two could communicate man to man. Reading from the letter, Nixon said the war had gone on too long, expressed his solemn desire for peace, and offered again to negotiate. Nixon received a reply three days before Ho died in late August, which Nixon said only reiterated the same position North Vietnam was holding in the Paris peace talks. Sadly, there was no progress to report in the negotiations since even before Johnson halted the bombing the year before. Nixon said the blame belonged entirely to Hanoi.

Nixon had put into motion another plan, which he hoped would end the war—or at least end the United States' involvement some day—regardless of the lack of progress in the peace talks. "Let me briefly explain what has been described as the Nixon Doctrine—a policy which not only will help end the war in Vietnam, but which is an essential element of our program to prevent future Vietnams," he said. The doctrine consisted of three principles that would guide American foreign policy in Asia. First, the United States would keep all treaty commitments. Second, the United States would continue to provide a nuclear shield for our allies and any country we considered vital to American national security. Third, the United States would provide military and economic aid upon request, but the nation requesting U.S. aid would bear the primary responsibility for supplying troops.

Americanization of the war was over, and Vietnamization had begun, and the results were already evident. Air operations were down 20 percent and more than sixty thousand men, including 20 percent of all combat troops had been withdrawn. South Vietnamese troops were taking over combat responsibilities according to a specified timetable—though Nixon deliberately chose not to publicize it or reveal any particulars to Hanoi. As usual, Nixon warned Hanoi not to interpret his actions as a sign of weakness and said he would take action if American troops were in jeopardy.

●●●

In mid-December 1969, Nixon addressed the nation again to report progress on Vietnam.[5] He elaborated on his two approaches to reduce and eventually end American involvement in the war, either through a peace settlement or through Vietnamization. The purpose of Nixon's national address that evening was to report there was no progress. Hanoi's position remained unchanged: withdrawal of all American forces from Vietnam and unification of North and South Vietnam. Nixon regarded this as nothing but "defeat and humiliation" for the United States, and could not accept it. Despite his obvious frustration, he pledged to keep negotiating a peace settlement fair to all parties.

Regarding the progress of Vietnamization, Nixon reminded his listeners the rate of withdrawal would depend on several factors, including the progress of the peace talks, the training of South Vietnamese forces, and the level of enemy activity. The Paris peace talks were making no progress. The training program for Vietnamese troops was moving forward, but enemy activity and infiltration were increasing. Although Nixon was not concerned the North was preparing for a major offensive, he and his national security team were monitoring the situation carefully. Based on this, Nixon announced his decision to withdraw fifty thousand more U.S. troops by mid-April 1970, for a total reduction in force since his inauguration of one hundred fifteen thousand men. Finally, he issued his standard warning to North Vietnam not to interpret the troop withdrawals as a sign of weakness and recommended that Hanoi "abandon its dreams of military victory." Clearly, Nixon hoped the American people would take it as a sign that he was serious about ending the war.

•••

In his 1970 annual message, Nixon said his top foreign policy priority was to end the war in Vietnam and to negotiate a just and sustainable peace. Nixon wanted to base his foreign policy on an assessment of the world as it was then, not as it was at the end of WWII. "Many of the policies which were necessary and right then are obsolete today," he said. Because of the destruction caused by WWII, and the United States' overwhelming military and economic strength, the United States had the greatest responsibility to maintain peace and stability around the world. But Japan and most of Europe had recovered, many new nations had emerged from colonialism a decade before. Thus, America should not and could not be the driving force behind the defense or the development of other nations. "The nations of each part of the world should assume the primary responsibility for their own well-being" he said, "and they themselves should determine the terms of that well-being."[6]
Nixon pledged the United States would keep its treaty commitments, but reduce its involvement in the affairs of other nations. Nixon believed his new policy would strengthen our alliances and initiate a renewed sense of common purpose. In Europe, the foundation of our relations would be mutual consultation. In Latin America, we would be partners rather than patrons. In Asia, we would expand peace and prosperity in the region through our relationship with Japan. We would work to develop a new relationship with the Soviet Union, moving away from confrontation, and toward negotiation. In a phrase epitomizing practical idealism, Nixon said, "Our negotiations on strategic arms limitations and in other areas will have far greater chance for success if both sides enter them motivated by mutual self-interest rather than naive sentimentality." Finally, he announced his administration had quietly resumed discussions with the PRC.

In mid-April 1970, Nixon addressed the nation again on the situation in Vietnam. Nixon restated the three factors that would affect the rate at which he would withdraw troops: training South Vietnamese troops, progress in the peace talks, and the level of enemy activity. Once again, there was a stalemate in the negotiations taking place in Paris. Hanoi was still demanding the United States withdraw all forces from Vietnam unilaterally and unconditionally. If we agreed to this, we would be helping to overthrow the South Vietnamese government, and in effect, forcibly replacing it with a communist dictatorship. "That would mean humiliation and defeat for the United States," he said, "This we cannot and will not accept."[7]

Nixon reported there were thousands of North Vietnamese soldiers in Laos and Cambodia launching attacks into South Vietnam, and the North continued to send men, materiel, and supplies down the Ho Chih Minh Trail. Because good progress in training South Vietnamese troops was taking place, however, Nixon pledged to continue withdrawing American forces. An additional one hundred fifty thousand would be withdrawn in the next twelve months, totaling two hundred sixty-five thousand since Nixon took office a little more than fifteen months earlier. Again, Nixon repeated his customary warning to the North not to take advantage of his Vietnamization program. There was a shorter path to peace, he said, through negotiation and compromise.

Nixon's primary objective remained a political solution ensuring South Vietnam would be able to exercise its self-determination while maintaining the stability and political representation of various groups within South Vietnam. If only Hanoi responded positively to his offer in Paris, most American troops would be already home. According to Nixon, Hanoi demanded we stop the bombing and withdraw our troops as a precondition to the peace talks, and he was frustrated because he was no closer to a political solution. "It is Hanoi and Hanoi alone that stands today blocking the path to a just peace for all the peoples of Southeast Asia." However, he also claimed that pacification was succeeding and peace was within reach. He made the carefully worded assertion that South Vietnam "can develop the capability for their own defense," which is short of saying the South could actually defend itself.

Somewhat carelessly, he said North Vietnam failed to win because they made three basic mistakes. First, they failed to win a military victory against American and South Vietnamese forces. Second, they failed to win a political victory in the South. Third, they failed to win a political victory in America. "This proved to be their most fatal miscalculation," he said. Only time would tell Nixon was wrong on the second and third counts. Technically, he was right on the first count but it was irrelevant.

•••

In late April 1970, U.S. forces invaded Cambodia on a search and destroy mission against Viet Cong troops and bases across the border. On April 30—just ten days after he last spoke to the nation about Vietnam— Nixon delivered another address.[8] Because of increased military activity, particularly in Cambodia, Nixon decided to take "strong and effective measures" in order to protect our troops and continue the process of Vietnamization.

The problem according to Nixon was that the North Vietnamese were not respecting Cambodia's neutrality. For several years, the North maintained camps along Vietnam's border with Cambodia. North Vietnamese and Viet Cong troops used the camps as training and storage facilities— ammunition, weapons, and prisoners of war—and to stage raids into South Vietnamese territory. Even though this practice had been going on for several years, Nixon said he never took action before because he did not wish to violate the sovereignty of a neutral nation. During the last two weeks, however, the North was using these camps for more than guerilla raids, they were surrounding Phnom Penh (Cambodia's capital approximately one hundred thirty miles northwest of Hanoi) and concentrating their forces perhaps in advance of a major operation. Subsequently, said Nixon, Cambodia requested assistance from the United States.

Faced with this situation, Nixon considered three options. First, he could do nothing, which meant North Vietnam would go on using Cambodian territory to attack South Vietnam with impunity. Doing nothing might also interrupt the troop withdrawal schedule and endanger the lives of American troops. Second, he could furnish Cambodia with "massive military assistance." Nixon rejected this option because it was unrealistic to expect Cambodia to use the military assistance effectively given the time constraints and the urgency of the threat. Third, he would "go to the heart of the trouble," meaning clean out the North Vietnamese and Viet Cong camps along the border—and that was what Nixon chose to do.

Nixon assured the audience South Vietnamese troops were taking "major responsibility" for the invasion into Cambodia, but the United States was providing air and logistical support. Then Nixon announced American and South Vietnamese troops would launch a major attack—that night—against North Vietnamese and Viet Cong forces in Cambodia. "This is not an invasion of Cambodia," he said. His goal was not to occupy Cambodian territory, but to drive enemy forces out of positions from which they could threaten U.S. troops.

In addition, Nixon said invading Cambodia was indispensable to the troop withdrawal program. He was not expanding the war, he said, but helping to end the war and minimize American casualties. Yet again, Nixon blamed Hanoi for the conflict and for the lack of progress putting an end to it, decrying their intransigence, belligerence, and aggression. Nixon issued yet another warning: if Hanoi persisted in escalating the violence, he would take whatever action was necessary to protect American troops.

•••

In May 1970, the Ohio National Guard killed four student demonstrators at Kent State University. In June, the U.S. Senate repealed the Gulf of Tonkin Resolution. In September, former naval officer and Vietnam combat veteran John Kerry attended a rally in Valley Forge, Pennsylvania to protest the war.

In early October 1970, Nixon went before the nation again to discuss his latest peace initiative.[9] When Nixon ordered the invasion of Cambodia, he also began negotiating a cease-fire throughout Indochina. He called this a "cease-fire-in-place" because the various combatants would remain in the positions they then held. This would not end the war, but create an opportunity to renew peace talks, an unusual approach, but appropriate and necessary because this was a guerilla war with ambiguous front lines. His proposal included several principles. First, international observers must monitor it. Second, none of the participants could take advantage of the cease-fire to reinforce their combat forces. Third, it must include all kinds of warfare, including terrorism and bombing. Fourth, it must include all of Indochina, not just Vietnam. Fifth, the cease-fire should be a step toward negotiating an end to the war.

Approximately half of the total number of American troops stationed in Vietnam had been withdrawn since Nixon took office. Because his Vietnamization program was proceeding, he pledged his willingness to negotiate a complete withdrawal as part of a comprehensive peace settlement, though his position was almost identical to his previous statements. He said the North's intention to dismantle South Vietnam's government and political structure violated their right to self-determination. Thus, any settlement had to reflect the will of the South Vietnamese, including the relationships between existing political forces. Finally, Nixon proposed (he practically begged) all participants to release their prisoners of war.

In his 1971 annual message, Nixon did something no president had done since the second half of the nineteenth century. Amazingly, he devoted all of his state of the union speech to domestic policy and omitted foreign policy completely.

•••

In April 1971, Nixon delivered another address to the nation. First, Nixon announced he was increasing the rate of troop withdrawals from Vietnam. He then launched into another review of the situation he found when he came into office. As a matter of principle, it is a good thing for a president to communicate his policies and keep his constituents informed. By April 1971, however, Nixon was in office more than two years. Like every president in American history, Nixon inherited many policies from previous administrations. The situation *he found* was no longer relevant.

Nonetheless, Nixon began his review of the Vietnam situation by going back to 1961, when he left Washington after serving two terms as vice president under Dwight Eisenhower. By the time he returned to Washington eight years later, there were more than half a million Americans in Vietnam and more than thirty thousand killed. (By the time of this speech, the number killed was over fifty thousand.) However, his Vietnamization program was moving in the right direction. More than half the American troops stationed in Vietnam—two hundred sixty-five thousand men—would be home by the following month.

Nixon reiterated the reasons behind his decision to invade Cambodia the previous year. Despite the possibility of widening the war, increasing U.S. casualties or slowing down the troop withdrawals, Nixon reported he withdrew our forces from Cambodia less than two months after the initial invasion. He also provided his assessment of the Laotian operation, in which South Vietnamese forces received air support from the United States. First, the operation demonstrated the South could fight successfully against the North without American advisors. The Laotian operation also disrupted the North's supply lines, consumed ammunition, and weakened their ability to sustain an attack. As a result, Nixon declared his Vietnamization program a success and announced he was increasing the rate of troop withdrawals. One hundred thousand more troops would be coming home by December that year, which would mean more than two-thirds of the total since he took office.

His offer (from the previous October) of an immediate cease-fire, followed by a regional conference to discuss peace in Indochina was still on the table. As long as it was still on the table, Nixon preferred not to announce a specific date when American involvement in Vietnam would end because he was concerned about losing his advantage in the peace talks and perhaps endangering the release of American prisoners of war. The change in his stated goal ("total American withdrawal from Vietnam") was conspicuous. In Nixon's words:

> The issue very simply is this: Shall we leave Vietnam in a way that—by our own actions—consciously turns the country over to the Communists? Or shall we leave in a way that gives the South Vietnamese a reasonable chance to survive as a free people? My plan will end American involvement in a way that would provide that chance. And the other plan would end it precipitately and give victory to the Communists.[10]

One year earlier, he said his primary objective was a political solution that would ensure South Vietnamese self-determination. A year later, his motive was to end the war in a way that did not resemble a defeat, and his objective was to ensure South Vietnam would have *a reasonable chance to survive*. Nonetheless, American involvement in Vietnam was slowly but surely ending.

•••

In June 1971, the *New York Times* began publishing the Pentagon Papers, after Daniel Ellsberg, a civilian employee at the Rand Corporation copied thousands of classified documents regarding the government's management of the Vietnam War, and then leaked them to the *Times*. The Pentagon Papers included many classified Defense and State Department documents, and revealed government officials realized the war was unwinnable. The revelation destroyed public trust and embarrassed the Nixon administration.

In mid-August 1971, Nixon announced the gold standard would no longer determine the exchange rate of the U.S. dollar, essentially ending the Bretton Woods system of floating/fixed monetary exchange rates created following WWII. That fall, the PRC became a member of the United Nations and the UN Security Council.

In his 1972 annual message, Nixon announced he would be traveling to China and the Soviet Union that year. He remarked there were "great differences" between us, but world peace depended on the great powers finding a way to coexist peacefully. He predicted the new year would mark the beginning of the greatest progress toward peace in twenty-five years. Because American involvement in Vietnam was ending, we now had the opportunity to "build a generation of peace." To accomplish that we would need to maintain a strong national defense—and therefore increase defense spending.

The world had changed dramatically since 1961 when John Kennedy pledged to pay any price, bear any burden, meet any hardship, support any friend, and oppose any foe. The world had entered a new era he said, and the time came to adjust our foreign policy to "meet the new realities" of the era. Although the country's commitment to freedom would remain unshakable, the United States would no longer make commitments we were unwilling or unable to keep. Our friends and allies would have to start contributing a greater share of their self-defense.

Again, this is not as radical a departure as Nixon believed. In Eisenhower's 1953 annual message, he explicitly stated mutual security means America's allies have to contribute their full share. According to Nixon's "new" foreign policy framework, the United States would maintain a nuclear force capable of deterring or meeting any threat to our (and our allies') national security. The United States would also help other nations develop defensive capabilities, honor all treaty commitments, and protect American interests if they were threatened anywhere in the world. If our interests were not threatened and our treaty commitments were not at stake, then we would not intervene militarily. We would use our influence to prevent war, but if war came, we would use our influence to stop it. After the war, we would provide assistance to help the participants recover.

In late January 1972, Nixon announced a plan he said could end the war almost immediately, bring home all American troops—and all prisoners of war—within six months.[11] Nixon recounted a series of secret negotiations between his envoys and the North Vietnamese, spanning a period of eighteen months. By going public with the proposals at that time, he hoped to break the deadlock and make a deal.

The essence of Nixon's peace plan included familiar elements: first, within six months of the agreement, the United States would withdraw all troops from South Vietnam. Second, there would be a cease-fire throughout Indochina. Third, there would be an exchange of all prisoners of war. Fourth, South Vietnam would hold a presidential election supervised by an independent, international body. Nixon's offer would allow all political parties—including the communists—to participate in and help run the elections. Nixon had made this offer more than three months before, but the North Vietnamese were stalling. He tried to assure his audience this was a settlement, not surrender. Regardless, Nixon promised American troop withdrawals would continue even if Hanoi refused to accept his plan.

•••

In late February 1972, Nixon made a one-week visit to the PRC, unprecedented for a sitting American president. Nixon met with Communist Party Chairman Mao Zedong and had a series of meetings with Premier Zhou Enlai. Nixon and Zhou discussed a wide variety of regional issues, the substance of which would remain classified decades later. At the end of Nixon's trip, the United States and China issued the joint Shanghai Communiqué, in which the United States made a commitment to self-determination for all the people of Indochina, and pledged to continue negotiating an end to the conflict in Vietnam. Most important—because it epitomizes the practical side of practical idealism—the communiqué acknowledged "there is but one China and that Taiwan is a part of China."[12] Ultimately, Nixon's rapprochement with China following decades of estrangement would be his most significant foreign policy accomplishment.

•••

In late March 1972, North Vietnamese forces launched a massive offensive (with more than one hundred thousand troops) across the demilitarized zone into South Vietnam. In late April, Nixon went before the nation again to discuss the war and the status of the peace talks. Nixon said that even though Hanoi's response to his recent offer was to escalate their military activities, he would commit no American ground troops. However, Nixon did order American naval and air forces to attack North Vietnamese military installations and other targets. Furthermore, Nixon announced the withdrawal of American troops would continue.[13]

In an address to the nation that May, Nixon recounted North Vietnam's recent military activity—and this time noted they received tanks and artillery from the Soviets.[14] In response to North Vietnam's offensive, Nixon had only three alternatives. First, he could order the immediate withdrawal of American forces. Second, he could continue trying to negotiate a settlement. Third, he could take decisive military action. Once again, he said the "easy" thing politically would be to order the immediate withdrawal of all American troops. After all, it was Lyndon Johnson, not him, who sent half a million Americans to Vietnam. Nixon chose the third alternative, decisive military action and announced his order to mine Haiphong Harbor and bomb the Hanoi–Haiphong region from the air.

His short-term goal was to close access to the ports and stop the flow of supplies. Nixon also said he would continue naval and air strikes against rail and communication lines and other military targets. His ultimate objective was to persuade Hanoi to agree to his terms permitting the United States to "withdraw with honor." Arguing that his proposal was "the maximum of what any President of the United States could offer," he called the North Vietnamese insolent and arrogant. Toward the end of his speech, Nixon issued a thinly veiled warning to the Soviets not to intervene because it could hinder the new arms limitation agreement underway. One month later, Nixon and Leonid Brezhnev signed a treaty to limit antiballistic missile systems.[15]

•••

On June 17, 1972, police arrested five men after they broke into the offices of the Democratic National Committee at the Watergate Hotel in Washington, DC. During the Olympic Games that summer, an Arab terrorist group murdered eleven Israeli athletes at the Olympic Village in Munich, West Germany. In November, Richard Nixon won the presidential election in a landslide, defeating George McGovern, former WWII bomber pilot, congressman, and senator from South Dakota.

In his 1973 inaugural address, Nixon predicted the country was standing on the threshold of peace. He cautioned against retreating into isolation as we had done so often in "other postwar periods." Nixon used his second inaugural to announce his "new policies for peace," which would give the United States greater international responsibilities than ever before, particularly regarding Beijing and Moscow. He pledged to fulfill our treaty obligations, support self-determination, work to limit nuclear arms, and reduce tensions between the super powers. He said the United States would contribute its share to the common defense, and he expected our allies to contribute theirs. In Nixon's words:

> And let us be proud that by our bold, new initiatives, by our steadfastness for peace with honor, we have made a breakthrough toward creating in the world what the world has not known before—a structure of peace that can last, not merely for our time, but for generations to come. We are embarking here today on an era that presents challenges as great as those any nation, or any generation, has ever faced.[16]

As stated earlier, this framework was very similar to the one Eisenhower presented in 1953, and thus was not as innovative as Nixon believed. However, 1973 was destined to be a watershed year for Vietnam and the cold war. In late January, Nixon would deliver an address to announce he reached an agreement to end the Vietnam War, and bring "peace with honor." The people of South Vietnam, he said, would have the right of self-determination and continue to receive American aid. A cease-fire would take place, and all American troops would be coming home within sixty days.[17]

In late March, Nixon made the following announcement: "For the first time in 12 years, no American military forces are in Vietnam. All of our American POW's are on their way home."[18] What a difference this was from as recently as four years ago when there were more than half a million American troops in Vietnam, getting killed in action at a rate of three hundred per week. Our challenge now, said Nixon, was winning the peace.

Despite having just announced the end of the longest war in American history, he argued now was not the time to starting cutting our defense budget. "There is one unbreakable rule of international diplomacy" he said, "You can't get something in a negotiation unless you have something to give. If we cut our defenses before negotiations begin, any incentive for other nations to cut theirs will go right out the window." (Years later, Ronald Reagan would base his military buildup on the same "unbreakable rule.") If we unilaterally cut our defense budget, if the United States ever became the world's *second* most powerful nation, Nixon predicted the world would suffer irreparable harm.

●●●

In May 1973, the U.S. Senate began holding hearings on the developing Watergate scandal. In October, the Yom Kippur War began. Anwar Sadat of Egypt and Hafez al-Assad of Syria, wanted to win back the territory they lost to Israel in the 1967 Six-Day War. They launched a coordinated surprise attack on the Jewish holy day Yom Kippur. Syrian forces attacked the Golan Heights while Egyptian forces attacked around the Suez Canal and the Sinai Peninsula. The Syrians surprised the Israelis in the Golan Heights and moved toward the Sea of Galilee. The Israelis brought in reinforcements and pushed the Syrians back across the 1967 frontier, and then to the outskirts of Damascus. The Egyptians attacked Israeli fortifications, but their rapid forward movement into the Sinai desert stretched their supply lines. Israeli forces counterattacked and virtually surrounded Egyptian forces. By late October, the belligerents reached a cease-fire agreement and Israel agreed to withdraw its troops from the Suez Canal. The United Nations would later establish a demilitarized zone in the Sinai.

Back in August 1971, Nixon announced the gold standard would no longer determine the exchange rate of the U.S. dollar. Partly because of the dollar's subsequent devaluation, and partly because of the United States' support for the Israelis during the Yom Kippur War, several Arab members of OPEC (Organization of Petroleum Exporting Countries) declared an embargo and drastically raised the price of oil. This created an energy crisis in the United States and every other industrialized country, all of whom had grown dependent on inexpensive oil. As the retail price of gasoline increased, the U.S. government urged consumers to conserve energy—and later would order gasoline rationing and reduce the maximum speed limit nationwide. In addition, the crisis created an economic anomaly in which inflation and recession occurred simultaneously. The oil embargo would end in March the following year.

•••

In October 1973, Vice President Spiro Agnew resigned from office after pleading no contest to a charge he accepted bribes while serving as governor of Maryland. Nixon named Michigan congressman Gerald Ford to succeed Agnew.

In November, Congress passed the War Powers Resolution (overriding Nixon's veto), which limited presidential power to wage war without congressional approval.[19] The stated purpose of the resolution was "to fulfill the intent of the framers of the Constitution." The War Powers Resolution now required the president to consult with Congress before sending U.S. armed forces into any situation outside U.S. territory "where imminent involvement in hostilities is clearly indicated by the circumstances," and required the president to consult with and report to Congress on a regular basis as long as U.S. troops were in a combat zone.

To fulfill the reporting requirement, the president now had forty-eight hours to submit to Congress—in writing—an explanation of why the use of armed forces was required, an estimation of the scope and duration of the fighting, and any other information Congress requested. Furthermore, the president was required to terminate the use of any armed forces within sixty days of submitting the report unless Congress issued a formal declaration of war, issued a sixty-day extension or because the president was unable to comply because the United States was under attack.

In his 1974 annual message, Nixon reported the United States was at peace with the world for the first time in twelve years, all of our troops were home from Southeast Asia, our prisoners of war were back on American soil, and there was no draft. Nixon touted his recent arms limitation treaty with the Soviet Union, as well as his rapprochement to China. After more than two decades of hostile isolation, Nixon hoped to launch an era of "peaceful exchange and expanding trade" with the PRC.

One of Nixon's foreign policy goals for the new year was to "break the back" of the energy crisis, and contribute to world peace by helping negotiate "a just and lasting settlement in the Middle East." Nixon said the United States was committed to playing "an active role" in the region.

In fact, the United States was already playing two very active roles in the region—supplying weapons and buying oil—that would make playing the role of peacemaker problematic for decades to come.

•••

In May 1974, the Judiciary Committee of the U.S. House of Representatives held hearings to discuss Richard Nixon's impeachment based on his involvement in the Watergate scandal. In July, the Judiciary Committee charged Nixon with obstruction of justice, abuse of power, and contempt of Congress. On August 9, facing certain impeachment, Nixon resigned as president. Vice President Gerald Ford took the oath of office the following day.

During the 1976 presidential election, Gerald Ford won the Republican nomination after fending off a challenge from conservative Republican Ronald Reagan, former governor of California. The Democrats nominated Jimmy Carter, the former one term governor of Georgia. Many voters lost faith in the government because of the cover-ups during the Vietnam War and the Watergate scandal, and perhaps because of Ford's pardon (in September 1974) of Richard Nixon for any crimes he may have committed as president. Carter defeated Ford in a close election.

10

Arms Control III
and Strategic Defense II
Camp David Accord; Iran Hostage Crisis; Soviets Invade Afghanistan; Strategic Defense Initiative; Terrorist Attack in Lebanon; Invasion of Grenada; Iran-Contra Affair

In his 1977 inaugural address, Jimmy Carter said our foreign policy should be consistent with the same rules and principles that would apply at home, an observation Calvin Coolidge probably would have admired. The United States was so strong he said, that we did not need to rely on our military strength, but could demonstrate it quietly though the "nobility" of our ideas. The enemies we would fight against were poverty, ignorance, and injustice. According to Carter, the United States was "a purely idealistic nation" with a powerful moral compass and a preference for other nations who respected human rights as deeply as we did. Carter said the principles we held most deeply would drive his foreign policy, and he pledged to work for arms limitation as a step toward his ultimate goal: the elimination of all nuclear weapons.[1]

In a March 1977 speech at the United Nations, Carter said he believed the demand for human rights was a powerful force in the world.[2] Echoing the first of Wilson's fourteen points, he promised U.S. foreign policy in his administration would be more open. He pledged to end the arms race, asserting that accumulating thousands of nuclear weapons increased the threat of war and actually made both the Americans and the Soviets less secure, not more. Carter gave a brief description of what he hoped to accomplish with respect to each of the world's geographic regions: he would move forward with multilateral trade negotiations in Geneva, help strengthen democratic institutions in Portugal and Spain, work for a long-term peace settlement in the Middle East, and help bring about a peaceful end to apartheid in South Africa. He pledged a more constructive relationship between the United States and Latin America, particularly concerning the future of the Panama Canal, and looked forward to improving the United States' relationships with China and Vietnam. Carter wanted to continue pursuing SALT (strategic arms limitations) talks with the Soviets "with determination and with energy." Carter favored deeply reducing nuclear weapons on both sides, freezing production, halting their proliferation, and completely discontinuing nuclear testing.

"The basic thrust of human affairs," said Carter "points toward a more universal demand for fundamental human rights." Every country that joined the United Nations first had to sign the UN Charter, and thus took a pledge to respect human rights. That meant no member of the United Nations could mistreat its own citizens and then claim it was exclusively an internal matter. Another of his challenges was to mold a global economic system to bring prosperity to people in every country. Carter announced he would ask Congress for more foreign aid, try to increase the United States' financial contributions to the UN Development Program, International Development Association, and the World Bank, and try to increase the number of developing countries participating in the International Monetary Fund. He also pledged his commitment to "an open international trading system" in which American exporters would enjoy reciprocity and equal access to foreign markets that importers had to the huge American market.

•••

In May 1977, Carter gave the commencement address at Notre Dame University. With this speech, Carter attempted to present a comprehensive foreign policy framework for the first time, promising the fundamental values of democracy and human rights would be his guide.[3] Because of the common sense of the American people, Carter believed they should "share in the process of making foreign policy decisions." Carter reiterated his post-Watergate promise of openness, implying a democratic foreign policy would be inherently superior to one made by "an isolated handful."

Over the years, this "isolated handful" of policy-makers abandoned America's principles and adopted the "flawed and erroneous principles" of our enemies. Vietnam was the best example of the "intellectual and moral poverty" of this failed approach. According to Carter, two principles guided America's foreign policy since WWII. The first was containment of Soviet expansion. The second principle, which reinforced the first, was maintaining a strong alliance of noncommunist nations on both sides of the Atlantic. Carter then implied the cold war had lost some of its vitality. "That system could not last forever unchanged," he said, "Historical trends have weakened its foundation. The unifying threat of conflict with the Soviet Union has become less intensive, even though the competition has become more extensive."

Regardless of one's opinion of Jimmy Carter's presidency—or his postpresidential career for that matter—the record states he detected the same historical trends as several of his predecessors, as recently as Richard Nixon and as far back as Harry Truman. Carter saw dramatic change taking place; where colonialism was finished, new forms of nationalism that had been dormant for decades were stirring. He acknowledged there was still plenty of danger in the world, with ideological disagreements, and racial, tribal, and regional conflicts. The dramatic changes in the world called for a new vision of American foreign policy. Sounding similar to both Truman and Eisenhower, his new vision would be global in scope, rather than limited to the narrow interests of industrialized nations.

Carter's foreign policy rested on five cardinal principles. First, he would promote human rights, but not necessarily conduct his foreign policy according to "rigid moral maxims." Second, he would reinforce our alliances with the world's democracies in terms of economic cooperation, trade, and defense. Third, he would pursue an agreement with the Soviets to stop the dangerous and "morally deplorable" arms race. His goals in this area were to freeze production of nuclear weapons and substantially reduce their numbers, ban testing, prohibit all chemical warfare—and ultimately—sign an agreement to eliminate all nuclear weapons. Fourth, he would work for peace in the Middle East, particularly involving Israel, Syria, Jordan, and Egypt. In particular, Carter would focus on several key issues: articulating what peace meant to the Israelis and Arabs, increasing security for all parties, resolving border disputes, and establishing a Palestinian homeland. Fifth, Carter would lead a global effort to reduce the proliferation of nuclear and conventional weapons.

●●●

In his 1978 annual message, Carter said the government's disconnection from the American people weakened our foreign policy. Carter restated Wilson's first principle of diplomacy, arguing openness was one of the foundations of democracy, because decisions made after public debate would withstand the test of public scrutiny and be less prone to error.[4] Carter also brought up the Middle East conflict, the global economy, and the Panama Canal. In the Middle East, he clearly felt some urgency and hoped to negotiate a peaceful settlement of the long-standing conflict. Carter then turned his attention to the controversial business of transferring the Panama Canal. He said the new treaty would guarantee the canal would always be neutral and open to American ships, and in an emergency, our ships would have the right to go to the head of the line. Finally, Carter predicted the Panama Canal Treaty would demonstrate the United States' good faith, contribute to American national security and economic well-being, and "discourage the spread of hostile ideologies in this hemisphere."[5]

•••

In September 1978, Carter brokered the Camp David Accords between Egyptian president Anwar Sadat and Israeli prime minister Menachem Begin. The accord reaffirmed UN Security Council Resolution 242, which in 1967 acknowledged the sovereignty, territorial inviolability, and political independence of all states in the region, including Israel. The accord's ambitious goal was to create a framework for the entire region, not limited exclusively to Egypt and Israel.

The accord encouraged (but did not compel) the signatories, plus representatives from Jordan and the Palestinians to resolve "the Palestinian problem in all its aspects." Israel agreed to withdraw its troops and to give "full autonomy" to the inhabitants of the West Bank and Gaza. The accord encouraged various countries in the region, particularly Egypt, Jordan, Syria, and Lebanon to give full recognition to one another, end economic boycotts, grant equal protection under the law to each country's citizens, and explore opportunities for economic development. Under the terms of the accord, Israeli ships would have access to the Suez Canal, Israel would withdraw its forces from the Sinai, and there would be a demilitarized zone in the Sinai (east of the Gulf of Suez and west of the Gulf of Aqaba) with UN observers and limits on the size and location of armed forces. Most importantly, Egypt and Israel agreed to establish normal relations, including full diplomatic recognition.[6]

At the signing ceremony, Carter noted Anwar Sadat and Menachem Begin were actually signing two agreements. One was a peace treaty between Egypt and Israel and the other was a framework for peace in the Middle East. The peace treaty between Israel and Egypt was relatively straightforward. A few maps would have to be redrawn, but it resolved most of the disputes between the two countries. The other treaty was much more comprehensive, and encompassed a framework within which Israel could negotiate other treaties with Lebanon, Syria, and Jordan later on. Though he acknowledged great difficulties remained, Carter said together, the two agreements would assure Israel's security and help resolve "the Palestinian problem in all its aspects."[7]

Carter addressed a joint session of Congress the day after the signing ceremony. He said the Middle East was a "textbook for pessimism" and remarked it was 2,000 years since there was peace between Egypt and a free Jewish nation. As Carter acknowledged, "diplomatic ingenuity was no match for intractable human conflicts." Ignoring Calvin Coolidge's observation that humans would always outsmart any *human-made* formula for peace, Carter said the United States had no choice but ignore the barriers of ancient history, nationalism, and skepticism, and try to broker a peace settlement. Why did the United States have no choice? Carter began by referring to our deeply rooted values and "profound moral commitments." Then he got closer to the point: although there is no oil in Israel or Egypt, no region in the world had greater natural resources than the Middle East. "The strategic location of these countries and the resources that they possess mean that events in the Middle East directly affect people everywhere."[8]

•••

In his 1979 annual message, Carter said the primary goal of his presidency was to build world peace on a foundation of "our oldest American ideals," along with U.S. military power and a network of friendships and alliances, a fine conceptual summary of practical idealism. Carter praised America's armed forces, and urged Congress to support his defense budget, which he promised would increase the military's readiness, modernize its equipment, and strengthen the NATO alliance. However, said Carter, military power alone would be insufficient to guarantee our national security because people around the world were hungry for human rights. Carter called human rights the "wave of the future," and said the issue would not be which superpower would dominate the world ("None can and none will"), but how to create world peace.

Carter observed the United States did not seek to stifle change, but to protect its interests and promote peace in helpful, constructive ways. "We have no desire to be the world's policeman" he said, "But America does want to be the world's peacemaker." Carter believed the Panama Canal Treaty earned respect for the United States in Latin America, and his commitment to human rights and democracy—and opposition to apartheid—earned trust for the United States in Africa. He hoped to continue normalizing relations with China as long as it did not threaten Taiwan's security. He was pleased the United States was helping to find peaceful solutions to the dangerous conflicts in Nicaragua, Cyprus, Namibia, and Rhodesia—as well as Iran.

Carter restated his goal to control nuclear and conventional arms proliferation, and renewed his commitment to work with the Soviet Union. By then the second round of Strategic Arms Limitations Talks (or SALT II) had been going on for six years, and the cold war had been going on for thirty-three years. Although the conflict between the Jews and Arabs had been going on for 2,000 years, there is a notable difference between Carter's hopes for the Camp David Accord and SALT II. No treaty could replace a strong deterrent, he said, no treaty could end the threat of nuclear war, but only reduce the threat. For the benefit of any Soviet officials listening in, Carter said one example of the United States' deterrent capability was the Poseidon submarine. Although Poseidon submarines comprised less than 2 percent of our total nuclear force (which also included aircraft, land-based missiles, and other classes of submarine), just one of these relatively invulnerable vessels carried "enough warheads to destroy every large- and medium-sized city in the Soviet Union."[9]

•••

In January 1979, Mohammed Reza Pahlavi, the shah of Iran fled the country. In February, Ayatollah Ruhollah Khomeini returned to Iran after spending several years in exile. In March, Iran became an Islamic Republic. In May, Conservative Margaret Thatcher became prime minister of Great Britain. In June, Carter and Leonid Brezhnev signed "SALT II," and agreed to limit long-range, land-based intercontinental ballistic missile launchers. (Although the Senate never ratified the treaty because of the Soviet invasion of Afghanistan, both sides adhered to the terms.)[10] In late June, OPEC exacerbated the energy crisis by raising the price of crude oil again.

In mid-July 1979, Carter delivered his notorious *Crisis of Confidence* speech. The speech contained substantial foreign policy issues, but they received less attention than they deserved. Although inflation and unemployment were high and economic growth was sluggish, Carter said the country's real problem was neither the economy nor the energy crisis. "It's clear that the true problems of our Nation are much deeper," he said, deeper than gasoline shortages, deeper even than inflation or recession. What the country was experiencing, he said, was a crisis of confidence.[11]

Given the unreliability of most of the world's oil producing countries, Carter believed it was imperative for the United States to reduce its dependency on foreign oil. Toward that end, he presented a six-point plan to achieve energy independence. First, he pledged the United States would "never use more foreign oil than we did in 1977—never." Second, he pledged to establish import quotas on foreign oil. Third, Carter would launch a program to explore and develop alternate sources of energy. Fourth, he would ask Congress to compel utility companies to reduce their oil consumption. Fifth, he would ask Congress to create an Energy Mobilization Board (analogous to Franklin Roosevelt's WWII-era War Production Board). Sixth, he would institute a conservation program involving every city, county, and state in the country. Two days later, Carter asked his entire cabinet to resign, and would accept resignations from five, including Treasury, Justice, Transportation, Energy, and Health, Education and Welfare.

•••

The second half of 1979 was full of events that would influence U.S. foreign policy for decades. In July, Saddam Hussein came to power in Iraq. Nicaraguan president Anastasio Somoza fled to the United States. In November, Iranian militants took over the U.S. embassy in Teheran and captured more than sixty American hostages. Carter's initial response was to order an embargo of Iranian oil and freeze billions of dollars of Iranian assets in the United States. In mid-November, the Ayatollah Khomeini would order the release of thirteen hostages. And in late December, the Soviet Union invaded Afghanistan.

In his 1980 annual message, Carter said because of the hostage situation in Iran and the invasion of Afghanistan, the last few months had not been an easy time. Faced with two crises, Carter said something best described as nonresponsive. In his words: "I'm determined that the United States will remain the strongest of all nations, but our power will never be used to initiate a threat to the security of any nation or to the rights of any human being. We seek to be and to remain secure—a nation at peace in a stable world. But to be secure we must face the world as it is."[12]

Although the principle of self-restraint is admirable—and no realist could quibble with facing the world as it is—when American diplomats are being held hostage in one of our own embassies, the American people have a right to expect the president to say something a lot more potent. Rather than address the crisis at hand, Carter spoke about the "basic developments" influencing our foreign relations. These were Soviet aggression, the United States' dependence on foreign oil, and the social, religious, political, and economic pressures facing many developing countries—exemplified by what was happening in Iran. Carter called the hostage taking abhorrent, and said the nation—during peacetime at least—had never been so unified and "aroused."

Carter thought he could persuade the Iranians that the Soviet Union—with thousands of their troops next door in Afghanistan—was the real danger. Since 1945, the most critical factor determining the state of the world was the relationship between the United States and the Soviet Union. It was a complex relationship, sometimes cooperative and sometimes competitive. Occasionally it was confrontational: in the 1950s, it was Korea and the Middle East; in the 1960s, it was Berlin and Cuba. In the 1970s, however, three American presidents sought to move beyond the cold war by ending the nuclear arms race and reducing the risk of conflict. (However, Carter's analysis omitted the Vietnam War, which transcended decades, killed more than fifty-eight thousand Americans and an unknown number of Vietnamese, Cambodians, and Laotians—more than a million and perhaps as many as five million combatants and civilians.)

Carter said the Soviet invasion of Afghanistan was perhaps the most serious threat to peace since WWII. Was it more serious than the Cuban missile crisis? Was it more serious than the Vietnam War? According to Carter, "The vast majority of nations on Earth have condemned this latest Soviet attempt to extend its colonial domination of others and have demanded the immediate withdrawal of Soviet troops." Unfortunately, however, Carter stopped short of demanding it himself on that particular occasion. Instead, he announced the "stiff economic penalties" he would impose on the Soviets, such as revoking their fishing permits in U.S. coastal waters, blocking their access to high-tech equipment, and refusing to send a team to the Moscow Olympics.

Carter then advanced the theory that the Soviet Union's real motive for the invasion was to "consolidate a strategic position" in the region containing the majority of the world's oil. In Afghanistan, the Soviets were only a few hundred miles away from the Straits of Hormuz, the waterway connecting the Persian Gulf and the Gulf of Oman, through which most of the world's oil flowed. The westernmost tip of Afghanistan is approximately three hundred miles from the Straits of Hormuz. Between Afghanistan and that strategic shipping channel is Iran, which recently staged an Islamic revolution and deposed a government friendly to the United States. Carter said the crises in Iran and Afghanistan taught us a valuable lesson: we were too dependent on foreign oil. Finally, he finally made his position clear: "An attempt by any outside force to gain control of the Persian Gulf region will be regarded as an assault on the vital interests of the United States of America, and such an assault will be repelled by any means necessary, including military force."

•••

In February 1980, Abolhassan Banisadr became president of Iran. Ayatollah Ruhollah Khomeini announced the Iranian parliament would decide the outcome of the American hostage crisis. In April, the United States severed diplomatic ties with Iran. In late April, the United States launched a mission to rescue the hostages called Operation Eagle Claw, but the mission failed, and several service personnel died in the attempt. A few days later, U.S. Secretary of State Cyrus Vance resigned in protest. In September, the Iran–Iraq War began.

During the 1980 presidential election, the Democrats renominated Jimmy Carter after he fended off a challenge from the left by Massachusetts senator Ted Kennedy. The Republicans nominated Ronald Reagan, the charismatic former governor of California and well-known film and television star. Because of Carter's ineffective response to the Iranian hostage crisis, the energy crisis, and the economy, Reagan won in a landslide.

•••

On January 19, 1981, the United States and Iran signed an agreement to release the fifty-two Americans being held hostage in Iran. In his 1981 inaugural address the following day, Ronald Reagan did not mention this or say anything significant regarding foreign policy. In February, Wojciech Jaruzelski came to power in Poland. (In December, Jaruzelski would declare martial law.) In March, Reagan survived an assassination attempt. In June, the Israeli Air Force bombed a nuclear reactor in Iraq. In October, Egyptian president Anwar Sadat died in an assassination.

In Reagan's 1982 annual message, he said his two highest budget priorities would be a strong national defense and a "reliable safety net of social programs." Sounding like a slogan for cable news, Reagan said his foreign policy would always be strong, fair, and balanced. During his first year in office, Reagan took credit for strengthening the United States as "a force for peace and progress in the world," restoring the country's "military credibility," pursuing peace at the negotiating table, and thus regaining the respect of our friends and enemies alike.[13]

He proposed higher defense spending and a tougher foreign policy, asserting, "Our foreign policy must be rooted in realism." Like Carter, however, Reagan pledged to work with the Soviets toward an agreement that would reduce military forces on both sides, particularly intermediate-range nuclear missiles. In order to protect our national security—and get the Soviets to take the negotiations seriously—we had to negotiate from a position of strength, and that meant making substantial increases in defense spending.

•••

In April 1982, Argentinean troops invaded the Falkland Islands, an isolated British dependency in the South Atlantic, approximately eleven hundred miles south of Buenos Aires. Attacking without warning, Argentinean forces easily routed the token British garrison stationed there. In response, Prime Minister Margaret Thatcher deployed a naval task force of more than a hundred ships and twenty-seven thousand troops. As attempts to negotiate a peaceful end to the conflict failed, the British routed the Argentineans in a series of engagements. By mid-June, British troops reached the Falkland Islands capital Port Stanley, forcing the Argentineans to surrender, and capturing ten thousand prisoners of war. A few days later, the head of Argentina's military junta resigned—and Prime Minister Margaret Thatcher's popularity soared.

In early June 1982, while the war was not over yet, Ronald Reagan addressed the British parliament. He traveled to London between stops at an economic summit in Versailles and a NATO summit in Bonn. Reagan pointed to Poland's struggle for independence as a reminder never to take our own freedom for granted. Reagan said he was optimistic, however, because even after thirty years, none of the Soviet-style regimes in Eastern Europe had yet to establish their legitimacy or even hold free elections. From the Balkans to the Baltic Sea, none of the regimes "planted by bayonets" had taken root.[14]

However, said Reagan, we now faced threats to our freedom unimaginable to previous generations. The first was the threat of nuclear war, which could be the end of civilization. This was why the United States was negotiating with the Soviets on the START (Strategic Arms Reduction Talks) to reduce the risk of war. The second was the threat to freedom imposed "by the enormous power of the modern state." In Reagan's foreign policy, there was a relationship between these two threats, because the power of the state invariably led to the abuse of power. In Reagan's mind, there was no difference between Nazi Germany, the Soviet Union, or Cambodia under the Khmer Rouge party.

Reagan praised the British troops fighting the Falkland Islands War. They were not fighting for "lumps of rock," he said, but for democracy in the face of armed aggression. "If there had been firmer support for that principle some 45 years ago" he said, "perhaps our generation wouldn't have suffered the bloodletting of World War II." What did he mean when he said "that principle"? Although he used the passive voice, no doubt he meant what Harry Truman called the lesson of Munich: "Appeasement leads only to further aggression and ultimately to war."[15] If that is what Reagan meant, then he could not have chosen a more receptive audience.

Echoing one of Jimmy Carter's favorite themes, Reagan said people all over the world were rejecting the arbitrary power of the state and refusing to subordinate the rights of the individual. (If the reader is looking for the definition of human rights, it means rejecting the arbitrary power of the state and refusing to subordinate the rights of the individual.) Reagan said the Soviet Union was running against the tide of history because it denied freedom to its citizens. Reagan noted the steadily declining growth rate of the Soviet economy and its inability to feed itself even though 20 percent of its population worked in the agriculture sector. Meanwhile, Moscow continued to spend a disproportionate percentage of its resources on armed forces.

As stated, Lyndon Johnson, Richard Nixon, and Jimmy Carter were aware the cold war was winding down. Ronald Reagan detected the same historical trend. "The constant shrinkage of economic growth combined with the growth of military production is putting a heavy strain on the Soviet people," he said, "What we see here is a political structure that no longer corresponds to its economic base, a society where productive forces are hampered by political ones. The decay of the Soviet experiment should come as no surprise to us."[16]

Reagan said freedom was an inalienable and universal human right, and stated his objectives as follows: "to foster the infrastructure of democracy, the system of a free press, unions, political parties, universities, which allows a people to choose their own way to develop their own culture, to reconcile their own differences through peaceful means." This was the surest way he said, to protect diversity and establish genuine self-determination. Because democracy flourished in countries with different cultures and histories, it would be condescending or worse, to suggest anybody could prefer dictatorship to democracy. Over the long term, said Reagan "the march of freedom and democracy...will leave Marxism-Leninism on the ash-heap of history."

This strongly resembles two observations George W. Bush would make several years later. In his September 2001 speech to Congress, Bush said, the [al-Qaeda] terrorists, like the Nazis, would end up "in history's unmarked grave of discarded lies."[17] In Bush's 2004 annual message he said, "We also hear doubts that democracy is a realistic goal for the greater Middle East, where freedom is rare. Yet it is mistaken, and condescending, to assume that whole cultures and great religions are incompatible with liberty and self-government."[18]

Later in Reagan's speech to British Parliament, he said, "Since 1917 the Soviet Union has given covert political training and assistance to Marxist-Leninists in many countries. Of course, it also has promoted the use of violence and subversion by these same forces." This was slightly disingenuous because Reagan signed an order earlier in 1982 authorizing the U.S. government to help defeat the insurgency in El Salvador and oppose actions by Cuba, Nicaragua, or others to introduce foreign troops, weapons, or military supplies into Central America.[19] However, Reagan pledged to continue negotiating with the Soviets to reduce ballistic missiles, and repeated his conviction that strength was a prerequisite to peace, meaning substantial increases in defense spending would induce the Soviets to take the negotiations seriously. What would ultimately decide the outcome of the great struggle? It would not be military power, he said but "the values we hold, the beliefs we cherish [and] the ideals to which we are dedicated."

One day after his speech to British parliament, Reagan spoke to the West German Bundestag. Tacitly acknowledging the comprehensive cold war strategy launched during the Truman administration, Reagan expressed his satisfaction the United States had deterred nuclear war for almost forty years. "Our method has been to organize our defensive capabilities, both nuclear and conventional, so that an aggressor could have no hope of military victory," and our continued success would depend on keeping a strong alliance with well-equipped and trained military forces on both sides of the Atlantic.

Reagan said he was committed to maintaining NATO's nuclear deterrent —and equally committed to ending the arms race. His policies, he said were "based on the conviction that a stable military balance at the lowest possible level will help further the cause of peace." If the goal of his military buildup was to destroy the Soviet Union—rather than negotiate an arms control agreement—he gave no indication in this speech. "I'm optimistic about our relationship with the Soviet Union if the Western nations remain true to their values and true to each other. I believe in Western civilization and its moral power. I believe deeply in the principles the West esteems," he said, "And guided by these ideals, I believe we can find a no-nonsense, workable, and lasting policy that will keep the peace.[20]

•••

In September 1982, approximately twelve hundred U.S. Marines arrived in Beirut, Lebanon. Their mission was not well defined, but they were part of a multinational force (alternately described as an interposition, peacekeeping, or deterrent force) to protect the civilian population and keep the combatants apart during the Lebanese Civil War. In October, Helmut Kohl became chancellor of Germany, and the Solidarity movement was outlawed in Poland. In November, Yuri Andropov came to power in the Soviet Union.

In his 1983 annual message, Reagan's remarks on American foreign policy were quite brief. He reported the United States was "prosperous at home, strong and respected abroad, and at peace in the world." He said our leadership in the world *came to us* because of our strength and the values that guide our society, specifically "free elections, a free press, freedom of religious choice, free trade unions, and above all, freedom for the individual and rejection of the arbitrary power of the state." These values would serve as the cornerstone for the United States' foreign policy, which Reagan called a "comprehensive strategy for peace with freedom." He said military and economic strength would support the development of a worldwide infrastructure of democracy, and that "The restoration of a strong, healthy American economy has been and remains one of the central pillars of our foreign policy."[21]

Acknowledging the interdependence of the global economy, Reagan pledged to cooperate with Japan, Western Europe, and the International Monetary Fund to promote economic growth, low inflation, and free trade. Regarding defense policy, Reagan reported his administration developed "a realistic military strategy" and implemented a defense program that redeemed years of neglect. Sounding remarkably similar to many of his predecessors—Carter in particular—Reagan said his foreign policy was "based on bipartisanship, on realism, strength, full partnership, in consultation with our allies, and constructive negotiation with potential adversaries." Reagan then pledged his commitment to "carry on the peace process begun so promisingly at Camp David."

Echoing John Kennedy's *Alliance for Progress,* Reagan said the United States was "engaged in a partnership for peace, prosperity, and democracy" in the Western Hemisphere, particularly Central America and the Caribbean. "The security and economic assistance policies of this administration in Latin America and elsewhere are based on realism and represent a critical investment in the future of the human race." This undertaking is a joint responsibility of the executive and legislative branches," he said "and I'm counting on the cooperation and statesmanship of the Congress to help us meet this essential foreign policy goal." This was where Reagan planted the seeds of the Iran-Contra affair.

Finally, Reagan said the heart of his foreign policy was the United States' relationship with the Soviet Union. He restated his commitment to negotiate arms reductions, but insisted he would sign an agreement only if the reductions were verifiable. Because of the new Soviet leadership, Reagan looked forward to an improvement in Soviet–American relations. Admonishing the Soviets to respect the sovereignty of other nations he said, "Responsible members of the world community do not threaten or invade their neighbors. And they restrain their allies from aggression."

•••

In March 1983, Reagan delivered his famous "evil empire" speech. Just because class warfare and world revolution were the driving forces behind Soviet doctrine, he saw no reason why the United States should isolate itself and refuse to negotiate. Reagan pledged never to stop searching for peace, and asked his audience to pray for those living in "totalitarian darkness." In this speech, Reagan also said something reminiscent of Theodore Roosevelt's 1904 annual message, when Roosevelt cautioned against hypocrisy. "There must be no effort made to remove the mote from our brother's eye," said Roosevelt, "if we refuse to remove the beam from our own."[22] Although the Soviet Union was "the focus of evil in the modern world," according to Reagan, America had its own "legacy of evil." In Reagan's words:

> Our nation, too, has a legacy of evil with which it must deal. The glory of this land has been its capacity for transcending the moral evils of our past. For example, the long struggle of minority citizens for equal rights, once a source of disunity and civil war, is now a point of pride for all Americans. We must never go back. There is no room for racism, anti-Semitism, or other forms of ethnic and racial hatred in this country.[23]

If the ultimate goal of Reagan's military buildup was to destroy the Soviet Union, he gave no indication in this speech. Reagan said his goal was to achieve substantial reductions in nuclear weapons, and thus vowed to reject any agreement that would freeze Soviet and American nuclear weapons at their current levels. He argued a nuclear freeze would create a disincentive for the Soviets to keep negotiating and would actually reward their recent military buildup. Perhaps more importantly, it would prevent the United States from modernizing its aging nuclear forces. According to Reagan, the struggle between the United States and the Soviet Union was a struggle between good and evil. If we were to agree to a nuclear freeze with the Soviet Union, we would be ignoring "the facts of history and the aggressive impulses of an evil empire." Finally, Reagan said, "I believe that communism is another sad, bizarre chapter in human history whose last pages even now are being written."

Reagan was right: the Soviet Union would not last long. Reagan recognized the same historical trend as Lyndon Johnson, when he reported—eighteen years earlier—the communist empire was beginning to crumble.[24] As a reminder, Iran became an Islamic Republic in March 1979. By the end of 1979, when the Soviets invaded Afghanistan they were not expanding, but trying to hold on to their southern republics. By the time Ronald Reagan took office, the potential danger was not Soviet expansion, but disintegration.

•••

In an address to the nation on defense and national security in late March 1983, Reagan announced a decision he believed would bring peace and security to the United States well into the twenty-first century. Reagan said his efforts to rebuild the United States' neglected defenses began two years earlier with his request to Congress for a major increase in military spending. Although the defense budget then before Congress was substantially less than the one Reagan proposed two years before, he assured his audience it was still within safe limits.[25]

Reagan based his defense policy on a simple premise: strength was the best way to deter aggression and preserve the peace, while weakness only invited aggression. Reagan's definition of deterrence was to ensure any potential adversary reached the rational conclusion the costs of any attack —on the United States, its allies or vital interests—would outweigh the benefits. The Soviets were building up their military power (particularly long-range nuclear weapons capable of making a direct strike on American territory) he said, far beyond the legitimate requirements of national self-defense. According to Reagan, the Soviet Union's spreading military influence was directly challenging the vital interests of the United States and its allies. Reagan showed photographs of an intelligence station, a military airfield, and Soviet-made aircraft in Cuba, and claimed this military buildup was comparable to the one that precipitated the 1962 Cuban missile crisis. Reagan also displayed photographs, which he claimed showed Soviet military shipments to facilities in Nicaragua and the island of Grenada. Citing the Monroe Doctrine, Reagan said the rapid military buildup of Grenada looked very suspicious.

Reagan then proposed building a defensive weapons program to counter what he considered believed was "the awesome Soviet missile threat." It was in this speech that he proposed the Strategic Defense Initiative (though he did not use that exact phrase), a program to develop a high-tech shield capable of intercepting and destroying strategic ballistic missiles launched against the United States and its allies. Reagan announced he was launching a "comprehensive and intensive effort" to develop technologies that would make nuclear weapons obsolete. He acknowledged the task was formidable and could take decades to accomplish, but convinced himself recent technological advances made it reasonable to begin. Finally, Reagan said while we pursue the development of these new defensive technologies we should continue to pursue arms reductions and maintain the effectiveness of our conventional and nuclear forces.

•••

In September 1983, a Soviet military aircraft shot down Korean Airlines Flight 007, killing more than two hundred fifty civilians onboard.

A few days later, Reagan spoke to the nation. He charged the Soviet Union with violating "every concept of human rights," and said the world should never forget the "savagery" of this "crime against humanity."[26] Reagan said this was not just an attack against the United States or South Korea, but an attack against the world, and the Soviet Union owed the world an apology. "It was an act of barbarism," he said, "born of a society which wantonly disregards individual rights and the value of human life and seeks constantly to expand and dominate other nations." Reagan said the attack (which he also called an atrocity and a massacre) reminded him of Czechoslovakia, Hungary, Poland, and Afghanistan.

•••

In October 1983, a suicide bomber attacked the U.S. Marine Corps barracks at Beirut International Airport, in Lebanon, killing almost two hundred fifty. On October 25, two days after the suicide bombing in Lebanon, the United States invaded the southern Caribbean Island of Grenada, one of the world's smallest countries.

On October 27, Reagan addressed the nation on the events in Lebanon and Grenada. Regarding Lebanon, Reagan said the sixteen hundred U.S. troops deployed there were part of a multinational force trying to help restore order and keep the peace. Reagan recounted the details of the "hideous, insane attack" which killed so many marines in their sleep on a Sunday morning. Reagan then asked the question he knew was on everyone's mind: "Why should our young men be dying in Lebanon? Why is Lebanon important to us?" First, the Arabs and Israelis had already fought four wars in thirty years. Second, the Middle East was strategically important because of the region's oil resources and the Suez Canal. Third, America's interests would be at risk if the region fell into the hands of a rival power. Fourth, the United States consistently supported Israel's right to exist since 1948, and an unstable Lebanon put Israel's security at risk. Reagan then turned to the other question: why should American troops be in Lebanon? Amazingly, Reagan tried to bask in Jimmy Carter's glow, and said he was building on the 1978 Camp David Accord, and that required armed intervention by American, British, French, and Italian forces to convince Israeli and Syrian troops to withdraw from Lebanon.

Regarding Grenada, Reagan said the trouble began two years earlier when Grenada's democratically elected government fell to a communist coup. That government did not last long, and was itself toppled in October 1983. Since then, Granada really had no government, except for what Reagan called, "a self-proclaimed band of military men." There were approximately a thousand Americans in Grenada, and Reagan was concerned for their safety, worried they might be injured or taken hostage or worse. "The nightmare of our hostages in Iran must never be repeated," he said.

Reagan then explained the difference between U.S. foreign policy in 1793 and 1983. In his words:

> You know, there was a time when our national security was based on a standing army here within our own borders and shore batteries of artillery along our coasts, and, of course, a navy to keep the sealanes open for the shipping of

things necessary to our well-being. The world has changed. Today, our national security can be threatened in faraway places. [Grenada is approximately fifteen hundred miles southeast of Miami, Florida.] It's up to all of us to be aware of the strategic importance of such places and to be able to identify them.[27]

•••

In Reagan's 1984 annual message, he said very little about foreign policy. The goals he briefly listed were to stabilize relations with the Soviet Union, strengthen the United States' alliances, negotiate equitable reductions in nuclear weapons, develop democratic institutions throughout the world, and help keep the peace in the Middle East, Central America, and southern Africa. He said Americans have "never been aggressors" and "resort to force only when we must."[28] Reagan mentioned Grenada just once, when he introduced an army medic who rescued several of his wounded comrades after their helicopter crashed. Regarding the situation in Lebanon, he said we were making progress, and should not allow state-sponsored terrorism to prevent us from establishing Lebanon as a free, independent and sovereign nation—exactly the same thing George W. Bush would say twenty years later to rationalize invading Iraq.

•••

In February 1984, Konstantin Chernenko became general secretary of the Communist Party of the Soviet Union. In September, Brian Mulroney became prime minister of Canada. In October, British prime minister Margaret Thatcher survived an assassination attempt. In the 1984 presidential election, the Democrats nominated Walter Mondale, vice president under Jimmy Carter and former senator from Minnesota. Reagan remained wildly popular and defeated Mondale in a huge landslide.

•••

In his 1985 inaugural address, Reagan said his second administration would work toward arms reduction and continue rebuilding our defenses. Reagan said his other foreign policy goals would be to promote peace, freedom, democracy, and free enterprise in the world. He accused the Soviet Union of conducting the largest military buildup in history, but pledged to negotiate with them to reduce arms, and thus reduce the threat of nuclear war. He renewed his call for a program to develop a defensive shield to intercept and destroy nuclear missiles before they reached their target. According to Reagan, "It would render nuclear weapons obsolete," though what he probably meant was it would render nuclear *missiles* obsolete. Like Jimmy Carter, Reagan said he hoped one day to eliminate all nuclear weapons from the face of the earth.[29]

In his 1985 annual message, Reagan pledged to continue rebuilding the nation's armed forces, arguing that defense spending was an investment in peace and freedom. "You know," he said, "we only have a military-industrial complex until a time of danger, and then it becomes the arsenal of democracy."[30] He reported the American economy was stronger than ever, its alliances were stronger than ever, and the country had resumed its "historic role as a leader of the free world." Reagan remained committed to reducing the threat of nuclear war through verifiable agreements with the Soviets for mutual arms reductions—and stated his belief that increases in the United States' defense spending during his administration influenced the Soviets to keep negotiating.

Reagan restated his dream of forever banning all nuclear weapons, and predicted the SDI (Strategic Defense Initiative) would eventually eliminate the threat of nuclear war by rendering nuclear missiles obsolete. Reagan acknowledged the SDI research program would be expensive and take years to produce results, but said such a nonnuclear missile defense system could potentially save millions of lives. Arguing that America's mission was to defend freedom and democracy around the world, Regan said we had no choice but to stand by our democratic allies—and anyone else who defied Soviet-supported aggression. According to Reagan, our support for freedom fighters in Afghanistan and Nicaragua was "self-defense." He urged Congress to continue providing support to Central America and said, "I want to work with you to support the democratic forces whose struggle is tied to our own security."

•••

In March 1985, Mikhail Gorbachev came to power in the Soviet Union. In November, Gorbachev and Reagan met in Geneva, Switzerland to discuss Reagan's SDI and the reduction of nuclear weapons.

In his 1986 annual message, Reagan said national defense was more than just a budget line item. It was the federal government's highest priority. With no trace of irony Reagan said, "We have devoted 5 years trying to narrow a dangerous gap born of illusion and neglect, and we've made important gains."[31] As a reminder, in Jimmy Carter's 1979 annual message, he said one Poseidon submarine carried enough warheads to destroy every large and medium sized city in the Soviet Union. Another reminder: Carter graduated from the U.S. Naval Academy and served as Engineering Officer on the nuclear submarine USS *Seawolf* and other submarines in the Atlantic and Pacific fleets. In addition, the Berlin Wall would fall in November 1989, less than four years later. The Soviet Union's Communist Party would relinquish its monopoly on power in November 1990. By December 1991, the Soviet Union would cease to exist.

According to Reagan, however, the Soviet threat was as bad as ever, and we could not make it go away by ignoring it. In Reagan's words, "the threat from Soviet forces, conventional and strategic, from the Soviet drive for domination, from the increase in espionage and state terror remains great. This is reality. Closing our eyes will not make reality disappear." It is difficult to reconcile this with Reagan's assertion almost three years earlier (in his March 1983 Evil Empire Speech), that communism was another sad, bizarre chapter in human history whose last pages even then were being written.

Nonetheless, Reagan restated his enthusiasm for a missile shield that would some day render nuclear weapons obsolete and "free mankind from the prison of nuclear terror." He renewed his commitment to verifiable arms reductions, and said all of the responsibility for the success or failure of the negotiations belonged to the Soviets. "If the Soviet Government wants an agreement that truly reduces nuclear arms, there will be such an agreement," he said. He pledged the United States would continue to support liberty, democracy, and free markets around the world, and support the people fighting for freedom in Afghanistan, Angola, Cambodia, and Nicaragua. Finally, he said peace in the Western Hemisphere was a vital American interest, and asked Congress for funds to establish democracy in Nicaragua.

•••

In February 1986, Haitian president Jean-Claude Duvalier fled his country. The same month, Philippine president Ferdinand Marcos fled his country. In April, an explosion at the Chernobyl nuclear reactor in the Ukraine caused the world's worst nuclear disaster. In October, Ronald Reagan met Mikhail Gorbachev in Reykjavik, Iceland to negotiate an arms control agreement. In November, journalists reported a story that the United States secretly sold weapons to Iran (which was then at war with Iraq) and illegally diverted the proceeds to anticommunist insurgents in Nicaragua. Soon after the story broke, Reagan announced the formation of a special commission to investigate the so-called Iran-Contra affair.

In his 1987 annual message, Reagan reported the United States had made great progress rebuilding its armed forces, and was at peace with the world. Despite the progress, Reagan said he regretted the risk he took with regard to "our action in Iran." In his words:

> It did not work, and for that I assume full responsibility. The goals were worthy. I do not believe it was wrong to try to establish contacts with a country of strategic importance or to try to save lives. And certainly it was not wrong to try to secure freedom for our citizens held in barbaric captivity. But we did not achieve what we wished, and serious mistakes were made in trying to do so. We will get to the bottom of this, and I will take whatever action is called for.[32]

It is admirable any time the president takes responsibility for the failure of one of his policies. However, this was more than a policy failure. When the Prussian military strategist Carl von Clausewitz said war was the continuation of politics by other means, he was not talking about secret war. Rather than acknowledge that, Reagan said we should not dwell on the past, and then launched into a digression how important it was to take risks. He then said, "And let there be no mistake about American policy: We will not sit idly by if our interests or our friends in the Middle East are threatened, nor will we yield to terrorist blackmail."

Reagan then turned his attention to the Soviet threat. He said emphatically the United States must not permit the Soviet Union to establish a beachhead in Central America. He cautioned against losing our resolve to support anticommunist forces in Nicaragua. To make his case he quoted the Monroe Doctrine, and with impressive audacity, called Presidents Roosevelt, Truman, and Kennedy (all Democrats) as witnesses. In Reagan's words:

> Our commitment to a Western Hemisphere safe from aggression did not occur by spontaneous generation on the day that we took office. It began with the Monroe Doctrine in 1823 and continues our historic bipartisan American policy. Franklin Roosevelt said we "are determined to do everything possible to maintain peace on this hemisphere." President Truman was very blunt: "International communism seeks to crush and undermine and destroy the independence of the Americas. We cannot let that happen here." And John F. Kennedy made clear that "Communist domination in this hemisphere can never be negotiated." Some in this Congress may choose to depart from this historic commitment, but I will not.[33]

One of Reagan's highest priorities was to get the Soviets to behave more responsibly around the world. Other items on his agenda for Soviet–American relations were human rights, arms reduction, and "more open contacts between our societies." Reagan blamed the Soviets for the lack of progress in Reykjavik because they wanted to cripple SDI. He pledged never to "let them do it now or in the future" and called SDI "the most positive and promising defense program we have undertaken." Finally, Reagan said his administration would continue to oppose protectionism, and work toward free and fair trade during the Uruguay round of trade negotiations.

In early March 1987, Reagan addressed the nation again on the Iran-Contra affair. Reagan said he had not commented publicly on news reports because the American people deserved the truth, and he felt it would only create more doubt and confusion if he spoke out before the special commission issued its report. Admirably Reagan took responsibility for his actions and those of his administration, including actions taken without his knowledge. He said the plan began as a way to develop relations with possible leaders in a post-Khomeini government, but deteriorated after that. He gave his word he would never knowingly trade arms for American hostages in the Middle East, offered no excuses, and said it was a mistake.[34]

●●●

In June 1987, Reagan delivered his famous speech at the Brandenburg Gate in West Berlin, Germany. Reagan said he hoped the Soviets were beginning to understand the importance of freedom, and wondered if Moscow's new policies of openness and reform marked the beginning of deeper changes in the Soviet state or if they were merely "token gestures, intended to raise false hopes in the West." Reagan said he welcomed change and openness, but also wondered aloud if Mikhail Gorbachev was just trying to strengthen the Soviet Union without really changing it. This is when the president uttered his famous quote: "General Secretary Gorbachev, if you seek peace, if you seek prosperity for the Soviet Union and Eastern Europe, if you seek liberalization: Come here to this gate! Mr. Gorbachev, open this gate! Mr. Gorbachev, tear down this wall!"[35]

The clock was ticking on the Soviet Union, but perhaps Reagan was the victim of bad intelligence the same way George W. Bush would be some years later when he ordered the invasion of Iraq. At the June 1987 West Berlin speech, Reagan restated his commitment to negotiating another arms control agreement with the Soviets, and briefly discussed his enthusiasm for the SDI program, predicting it would eventually increase the safety of Europe and the world. Because the technology did not exist, Reagan continued to cling to the *political theory* of SDI, particularly that it would deter an attack on the United States because it did not kill people, but targeted nuclear missiles.

•••

In Reagan's 1988 annual message, he boasted his administration achieved "a complete turnabout, a revolution" in international relations. Under his leadership, the United States rebuilt its defenses, negotiated arms reductions, proposed SDI, and led what Reagan called "the global democratic revolution." Reagan said his staff was close to concluding a free trade agreement with Canada, and proposed the idea of a North American Free Trade Agreement with Canada and Mexico, and eventually a hemisphere-wide free trade area, which would include all of Central and South America.[36]

Reagan envisioned "a swelling freedom tide across the world: freedom fighters rising up in Cambodia and Angola, fighting and dying for the same democratic liberties we hold sacred. Their cause is our cause: freedom." He said Nicaragua had special meaning for Americans because that nation was so near our border. (Nicaragua is eight hundred miles from Florida and more than a thousand from Texas.) He asked Congress to provide support for the "freedom fighters" resisting communist rule. He also said supporting the freedom fighters in Afghanistan was "the key to peace," and predicted there would be no peace until the Soviet troops withdrew and the Afghan people had self-determination. Finally, Reagan made another pitch for SDI, arguing it was similar to arms reduction because it too would reduce the threat of nuclear war for the entire world. Reagan called SDI "our insurance policy against a nuclear accident, a Chernobyl of the sky, or an accidental launch by some madman who might come along."

•••

In February 1988, the U.S. House of Representatives rejected Reagan's request for funds to aid Nicaraguan rebels. In July, an American naval vessel shot down Iran Air Flight 655, killing more than two hundred fifty civilians onboard.

•••

During the 1988 presidential election, the Democrats nominated Michael Dukakis, governor of Massachusetts. The Republicans nominated George H.W. Bush, former WWII navy pilot, congressman, ambassador to the United Nations, chief of the U.S. Liaison Office in China, director of Central Intelligence, and vice president under Ronald Reagan. After the Republican convention that summer, George Bush never trailed in the polls and easily defeated Michael Dukakis in the general election.

In January 1989, Reagan delivered his farewell address and described his vision of the "shining city upon a hill," a metaphor he used before in his 1988 annual message. In my mind, said Reagan, it is "a tall, proud city built on rocks stronger than oceans, windswept, God-blessed, and teeming with people of all kinds living in harmony and peace; a city with free ports that hummed with commerce and creativity. And if there had to be city walls, the walls had doors and the doors were open to anyone with the will and the heart to get here."[37]

Admittedly, this metaphor contains few foreign policy implications, unless we consider immigration policy. It conveniently disregards the shining city's "legacy of evil" called racism. On other issues, Reagan was optimistic—as usual—because Soviet troops were withdrawing from Afghanistan while Mikhail Gorbachev's reforms were moving forward. Reagan wished Gorbachev well, and expressed his satisfaction over successfully negotiating an agreement to reduce stockpiles of nuclear weapons. If the ultimate goal of Reagan's foreign policy was to destroy the Soviet Union, he gave no indication in this speech. Instead, he expressed his satisfaction at having "forged a satisfying new closeness with the Soviet Union" over the past few years.

PART IV

Global Supremacy and Global Stewardship, 1989–

11

New World Order II and Limited War IV: Iraq

Tiananmen Square; Berlin Wall Falls; Invasion of Panama; Iraq Invades Kuwait; Gulf War; Gorbachev Resigns; the Soviet Union Disintegrates

In his 1989 inaugural address, George Bush said nothing significant about foreign policy, except he would keep the United States' military forces strong enough to keep the peace. In his 1989 annual message (technically a speech on administration goals), he said it was a time of great change in the world—which presidents often say—but this time it was true. The year would indeed be full of great change, beginning with the Soviet Union withdrawing the last of their troops from Afghanistan, followed by much more than Bush or anyone else knew at the time. Like his inaugural address, Bush's remarks about foreign policy were brief. He pledged to continue pursuing Reagan's SDI, halt the proliferation of nuclear weapons, and work toward banning chemical weapons. Echoing Jimmy Carter, he said reducing our dependence on foreign oil would increase our national security.[1]

•••

In late May 1989, student protesters in Tiananmen Square in Beijing, China erected a statue, the "Goddess of Democracy." In early June, the People's Liberation Army murdered several thousand protesters and other civilians during their crackdown on Tiananmen Square. A lone anonymous protester stood in front of a column of tanks to block their advance, but to no avail. In early June, the spiritual leader of the Islamic revolution in Iran,

Ayatollah Ruhollah Khomeini died. In August, Solidarity activist Tadeusz Mazowiecki became Poland's first noncommunist prime minister since WWII. In September, the Hungarian government began to relax foreign travel restrictions and opened its borders to East German immigrants and refugees.

In late September 1989, Bush spoke to the UN General Assembly. "Freedom's advance is evident everywhere," he said, particularly in Hungary, Poland, and the Soviet Union. Unfortunately, said Bush, the trend was not universal, and some isolated regimes still denied people the right of self-government. Bush was too polite to mention China specifically, but the juxtaposition is clear. Whereas the Chinese Government murdered thousands of its citizens in and around Tiananmen Square—the actual number remains unknown—somewhere in Eastern Europe a general had the good judgment to order his troops to hold their fire.

In November 1989, East Germany opened checkpoints in the Berlin Wall and allowed East German citizens to travel into West Germany. In November and December, communist parties in several East European nations renounced their monopoly on power. In early December 1989, Bush met with Mikhail Gorbachev on the Mediterranean island of Malta, and for the first time ever, the two leaders of the United States and Union of Soviet Socialist Republics held a joint press conference. A reporter asked Gorbachev if he thought the cold war was finally over. In response, Gorbachev said the Soviet Union would never start a "hot war" against the United States. Gorbachev and Bush agreed the world was exiting one era and entering another, and the new era called for a new approach. Gorbachev said it was time to abandon many things characteristic of the cold war, such as the ideological competition, arms race and mutual mistrust. Gorbachev said, "All that should be things of the past."[2] Thus, the cold war ended.

•••

In December 1989, the United States invaded Panama, and Bush addressed the nation regarding the invasion. He said his goals were "to safeguard the lives of Americans, to defend democracy in Panama, to combat drug trafficking, and to protect the integrity of the Panama Canal treaty." Bush reported that General Manuel Noriega, Panama's military dictator declared war on the United States, and threatened the lives of thirty-five thousand American citizens living there. Because diplomacy and negotiation failed to solve the problem, Bush ordered U.S. forces to crack down on any organized resistance and extradite General Noriega to the United States to face charges in a criminal court. Bush assured his audience the United States would recognize any democratically elected Panamanian government and American troops would be withdrawn as soon as possible. In addition, he promised the United States would uphold the Panama Canal Treaties and turn the canal over to Panama on schedule in the year 2000.[3]

In January 1990, Manuel Noriega surrendered to American forces in Panama. In Moscow, McDonald's opened their first restaurant, another sign the cold war was over. In Bush's 1990 annual message, he compared the great changes taking place in the world to 1945—and then abruptly changed the subject to Panama. According to Bush, the liberation of Panama and the emergence of democracy in Poland, Czechoslovakia, and East Germany fulfilled the hope of the American people and validated the long-standing goals of U.S. foreign policy. Bush interpreted the changes taking place as "a new consensus" in the world, which would lead to the spread of democracy and free markets not just in Eastern Europe, but also in Latin America, Asia, and Africa. Ironically, the one region Bush excluded from the list—the Middle East—would be the one that tested and defined his foreign policy and his presidency, as well as the presidency of his eldest son.

It was a time of great change and therefore great hope, but Bush warned it was also a time of great uncertainty. Because of the uncertainty, plans for the SDI would move forward. Bush pledged to build stronger relations with the Soviets, to encourage political reform and economic development, and to continue arms control negotiations (conventional, chemical, and nuclear), but refused to lower the United States' defenses. Finally, Bush promised a "coherent defense policy" as long as there were still conflicts, animosities, and competing interests in the world.[4]

•••

In February 1990, the Communist Party of the Soviet Union gave up its monopoly on power. In early August, Iraq invaded and occupied Kuwait with hundreds of tanks and more than a hundred thousand troops. In the first week of August, Bush delivered a national address requesting support for his decision to deploy American troops to Saudi Arabia. Four principles guided his decision. First, Iraq must withdraw its forces from Kuwait immediately and unconditionally. Second, Kuwait's legitimate government must be restored. Third, Bush pledged his total commitment to the security and stability of the Persian Gulf region. Fourth, he pledged to protect the lives of American citizens. There was another principle Bush mentioned, but for some reason did not include it with the other four: it was unacceptable to acquire territory by force.[5]

Bush announced his decision only after exhausting every other diplomatic alternative, stating plainly, "appeasement does not work." He reported ordering all trade with Iraq embargoed and all Iraqi assets in the United States and other countries frozen. He listed numerous meetings and conversations he had with various world leaders, particularly British prime minister Thatcher and Canadian prime minister Mulroney, both of whom strongly condemned Iraq's action. There was equally strong condemnation from the Arab League and the Gulf Cooperation Council, Japan, France, the Soviet Union, China, and many other governments around the world.

In addition, the UN Security Council approved sanctions against Iraq. Saudi Arabia's sovereign independence was a vital American interest, and Bush said it was important for the United States to stand up for its principles and stand by its friends—practical idealism in a nutshell. In addition, Bush warned Americans of the need to reduce their dependence on foreign oil, reminiscent of Jimmy Carter's 1979 "malaise" speech.

In September 1990, Bush addressed Congress on new developments in the Persian Gulf. He said Iraq's invasion of Kuwait was a great test of our resolve and "the first assault" on the new world order. He said we had to continue to demonstrate our determination, stand up to aggression, and support the rule of law. "Our interest, our involvement in the Gulf is not transitory," he said. There were vital principles at stake because Saddam Hussein was trying to wipe Kuwait off the face of the earth. There were vital economic interests at stake because if we permitted Iraq to annex Kuwait, Iraq's economic and military power would dominate the other oil producing countries in the region.[6]

Bush noted the UN Security Council passed five resolutions condemning Iraq's aggression, calling for Iraq to withdraw from Kuwait, and for the restoration of Kuwait's government. In addition, he reported Saudi Arabia, Kuwait, the United Arab Emirates, Turkey, and Egypt agreed to help defray the costs of the military action. Other nations were contributing funds for humanitarian aid, and several oil producing nations agreed to increase their production to replace the lost output from Iraq and Kuwait's oil fields. Bush then called on Congress to enact "a prudent multiyear defense program" that would reflect the change in United States–Soviet relations, but also recognize the world was still a dangerous place. In addition, Bush asked Congress to take action on "measures to increase domestic energy production and energy conservation in order to reduce dependence on foreign oil." Finally, he praised the troops who were going overseas to defend the "principle and the dream of a new world order."

In early October 1990, Bush spoke to the UN General Assembly. "Two days from now" he said, "the world will be watching when the Cold War is formally buried in Berlin." (East and West Germany would reunify on October 3.) Bush praised the UN Security Council's response to Iraq's invasion of Kuwait, and said his goal was to give the economic sanctions time to work. Bush said the United States had no territorial ambitions in the region, and pledged American forces would not remain in Saudi Arabia one day longer than necessary. (American forces would stay in Saudi Arabia until August 2003.) Although Bush hoped it would not be necessary to use force to drive the Iraqis out of Kuwait, his highest priority was to demonstrate he would not tolerate Iraq's aggression. According to Bush:

Iraq's unprovoked aggression is a throwback to another era, a dark relic from a dark time. It has plundered Kuwait. It has terrorized innocent civilians. It has held even diplomats hostage. Iraq and its leaders must be held liable for these crimes of abuse and destruction. But this outrageous disregard for basic human rights does not come as a total surprise. Thousands of Iraqis have been executed on political and religious grounds, and even more through a genocidal poison gas war waged against Iraq's own Kurdish villagers.[7]

Bush renewed his call for a total worldwide ban on chemical weapons and pledged to continue his efforts to stop the proliferation of nuclear weapons. He then shared his vision of the post-cold war new world order: a global partnership dedicated to increasing democracy and prosperity, to keeping the peace and abiding by rule of law. He envisioned a global partnership not unlike Woodrow Wilson, who also fought a war ostensibly for high principle in the hope of establishing a new international order.

•••

In November 1990, the UN Security Council authorized military intervention and set January 15, 1991 as the deadline for Iraq to withdraw from Kuwait. Also in November, Margaret Thatcher stepped down as Britain's prime minister. In December, Chancellor Helmut Kohl led a coalition to victory in the first free elections in unified Germany since 1932.

In early January 1991, Bush delivered an address on events in the Persian Gulf. With the January 15 deadline only ten days away, Bush said we should obtain the full support of the United Nations before putting our service men and women in harm's way—and the *twelve* resolutions passed by the UN Security Council were proof of the United Nations' unequivocal support. Hussein was threatening every country in the Persian Gulf, and could potentially threaten Eastern Europe's emerging democracies if he cornered the world energy market and choked off their fragile economies. Finally, Bush said the truly "unprecedented coalition" which the United States was leading was ready to use force "to defend a new order emerging among the nations of the world—a world of sovereign nations living in peace."[8]

In January 1991, Congress passed a resolution authorizing the president to use military force to liberate Kuwait.[9] One day after Hussein's deadline elapsed, Bush delivered an address to announce the United States began launching air strikes against Iraqi forces, but that ground forces were not yet engaged. He wanted to reassure his audience he exhausted every diplomatic avenue to resolve the crisis peacefully before he ordered the attack. Bush's first priority was to knock out Iraq's alleged nuclear and chemical weapons, and then its tanks and heavy artillery. Bush restated his objectives as follows: expel Iraqi forces from Kuwait, restore Kuwait's legitimate government, and force Iraq to comply with all UN resolutions. Once again, Bush referred to his vision of a new world order in which the rule of law governed the conduct of nations.[10]

In his 1991 annual message at the end of January, Bush restated his objectives, this time emphasizing the stability and security of the Persian Gulf region. He asserted the United States did not seek to destroy Iraq, but to encourage Iraq to use its resources to improve the life of its people and its neighbors. Bush condemned Hussein's ruthless aggression, praised the coalition's rejection of appeasement, and then said what would become perhaps the most famous line of his presidency: "The world has said this aggression would not stand, and it will not stand."[11]

Turning his attention to Europe, Bush said his objective was to help the Baltic States achieve their aspirations. The Baltic States were trying to secede from the Soviet Union, and Bush promised to maintain a dialog with Moscow and monitor the situation as it developed. On trade policy, he pledged his support for the Uruguay round of world trade negotiations, arguing it would stimulate economic growth and create jobs in the United States and other nations. In passing, Bush said he would continue to fund the SDI.

•••

Shortly after Iraqi troops invaded Kuwait in August 1990, the United States began building up its forces in Saudi Arabia and the Persian Gulf region. By the time the air campaign started in January 1991, there were six hundred sixty thousand coalition troops, 75 percent of which (approximately five hundred thousand) were Americans. As stated, the massive air campaign began in mid-January. Flying more than a thousand sorties per day, coalition forces gained air supremacy almost immediately, and relentlessly attacked targets in Kuwait and Iraq. The air campaign killed or wounded tens of thousands of Iraqi troops. When the ground campaign began in February, coalition ground forces pounded the Iraqis again and took thousands of prisoners.

One hundred hours after the launch of the ground campaign, Iraqi troops began withdrawing from Kuwait causing as much destruction as they could, particularly to Kuwait's oil fields. Coalition forces lost fewer than a thousand wounded, and approximately four hundred killed (including almost three hundred Americans). Hussein claimed victory, asserting that Iraq's defeated forces were not withdrawing from Kuwait, they were merely retreating.

In late February, Bush announced he was ordering a cease-fire. The Iraqi army was defeated, combat operations were suspended, and all the United States' military objectives were accomplished. "Tonight the Kuwaiti flag once again flies above the capital of a free and sovereign nation" he said, "And the American flag flies above our Embassy." Bush said the victory belonged not only to the United States, but also to every member of the coalition. Bush then outlined the conditions for the cease-fire and gave Iraq forty-eight hours to respond. Iraq had to release all prisoners of war; inform the proper authorities of the location of all mines; comply with all UN Security Council resolutions, particularly renouncing their annexation of Kuwait; and pay compensation for property damages and injuries.[12]

•••

In early March 1991, Bush addressed a joint session of Congress and almost immediately turned his attention toward the postwar world, outlining four elements of his framework for peace in the Middle East. First, he wanted to create "shared security arrangements," which essentially meant assembling a smaller version of the Gulf War coalition to maintain regional stability. Second, Bush said we needed to control proliferation of weapons of mass destruction, particularly regarding Iraq. Third, Bush hoped (beyond hope) to end the Arab–Israeli conflict. Any long-term peaceful resolution of the bitter dispute would require all parties to compromise. Specifically, Bush said Israel's Arab neighbors must recognize Israel's right to exist, and Israel must recognize the legitimate rights of the Palestinian people. "We've learned in the modern age geography cannot guarantee security" he said, "and security does not come from military power alone." Fourth, we needed to promote economic development in the Persian Gulf and Middle East.[13]

•••

In early August 1991, Bush delivered a speech to Ukraine's Supreme Soviet. Bush said Gorbachev's policies of glasnost and perestroika had "achieved astonishing things," and pledged his support for Ukraine's exploration of "the frontiers and contours of liberty." He said the United States wanted closer ties with the republics, but would not choose between supporting Gorbachev and other "independence-minded leaders" in the republics. He said the American people would support moderates dedicated to political and economic reform, but not "those who seek independence in order to replace a far-off tyranny with a local despotism. They will not aid those who promote a *suicidal nationalism* based upon ethnic hatred."[14]

In September, Bush addressed the UN General Assembly. He said the post-cold war and post-Gulf War era presented both dangers and opportunities. The greatest opportunity was to promote economic development through free trade. In particular, Bush said the Uruguay Round of trade negotiations, and free trade in general was the best way for developing nations to increase living standards for their people. Another opportunity was to promote democratic reform and build political institutions that respected the rights of individuals and minorities.

There was another opportunity to help the United Nations fulfill its historic mission, to promote international cooperation and the peaceful resolution of international conflict. Bush called on the United Nations to revoke resolution 3379, passed in November 1975, which equated Zionism with racism. "This body cannot claim to seek peace and at the same time challenge Israel's right to exist," he said, and by repealing this resolution unconditionally, the United Nations could enhance its credibility and serve the cause of peace.

The greatest danger of the postwar world was proliferation of nuclear, chemical, and biological weapons—and Iraq was still a threat, according to Bush. Six months after the Gulf War ended, Saddam Hussein was still in power and still showing contempt for the United Nations by violating several UN resolutions. However, Bush pledged the United States would enforce the sanctions as long as Hussein remained in power or until Iraq destroyed all its weapons of mass destruction and the means to deliver them.[15]

Later that month, Bush delivered a national address on the Soviet nuclear arsenal. The Soviet Union's transition to democracy created an opportunity to reduce the threat of nuclear war or a nuclear accident. As the world watched the Soviet Union disintegrate—or what Bush called *the drama of democracy unfolding*—it was important to avoid the slightest appearance of provocation.[16]

In December 1991, the United Nations repealed resolution 3379. Ukraine voted to break away from the Soviet Union. On Christmas Day, Mikhail Gorbachev resigned as president of the Soviet Union. At midnight on New Year's Eve, the Union of Soviet Socialist Republics officially ceased to exist.

•••

In his 1992 annual message, Bush said the biggest thing ever to happen in his lifetime was when the United States won the cold war. For the first time in thirty-five years, the United States' strategic bombers were no longer on round-the-clock alert. With typical understatement, he said, "Much good can come from the prudent use of power." Bush mentioned he hosted Boris Yeltsin at Camp David earlier in the month, and discussed arms control among other topics. Finally, he issued a gentle caution. The United States still had leadership responsibilities even though the cold war was over, and as long as he was president the United States would maintain strong military forces and support freedom everywhere.[17]

•••

During the 1992 presidential election, the Republicans renominated Bush. The Democrats nominated Bill Clinton, the brilliant young governor of Arkansas. Texas billionaire Ross Perot ran as an independent. Despite Bush's popularity immediately following the Gulf War, Americans were worried the weak economy would slip back into recession. Because of Perot's generally conservative views, his candidacy split support among Republicans, and Clinton won the election.

In early December, the UN Security Council passed a resolution authoriz-ing the United States to provide security for humanitarian relief operations in Somalia. Bush announced he was ordering American troops to Somalia. Their "limited objective," he said was to open supply routes and secure the environment for a UN peacekeeping force. He promised the troops would be back home as soon as possible.[18]

In January 1993, two months after his defeat at the polls Bush delivered a speech at the U.S. Military Academy, which served as a kind of farewell address. Once again, Bush described his dream of a new world order as "one of governments that are democratic, tolerant, and economically free at home and committed abroad to settling inevitable differences peacefully, without the threat or use of force." Bush worried how easily his dream could turn into a nightmare of full of petty tyrants bullying their citizens or threatening their neighbors with weapons of mass destruction.

As the end of his presidency drew near, this was clearly on Bush's mind because he also mentioned it during another speech around the same time. "The new world could, in time, be as menacing as the old. And let me be blunt: A retreat from American leadership, from American involvement, would be a mistake for which future generations, indeed our own children, would pay dearly."[19] If the United States did not remain involved in international affairs, we risked squandering our victory in the cold war. "Two hundred years ago, another departing president warned of the dangers of what he described as 'entangling alliances'. His was the right course for a new nation at that point in history. But what was 'entangling' in Washington's day," said Bush, "is now essential."[20]

12

Dollar Diplomacy II
and Monroe Doctrine IV

Firefight in Mogadishu; NAFTA; Crisis in Haiti; Crisis in Mexico; Dayton Peace Accords; Air Strikes in Iraq and Serbia

In Bill Clinton's 1993 inaugural address, he said little of substance on foreign policy. He borrowed George Bush's *new world order* theme, and said the United States would continue to play a leadership role in the world, and would use force if necessary to defend its vital interests. In mid-February 1993, Clinton addressed a joint session Congress. He said economic growth depended on increasing international trade and penetrating new markets, and pledged his support for the North American Free Trade Agreement (NAFTA). He segued into defense policy by reminding people a strong military requires a strong economy. Regarding defense policy, Clinton proposed cutting the defense budget and restructuring American military forces to meet the threats of the post-cold war era. As long as the world was dangerous and uncertain, he said the American military would always have "the best trained, the best prepared, the best equipped fighting force in the world."[1]

•••

In late February 1993, Islamic terrorists detonated a bomb in the underground garage of the New York World Trade Center killing six people and wounding more than a thousand. In mid-April, former president George Bush traveled to Kuwait for a ceremony to commemorate the United States' Gulf War victory. Kuwaiti authorities uncovered a plot to assassinate the former president using a car bomb, and arrested more than a dozen conspirators before they could carry out their plan. American investigators later concluded the Iraqi Intelligence Service was behind the assassination attempt.

In late June 1993, Clinton addressed the nation on the unsuccessful assassination attempt in Kuwait against former president Bush. Clinton said the results of the investigation concluded it was an elaborate plot devised and directed by the Iraqi Intelligence Service. Their purpose was to retaliate against former president Bush specifically because of the actions he took as president. Thus, it was an attack against the United States. Clinton responded by launching cruise missiles at the Iraqi Intelligence Service's Baghdad headquarters. Pledging to combat terrorism, deter aggression, and protect American lives, Clinton remarked, "If Saddam and his regime contemplate further illegal provocative actions they can be certain of our response."[2]

•••

In early November 1993, Clinton delivered a speech at the White House on NAFTA. First, he commented on the agreement's numerous celebrity endorsements, including all the living former presidents, secretaries of state, defense, and commerce, plus former national security advisors and leaders of the Federal Reserve. On the merits, Clinton said NAFTA was above politics because it would facilitate international trade and investment, stimulate economic growth, create new jobs, increase incomes, and strengthen the democratic institutions of our allies. According to Clinton, the wide support for NAFTA was one of the lessons learned from the post WWI and WWII eras. It was a historic opportunity in the post-cold war era to remain engaged with the world and help strengthen the global economy. NAFTA would be an important element in the new post-cold war global system—part of the new framework that was (and still is) emerging to replace the old two-superpower system. NAFTA would take effect on New Year's Day 1994.[3]

In his 1994 annual message, Clinton focused mostly on his economic plan and glossed over foreign policy issues. He said the world was still dangerous because of arms proliferation, ethnic and regional conflicts, terrorism, and nationalism. Because the United States was "the world's greatest power" (as opposed to the only superpower), he pledged to maintain our defenses and fulfill our responsibilities. Taking into account the law-enforcement approach to terrorism prior to the attacks of September 11, 2001 Clinton said, "This year we secured indictments against terrorists and sanctions against those who harbor them." In the next sentence, however, Clinton touted his administration's achievements promoting environmentally sustainable economic growth.[4]

•••

In spring 1994, intertribal conflict, ethnic cleansing, and genocide resulted in the deaths of almost a million people in Rwanda. What was Clinton's response? When president Juvenal Habyarimana of Rwanda and president Cyprien Ntaryamira of Burundi died under suspicious circumstances, he issued a condolence statement, and then authorized the evacuation of American citizens. He ordered an arms embargo, issued a statement calling for a cease-fire and then expelled all Rwandan diplomats, claiming the United States could no longer permit "representatives of a regime that supports genocidal massacre to remain on our soil." Finally, after the genocide was over, Clinton authorized assistance to refugees.[5]

When reporters ask *former* president Clinton if he has any regrets, he has a ready answer. Long after the crisis, Clinton says his biggest regret is not intervening to stop the genocide. Of course, the question has nothing to do with foreign policy, but it is an attempt to get Clinton to talk about scandal in the Oval Office. The purpose of Clinton's response is to rebuke anyone more interested in scandal than serious policy issues. The purpose of Clinton's response is to change the subject.

A reminder on the significance of chronology and geography with regard to the doctrine of practical idealism: six months before ethnic cleansing began in Rwanda, the Battle of Mogadishu took place in Somalia, on the Indian Ocean coast eleven hundred miles to the east. In early October 1993, eighteen Americans died—plus more than a thousand Somali militia and civilians—in a firefight during the unsuccessful mission to capture Mohamed Farrah Aidid. At the time, Clinton said the United States should not "cut and run" from Somalia just because things got difficult. "Our own credibility with friends and allies would be severely damaged," he said, "Our leadership in world affairs would be undermined at the very time when people are looking to America to help promote peace and freedom in the post-cold-war world." Nonetheless, Clinton announced he was withdrawing all American combat troops from Somalia by the end of March 1994. "*We'll do what we can to complete the mission before then,*" he said.[6]

•••

In mid-September 1994, Clinton addressed the nation about a problem much closer to home, the deteriorating situation in Haiti (which is located on the western side of the Caribbean island of Hispianiola). Haiti's government was the most violent dictatorship in the Western Hemisphere, and Clinton announced the United States was going to lead a multilateral force to stop atrocities taking place there, restore democracy and preserve stability in the hemisphere. On this particular occasion, Clinton said the United States had a responsibility to *protect its interests and secure its borders.* To reassure his audience he was not exaggerating, Clinton quoted George Bush, who said the flood of thousands Haitian refugees during his previous administration was "an unusual and extraordinary threat to the national security, foreign policy, and economy of the United States." Clinton reported more than fourteen thousand refugees rescued by the Coast Guard were then living at the U.S. Naval base in Guantánamo Bay, Cuba.[7]

Clinton described his repeated efforts to resolve the crisis diplomatically, but Haiti's dictators were clinging to power, and massive amounts of food, medicine, and other humanitarian aid were not getting through to the people who needed it most. The UN Security Council recently approved a resolution authorizing the use of force to remove the dictators and install a democratic government. Although Clinton held out hope for a peaceful resolution, he said the time had come for the United States to act. Clinton said the country was nearby; our interests were clear, and the mission was achievable and limited—quite different from Rwanda. Clinton sought to demonstrate the continuity of his policy by comparing the limited and specific mission in Haiti to Panama and Grenada.

According to Clinton's plan, a large force would invade Haiti (which is located on the western side of the Caribbean island of Hispianiola), remove the dictators from power, and reinstall Haiti's democratically elected government. While this was taking place, U.S. forces would restore civil order and the international community would begin providing humanitarian assistance to rebuild their country. Once this phase was completed, most American troops would come home. Along with other UN troops, a small U.S. force would remain in the country until after the elections could take place and the new government could take office. Two days later, Clinton addressed the nation again, announcing Haiti's dictators had agreed to step down, "rather than to face imminent action" by coalition forces.

In a September 1994 speech to the UN General Assembly, Clinton said the end of the cold war placed the United Nations in a strong position to promote multilateral cooperation, and recent events in Haiti were a good example. Clinton said Haiti's military dictators agreed to step down because of creative diplomacy, the influence of economic power and the threat of force. In fact, more than sixty American warplanes were already in the air and on their way to Haiti when the Haiti's dictators agreed to step down.[8] He said Bosnia was another example of what the international community could accomplish when diplomacy was backed up by the threat of military force. Bosnian Serbs had the city of Sarajevo under siege since April 1992. The threat of NATO air strikes in Bosnia interrupted the centuries old ethnic conflict temporarily, but people living in Sarajevo were still facing shortages of food, drinking water, and medicine, not to mention the daily threat of sniper attacks.

• • •

As of October 1994, Saddam Hussein was still not cooperating with weapons inspectors. Not only had he not completely withdrawn his forces away from the Kuwait border, he recently moved more troops toward the border. In October 1994, Clinton addressed the nation to announce he ordered an aircraft carrier battle group, cruise missile ships, a marine expeditionary brigade, an army task force, and more than three hundred fifty aircraft to the Persian Gulf region. Clinton pledged his commitment to protect the stability of the Persian Gulf and said, "We will not allow Iraq to threaten its neighbors or to intimidate the United Nations as it ensures that Iraq never again possesses weapons of mass destruction."[9] A few days later, Iraq began withdrawing its troops from the Kuwait border.

In December 1994, the Mexican government decided to devalue the peso, permitting it to float freely against the U.S. dollar. The peso's value fell farther and faster than officials expected, and created an economic crisis in Mexico. Mexico's foreign debt—mostly to U.S. investors and banks—totaled more than thirty billion dollars, including approximately twenty-three billion dollars in short-term loans coming due in 1995. In response, the Clinton administration began putting together a bailout package of loans and loan guarantees to help stabilize the Mexican economy.

In his 1995 annual message, Clinton said even though the cold war was over, the United States still had leadership responsibilities in the world, and Mexico was a case in point. The reason we had to act was not for Mexico, but for the sake of Americans whose livelihoods depended on a strong Mexican economy. Clinton urged Congress to support the Mexican stabilization program, arguing it was not a loan, not foreign aid, and not a bailout. In an effort to explain in simple terms what was actually a complex transaction—like Franklin Roosevelt would do—Clinton compared it to cosigning a bank loan with good collateral to cover our risk.[10] It is interesting to consider why there would be opposition to providing financial support to Mexico. The United States had intervened militarily in Mexico and elsewhere in the hemisphere on numerous occasions. Part of the rationale to justify supporting "freedom fighters" in Nicaragua was because if we did not stop the spread of communism in Central America, Mexico could be next. If the Monroe Doctrine was a good idea, and NAFTA was a good idea, then so was stabilizing Mexico's economy. Early the following year, the United States would approve a bailout package to Mexico, which included funds from the International Monetary Fund and the U.S. Treasury.

•••

In October 1995, Clinton attended a symposium marking the fiftieth anniversary of the Nuremberg war crimes trials. His speech set no foreign policy precedents, but did include a brief explanation why practical idealism entails promoting democracy:

> Democracy is the best guarantor of human rights—not a perfect one, to be sure; you can see that in the history of the United States. But it is still the system that demands respect for the individual, and it requires responsibility from the individual to thrive. Democracy cannot eliminate all violations of human rights or

outlaw human frailty, nor does promoting democracy relieve us of the obligation to press others who do not operate democracies to respect human rights. But more than any other system of government we know, democracy protects those rights, defends the victims of their abuse, punishes the perpetrators and prevents a downward spiral of revenge. So promoting democracy does more than advance our ideals. It reinforces our interests.[11]

In November 1995, the Republic of Bosnia-Herzegovina, the Republic of Croatia, and the Federal Republic of Yugoslavia signed the Dayton Peace Accords. (Negotiations took place in Dayton, Ohio, thus the name.) The parties agreed to respect the sovereign equality of one another, settle disputes by peaceful means, and refrain from threatening or using force against Bosnia and Herzegovina or any other state. The parties also agreed to respect Bosnia-Herzegovina's boundaries, particularly the Serb Republic. Finally, the signatories agreed to respect Bosnia-Herzegovina's constitution and elections, and establish a commission on refugees and human rights.[12]

■■■

In his 1996 annual message, Clinton said one of the goals of his administration was "to maintain America's leadership in the fight for freedom and peace throughout the world." As memories of the cold war receded into the past, Clinton disagreed with the "voices of isolation" who asserted the United States should retreat from its global responsibilities. Positioning himself in opposition to "voices of isolation," he seems to suggest that the range of foreign policy alternatives consisted of choosing between isolation on the one hand and *having a foreign policy* on the other. The threats facing the world today, such as terrorism, weapons of mass destruction, organized crime, drug trafficking, ethnic and religious hatred, aggression by rogue states, said Clinton, were all global, and either we were going to address them or we were going to suffer the consequences.[13]

●●●

During a 1996 reelection campaign speech in Michigan, Clinton touted what he believed were his foreign policy successes. These included negotiating a freeze of North Korea's nuclear program, intervening to prevent the collapse of the Mexican peso, negotiating numerous new trade agreements, working to reduce the threat of weapons of mass destruction, tightening security in airports and airplanes, and adopting a so-called zero tolerance for terrorism policy.[14] He said we should not retreat into isolationism merely because the cold war was over, and pledged NATO would remain the "bedrock of our common security." He advocated enlarging NATO and pledged to reach out to the new democracies in Central Europe, the Baltic States, and the newly independent states of the former Soviet Union. He predicted there would be situations when only America could make the difference between war and peace. However, we should resist the temptation to become the world's policeman, and intervene only when our interests or values were at stake.

Clinton made an obscure reference to the 1648 Treaty of Westphalia, which formally ended the Thirty Years War and marked the beginning of the modern international system—the same treaty George W. Bush referred to in his *2002 National Security Strategy*. Praising the elder Bush's role in the reunification of Germany, Clinton said "And now, for the very first time since nation-states first appeared in Europe, we have an opportunity to build a peaceful, undivided, and democratic continent."

In the 1996 presidential election, Bill Clinton remained popular as he presided over a booming peacetime economy, and the Democrats renominated him unanimously. The Republicans nominated Bob Dole, WWII combat veteran, and former Congressman and senator from Kansas. The dynamics of the election were similar to 1992; Ross Perot ran as an independent again—though this time Perot failed to win half as many votes as he did in 1992—and Bill Clinton won reelection.

•••

In his 1997 annual message, Clinton said our first task was to help build an undivided, democratic Europe. "When Europe is stable, prosperous, and at peace, America is more secure," he said. Toward that end, Clinton recommended expanding NATO membership by inviting several Central and East European nations, and developing a partnership between NATO and Russia. Regarding Asia, Clinton recommended expanding trade relations, and continuing to negotiate with North Korea and "bridge the Cold War's last divide." Clinton pledged to continue developing U.S.–China relations, and engage China in a dialogue on several issues, particularly banning nuclear tests and improving human rights. Clinton said the United States needed to increase exports to Asia and Latin America, because expanding trade promoted economic development and democracy. Clinton renewed his call to eliminate land mines throughout the world and restated his support for the worldwide treaty to ban chemical weapons. He briefly mentioned his administration was working with other nations to prevent terrorists from attacking, and to hold them accountable if they did.[15]

•••

In May 1997, Tony Blair became prime minister of Britain. In July, the United Kingdom transferred sovereignty of Hong Kong to the PRC. In late October 1997, Clinton delivered an address outlining his foreign policy goals toward China. First, he wanted to promote peace, prosperity, and stability in the world, and achieving that goal was more realistic with China's cooperation than without it. Second, he hoped to promote peace, prosperity, and stability in Asia. The United States intended to maintain military forces in Asia, particularly on the Korean peninsula, and Clinton wanted China to play a constructive and cooperative role on that issue. Third, Clinton restated the United States' official "one-China" policy, and said "The Taiwan question can only be settled by the Chinese themselves peacefully." Fourth, the United States and China had a shared interest in limiting the proliferation of weapons of mass destruction. Clinton pledged to talk to President Jiang Zemin (who would travel to Washington the following week) about some of China's "troubling weapons supply relationships," and try to convince him it was in China's best interest to strengthen their controls on weapons exports. Fifth, the United States and China had a shared interest in fighting organized crime and international drug trafficking. Sixth, Clinton said he supported China's membership in the World Trade Organization, and wanted increased access for American goods and services to China's markets.[16]

In his 1998 annual message, Clinton predicted the worst threats to national security in the new century would be terrorism, international organized crime, and drug trafficking. "These 21st century predators feed on technology and the free flow of information and ideas and people, and they will be all the more lethal," he said, "if weapons of mass destruction fall into their hands." Clinton announced Hungary, Poland, and the Czech Republic would soon join NATO, and asked the Senate to continue supporting U.S. peacekeeping troops in Bosnia. He restated his commitment to a comprehensive nuclear test ban treaty and his commitment to limit the proliferation of weapons of mass destruction. Finally, Clinton reported Saddam Hussein was developing weapons of mass destruction and still preventing the UN weapons inspectors from doing their job. Clinton then spoke directly to Hussein: "You cannot defy the will of the world," he said, "You have used weapons of mass destruction before; we are determined to deny you the capacity to use them again."[17]

•••

In February 1998, Osama bin Laden issued a fatwa (a religious edict) declaring holy war against Jews and Americans. Fighting between Serbians and ethnic Albanians escalated in Kosovo. In March, Clinton traveled to Africa, with stops scheduled in Botswana, Ghana, Rwanda, Senegal, South Africa, and Uganda. Prior to his departure, Clinton listed four goals: show support for democracies, increase trade and investment, look for ways to prevent ethnic conflict, and promote sustainable development. In late March, during a speech in Kigali, Clinton blamed the Rwandan government for the methodical extermination of more than a million Tutsis and moderate Hutus in 1994. Referring to the international community and other African nations, he said, "We did not act quickly enough after the killing began. We should not have allowed the refugee camps to become safe haven for the killers. We did not immediately call these crimes by their rightful name: genocide."[18] If Clinton had any regrets he did nothing to stop the genocide four years earlier, he gave no indication in this speech.

In August, terrorists bombed American embassies in Dar es Salaam (Tanzania) and Nairobi (Kenya) killing more than two hundred and wounding thousands. In response, Clinton ordered missile attacks against al-Qaeda camps in Afghanistan and a pharmaceutical factory in Khartoum, Sudan. In late October 1998, Iraq announced its refusal to cooperate with UN weapons inspectors.

In mid-December 1998, Clinton addressed the nation on his decision to order air strikes on military targets in Iraq. The last straw was Hussein's announcement not to permit weapons inspections, which was one of the conditions of the cease-fire following the Gulf War. Clinton reminded his audience Saddam Hussein used chemical weapons before, particularly against Kurdish civilians in Northern Iraq. "The international community had little doubt then, and I have no doubt today, that left unchecked, Saddam Hussein will use these terrible weapons again," he said.[19]

Clinton admitted the efforts at diplomacy were ineffective. Hussein seemed only to understand force or the threat of force. According to Clinton, Iraq's persistent refusal to cooperate with the United Nations presented "a clear and present danger to the stability of the Persian Gulf and the safety of people everywhere." The previous month, Clinton cancelled an air strike against Iraq while the planes were in midair, and if he did not follow through this time, it would destroy the United States' credibility to check Saddam in the future. In our long-term plan to "contain" Iraq, he said we might have to use force again "if Saddam takes threatening actions, such as trying to reconstitute his weapons of mass destruction or their delivery systems, threatening his neighbors, challenging allied aircraft over Iraq, or moving against his own Kurdish citizens." Finally, Clinton said as long as Saddam was in power, he would be a threat to his people, to the Persian Gulf and to the rest of the world.

In his 1999 annual message, Clinton said he wanted to reach a new consensus on international trade, and listed the issues he believed business, labor, environmentalists, farmers, and the government should be able to agree on. First, we ought to increase trade and open markets, but we should make sure ordinary people actually benefit. Second, we should insist international trade organizations do business in the open. Third, we should enforce our trade laws uniformly to protect American consumers and exporters. Fourth, we should help American manufacturers hurt by the unfair trade practices of other countries. Yet again, he asked Congress for fast track negotiating authority.[20]

Clinton built the rest of his foreign policy framework around several themes: pursuing peace, fighting terrorism, renewing our alliances, and maintaining a strong military. Among the United States' successful interventions in regional conflicts, Clinton listed Ireland, Bosnia, Kosovo, and the

Middle East. In particular, Clinton asked Congress to support the 1998 Wye River Memorandum, which was another sincere attempt to promote Israeli–Palestinian cooperation, aimed at combating terrorism, outlawing terrorist organizations, prohibiting illegal weapons, and preventing violence.[21] Regarding the bombing of the American embassies in Kenya and Tanzania, Clinton said it was a reminder of the increased threats we faced from outlaw nations and terrorists. Regarding the missile strikes in Afghanistan and Sudan, Clinton said, "We will defend our security wherever we are threatened, as we did this summer when we struck at Osama bin Laden's network of terror."

Clinton repeated his support for limiting the spread of nuclear weapons, and mentioned North Korea, India, and Pakistan in particular. He pledged to continue working with Russia and former Soviet Republics to protect nuclear technology and materials. Clinton urged Congress to ratify the Comprehensive Test Ban Treaty (Congress would reject it in October 1999). He praised the troops who carried out the air strikes against Iraq, and said the United States would continue to contain Saddam Hussein and work for regime change in Iraq. Finally, he pledged his support for the United Nations, and asked Congress to pay the United States' delinquent dues. (By then, the United States owed more than a billion dollars, which Congress refused to pay because several members objected to what they considered waste, mismanagement, and corruption at the United Nations.)

●●●

In March 1999, Hungary, Poland, and the Czech Republic joined NATO. Ethnic conflict in the former Yugoslavia continued to escalate, and hundreds of thousands of ethnic Albanians fled Kosovo into Macedonia and Albania. American and British diplomats tried to reach an agreement under which NATO troops would serve as peacekeepers, but negotiations broke down while the fighting and refugee crisis deteriorated. In late March, NATO began bombing Serbian air defenses and other military targets. As the bombing campaign progressed, NATO began to target Serbian ground units and accidentally hit a convoy of Kosovo Albanian refugees and the Chinese embassy in Belgrade. The bombing campaign lasted until June, when Serbian leader Slobodan Milosevic agreed to accept a UN/NATO peacekeeping force in Kosovo.

On the day the bombing campaign ended, Clinton addressed the nation. For the first time in eleven weeks, "the skies over Yugoslavia are silent," he said "The Serb army and police are withdrawing from Kosovo. The one million men, women and children driven from their land are preparing to return home. The demands of an outraged and united international community have been met." The Kosovar people were victims of some of the worst atrocities since WWII, and when Clinton launched the bombing campaign, he had three goals in mind. First, he wanted to protect the Kosovar people and permit them to return to their homes. Second, he wanted to compel Serbian forces to withdraw from Kosovo. Third, he wanted to deploy a NATO force to keep the peace.[22]

Clinton said the widespread violence in Kosovo was the result of Serbian leader Slobodan Milosevic's ten-year campaign of ethnic cleansing in the former Yugoslavia. Hundreds of villages were burned and tens of thousands of people murdered. Clinton pledged the International War Crimes Tribunal would charge Milosevic with war crimes. Now that the first phase was complete, the next phase was to help the Kosovar refugees return home, help them rebuild their homes and villages, deliver food and medicine, and disarm the Kosovo Liberation Army. Finally, because all of this would require establishing and maintaining security, fifty thousand peacekeeping troops from more than thirty countries (including seven thousand Americans) would be deployed to Kosovo.

•••

In December 1999, Russian president Boris Yeltsin resigned, and was succeeded by Vladimir Putin. In his 2000 annual message, Clinton called globalization "the central reality of our time." Globalization was a revolution that would bring barriers down, and create new networks between nations, individuals, economies, and cultures. The forces of globalization would bring profound change, with new opportunities and new threats, he said, and in order for the United States to take advantage of the opportunities, "We must be at the center of every vital global network, as a good neighbor and partner."[23]

Then he outlined the steps he believed would position the United States for global leadership. First, he repeated his call to "forge a new consensus on trade." Clinton was convinced international trade was the key to economic development, but the forces of globalization were not limited to economics. Globalization also fostered the free flow of ideas and helped spread freedom and democracy. For this reason, the United States must continue to engage "our former adversaries" Russia and China, and help them maintain their stability, prosperity, and democracy.

In particular, Clinton said we should continue to reduce our nuclear arsenal, and help Russia safeguard its nuclear weapons and materials. We should help China develop economically by supporting its membership to the World Trade Organization and grant most favored nation trade status. China already had access to American markets, and taking these steps would ensure American manufacturers would have access to China's markets. In addition, Clinton said the United States should play the role of peacemaker, defend human rights and religious freedom, and whenever possible help prevent regional conflicts from spreading. Another challenge was preventing advanced weapons technologies from falling into the hands of terrorists and rogue nations. The United States needed to dissuade

North Korea and Iran from developing nuclear weapons and prevent Iraq from threatening the Persian Gulf. Although Clinton did not specifically say the words *Strategic Defense Initiative,* he did recommend developing a system to defend against missile threats.

•••

In March 2000, Vladimir Putin won Russia's presidential election. In October, terrorists bombed the *Cole,* a U.S. Navy destroyer in Aden, Yemen. In December, Clinton delivered an address at the University of Nebraska on "foreign policy for the global age." The forces of globalization, he said, created opportunities and challenges. One of the opportunities was greater access to foreign markets, so ordinary people such as Nebraska's farmers could benefit from trade. One of the challenges was to maintain our national security while international borders were opening. The movement of people, ideas, goods, and technology made us vulnerable to terrorists, which is why we needed to eradicate as many weapons of mass destruction as possible, and convince Russia and countries of the former Soviet Union to reduce their nuclear arsenals. This is also why we needed to strengthen our resolve never to permit Saddam Hussein to use, build, or acquire weapons of mass destruction. And this is why we needed to negotiate an agreement with North Korea to freeze their nuclear program.

Clinton then made some uncharacteristically candid observations about the United States' unique position as the world's only military and economic superpower:

> Now, nobody in the world benefits from stability more than we do. Nobody. Nobody makes more money out of it. Just think about pure, naked self-interest. Nobody. And when we pay for this peacekeeping…we get more than our money's worth out of it. And when we walk away from our responsibilities, people resent us. They resent our prosperity, they resent our power and, in the end, when a whole lot of people resent you, sooner or later they find some way to manifest it.[24]

Unfortunately, nobody was paying attention. Clinton delivered this speech a few days before the Supreme Court issued its opinion in the matter of Bush vs. Gore, reversing the judgment of the Florida Supreme Court and effectively terminating Florida's selective manual ballot recount. Thus, George W. Bush, Republican governor of Texas and eldest son of George H.W. Bush, narrowly won Florida's twenty-five electoral votes and the 2000 presidential election.

13

Limited War V: Iraq and the War on Terror
Defense Reform; 9/11 Attack; Invasion of Afghanistan; Disarmament Crisis; Iraq War and Occupation

In his 2006 annual message, George W. Bush said the goal of his foreign policy was to end tyranny in the world. "Some dismiss that goal as misguided idealism," he said, "In reality, the future security of America depends on it."[1] Before we dismiss anything, we should glance into the rearview mirror.

Of all the major themes in Bush's national security strategy, terrorism, homeland security, human rights, promoting democracy, international trade and economic development, only one originates in the twentieth century: weapons of mass destruction. The threat turned potentially catastrophic in 1962 when the Soviet Union attempted to install nuclear missiles on Cuba, a mere ninety miles from Florida. However, the move toward arms control did not begin with that incident; nor did it begin with the cold war or the advent of nuclear weapons, but with the Geneva Protocol prohibiting chemical and germ warfare, such as mustard gas used during WWI.[2]

Our problems with Cuba did not begin with the missile crisis or the 1961 Bay of Pigs invasion, or even with Fidel Castro's overthrow of the Batista government in 1959. The trouble began with the 1819 Adams-Onís Treaty —four years before the Monroe Doctrine—that ceded Florida to the United States, but left Cuba as a Spanish Colony. Although Cuba had been fighting for its independence from Spain since 1821, Ulysses Grant refused to intervene in 1875 because he did not consider the Cuban insurrection a full-fledged revolution. In 1898, the explosion on the USS *Maine* in Havana

Harbor precipitated the Spanish-American War. Following the war, the United States established a naval base at Cuba's Guantánamo Bay, ostensibly to protect the eastern approach to the Panama Canal. Guantánamo Bay is, of course, where the Bush administration has detained more than a thousand suspected terrorists.

The occupation of Guantánamo Bay, acquisition of the Philippines and Hawaii, and construction of the Panama Canal exemplify the way Theodore Roosevelt redefined the Monroe Doctrine and expanded its geographic scope. At the dawn of the twentieth century, the American sphere of influence would no longer be limited to the Western Hemisphere, but would include every region of the world. American foreign policy got a makeover when Woodrow Wilson envisioned a new world order based on open diplomacy, free navigation, free trade and of course, self-determination. Along with the Monroe Doctrine (and the Roosevelt corollary), self-determination is one of the most durable articles of practical idealism. Every president elected since Franklin Roosevelt has cited self-government and/or self-determination to support a wide range of policies:

- 1936: Franklin Roosevelt said the good neighbor policy was devoted to the ideal of self-government.

- 1946: Harry Truman said his foreign policy would be based on the principle that all people had the right to sovereignty and self-government without foreign interference.

- 1955: Dwight Eisenhower pledged his commitment to the principles of self-determination and self-government when he signed the Manila Pact and the Pacific Charter.

- 1963: John Kennedy said the central issue of the cold war was between those who imposed communism and those who believed in self-determination.

- 1965: Lyndon Johnson said one of the great unfinished tasks of American foreign policy was the reunification of Germany through self-determination.

- 1966: Lyndon Johnson said self-determination was one of the principles we were fighting for in Vietnam.

- 1969: Richard Nixon refused to accept any peace settlement that would arbitrarily deny South Vietnam's self-determination.

- 1979: Jimmy Carter said self-determination was part of the worldwide struggle for human rights and claimed it was one of the values on which our nation was founded.

- 1982: Ronald Reagan said the surest way to establish self-determination was to foster the infrastructure of democracy: labor unions, political parties, universities, and a free press.

- 1988: Ronald Reagan pledged to support Afghan freedom fighters and predicted there would be no peace in Afghanistan until the people had self-determination.

- 1989: George H. W. Bush said some regimes still denied their people the right of self-government, a polite reference to the Tiananmen Square massacre.
- 1993: Bill Clinton signed a resolution apologizing for the 1893 overthrow of the Kingdom of Hawaii, which deprived Hawaiians of their right to self-determination.
- 2003: George W. Bush said the Iraqi people were capable of self-government, and it would set a good example for the Middle East if Iraq established democracy.
- 2005: George W. Bush said advancing the ideal of democracy and self-government in Iraq "is the calling of a new generation of Americans."
- 2006: George W. Bush said voters in Afghanistan, Iraq, Palestine, and elsewhere in the Middle East were "writing a new chapter in the story of self-government."[3]

Of course, many of these appeared during the cold war, which unofficially began in 1947 when Harry Truman asked Congress to help contain communist influence in Greece and Turkey. Several other major cold war milestones followed the Truman Doctrine, including the Marshall Plan; the National Security Act which created the Central Intelligence Agency, Department of Defense, Joint Chiefs of Staff, and National Security Council; the Berlin airlift; Executive Order 9981 which desegregated the military; and the creation of the NATO. Then in 1989, the Soviets simply gave up, just as Harry Truman said they would.

Harry Truman is responsible for another of the most durable articles of practical idealism: limited war, a twentieth century variation of the Grant Doctrine's emphasis on using power with restraint. Truman deliberately chose to fight a limited war in order to preempt a general war when North Korea crossed the thirty-eighth parallel. Lyndon Johnson said Vietnam was a limited war. Richard Nixon disliked the negative connotations of limited war and described the limited objectives of his Vietnam policy. Later, George H. W. Bush described the limited objectives of the mission in Somalia, as did Bill Clinton regarding the mission in Haiti. All of which brings us to George W. Bush, who also disliked the connotations of limited war, and said the only way to limit the duration of the Iraq War was to use decisive force.[4]

•••

In George W. Bush's 2001 inaugural address, his remarks on foreign policy were brief, but to the point. He said the United States would build its defenses strong enough to deter any challenge. He pledged the United States would remain engaged in the world, defend its allies and interests, confront those who would use weapons of mass destruction, and change the balance of power to favor freedom. Finally, he said America would speak for the values that gave birth to our nation, an affirmation of practical idealism and a prediction of things to come.[5]

In an address to a joint session of Congress in late February 2001, Bush pledged to work with the United States' allies to be a force for good in the world, and to promote "a distinctly American internationalism." He pledged to restructure the nation's military forces to prepare for emerging threats, but did not promise to increase the defense budget. At this point, Bush envisioned a far-reaching transformation effort, but wanted to put strategy before spending. "Our defense vision will drive our defense budget, not the other way around," he said. He was determined to turn the military away from its cold war orientation toward a structure better suited to the twenty-first century. Bush also pledged his support for a missile defense system, and specifically mentioned the importance of defending against terrorists and tyrants in rogue nations.[6]

●●●

In April 2001, authorities arrested former president of Yugoslavia Slobo-dan Milosevic on charges of war crimes. In June, British prime minister Tony Blair's Labor Party won reelection. On September 11, nineteen men affiliated with Osama bin Laden and al-Qaeda hijacked four commercial jets and turned them into suicide bombs. They crashed two into the twin towers of New York's World Trade Center. They crashed another into the Pentagon building and another into a field in rural Pennsylvania. They killed almost three thousand people, including civilians, firefighters, police officers, and military personnel. As television cameras captured stunning images of the twin towers burning and then collapsing, international reaction condemning the attacks was swift and nearly unanimous.

Following the 9/11 attacks, Bush did not make his first major address until September 20. However, he did issue a series of statements. On September 11, Bush reported implementing the government's emergency response plans and ordered intelligence and law enforcement officials to launch an investigation. He said something about the United States being a beacon of freedom and opportunity, which supposedly explained the motive for the attacks. He also pledged to "win the war against terrorism."[7] The following day, Bush said the 9/11 attacks were more than acts of terror; they were acts of war. Based on incomplete intelligence to say the least, Bush said the enemy was unlike any other America ever faced. He pledged all the country's resources to win this "monumental struggle of good versus evil."[8] On September 15, he announced plans for "a comprehensive assault on terrorism." He predicted a broad and sustained campaign, which would take place "in a series of decisive actions against terrorist organizations and those who harbor and support them."[9] On September 17, Bush visited the Islamic Center of Washington, DC. He read from the Koran and called Islam a religion of peace.[10]

On September 20, 2001, Bush addressed a joint session of Congress. Only nine days after the attack, rescue crews and investigators were still digging through the rubble, but the country was beginning to recover from the shock. "Tonight, we are a country awakened to danger and called to defend freedom. Our grief has turned to anger and anger to resolution," he said, "Whether we bring our enemies to justice or bring justice to our enemies, justice will be done." British prime minister Tony Blair was in Washington for the speech, and Bush said, "America has no truer friend than Great Britain. Once again, we are joined together in a great cause."

Based on the best evidence available at the time, Bush said the people responsible for this "act of war" belonged to a loosely affiliated, worldwide terrorist organization called al-Qaeda, with more than a thousand members in sixty countries. Al-Qaeda is "a fringe movement" he said, and is the same group responsible for bombing the American embassies in Tanzania and Kenya and the USS *Cole* in Yemen. "We have seen their kind before" he said, "They're the heirs of all the murderous ideologies of the 20th century. By sacrificing human life to serve their radical visions, by abandoning every value except the will to power, they follow in the path of fascism, Nazism, and totalitarianism. And they will follow that path all the way to where it ends in history's unmarked grave of discarded lies."

Under the loose control of Osama bin Laden, al-Qaeda was using Afghanistan as a base to train its members and launch terrorist attacks. Bush issued an ultimatum to the Taliban regime, Afghanistan's brutal religious dictatorship. First, the Taliban must surrender all al-Qaeda leaders in Afghanistan. Second, they must release all illegally imprisoned foreign nationals. Third, they must protect all foreign journalists, diplomats, and aid workers in the country. Fourth, they must close all terrorist training camps, and surrender every person affiliated with the terrorist camps to proper authorities. Fifth, they must give American authorities full and unrestricted access to the camps. "These demands are not open to negotiation or discussion," he said.

Bush then spoke directly to Muslims around the world:

We respect your faith. It's practiced freely by many millions of Americans and by millions more in countries that America counts as friends. Its teachings are good and peaceful, and those who commit evil in the name of Allah blaspheme the name of Allah. The terrorists are traitors to their own faith, trying, in effect, to hijack Islam itself. The enemy of America is not our many Muslim friends. It is not our many Arab friends. Our enemy is a radical network of terrorists and every government that supports them.[11]

Bush then declared "war" on terror. He warned his listeners this war would look nothing like the Gulf War with its well-defined theater and quick victory, and nothing like the Kosovo air strikes, during which no American troops died in combat. This war would be *unlike* any other war we have ever fought, and involve "far more than instant retaliation and isolated strikes." He pledged every tool at his disposal—diplomacy, intelligence, law enforcement, financial influence, and "every necessary weapon of war" to win. In addition to pursuing terrorist organizations, the United States would consider any government that supported or harbored terrorist organizations a hostile regime. Thus, every nation in the world must make a choice: "Either you are with us or you are with the terrorists."

•••

At first, the Taliban refused to negotiate and demanded to see evidence of Osama bin Laden's involvement in the 9/11 attacks. Facing the increasing probability of an invasion, the Taliban then offered to extradite bin Laden to a neutral country, but Bush refused. With General Tommy Franks commanding, the invasion began with the insertion of American and British special forces on the ground, followed by an aerial bombing campaign in early October 2001, targeting Taliban and al-Qaeda forces, particularly around Kabul and Kandahar. The Taliban's defenses were no match for the allies' overwhelming technological superiority. In mid-November, the Taliban evacuated Kabul, and regrouped their remaining forces near Kandahar. Many of the remaining al-Qaeda forces retreated into the mountains near the Pakistan border, east of Kabul. By late November and early December, most of the remaining Taliban and al-Qaeda forces surrendered, but bin Laden's whereabouts remained unknown.

•••

In his 2002 annual message, Bush said the nation was at war and the economy was in recession, but the country was on the road to recovery. Except for failing to apprehend bin Laden, the military action in Afghanistan was a success. The United States killed or captured thousands of terrorists, destroyed Afghanistan's terrorist training camps, and reopened the American embassy in Kabul.[12] Putting his stamp on practical idealism, Bush pledged the United States would never impose its culture anywhere and never compromise its basic principles: human rights, the rule of law, limited state power, property rights, free speech, equal justice, respect for women, and religious freedom.

Bush listed two objectives in the war on terror. First, he pledged to shut down the terrorists' camps, disrupt their plans, and bring them to justice. Although the allies eliminated many terrorist training camps in Afghanistan, there were similar ones in other countries equally dangerous, and Bush reported American troops, intelligence, and law enforcement officials were active in countries such as the Philippines, Bosnia, Somalia, and Pakistan. Second, he pledged to prevent terrorists and hostile regimes from threatening the United States and its allies. Bush separated this objective into two parts: first, prevent terrorists from acquiring the materials, technology, or expertise to make weapons of mass destruction; and second, develop a missile defense shield to protect the United States and its allies from attack.

Bush called North Korea, Iran, and Iraq "an axis of evil" in this speech, but did not use the phrase preemptive action. The closest he came was to say, "I will not wait on events, while dangers gather. I will not stand by, as peril draws closer and closer. The United States of America will not permit the world's most dangerous regimes to threaten us with the world's most destructive weapons."

Moving on to the financial issues, Bush said his budget would support three goals: winning the war on terror, protecting our homeland, and reviving our economy. The high-tech weaponry used in Afghanistan defeated the enemy while minimizing casualties, but it was expensive, so Bush asked Congress for a substantial increase in defense spending. In order to protect the United States from another attack, his budget also called for major increases in spending for homeland security, particularly in terms of intelligence, bioterrorism, emergency response, port security, and border security. "America is no longer protected by vast oceans" he said, "We are protected from attack only by vigorous action abroad, and increased vigilance at home." Finally, Bush asked Congress to pass legislation to promote energy conservation and domestic energy production in order to make the United States less dependent on foreign oil.

•••

Throughout 2002, Iraqi president Saddam Hussein continued to defy the United Nations, refusing to grant UN weapons inspectors unlimited access, causing the confrontation over disarmament to escalate. In mid-September 2002, almost exactly one year after the 9/11 attacks, Bush addressed the UN General Assembly. Bush remarked how different the United Nations was from the League of Nations. In particular, when we created the United Nations, we also created the UN Security Council so "our deliberations would be more than talk, our resolutions would be more than wishes." Bush also announced the United States would rejoin UNESCO (the United Nations Educational, Scientific and Cultural Organization) and participate fully in its mission to promote human rights.[13]

Regarding the Middle East, he pledged his commitment to "an independent and democratic" Palestinian state. He then turned his attention to Iraq. Bush recounted Iraq's recent history, beginning with Saddam Hussein's invasion of Kuwait in 1990. For Bush, the single most important lesson from the Gulf War was the futility of appeasement. Because the United Nations was the "world's most important multilateral body," it was important all UN resolutions were enforced. He noted Iraq was required to comply with all UN Security Council resolutions as part of the February 1991 cease-fire, but repeatedly and flagrantly violated every one of them. He presented a list of Hussein's most egregious violations, including the 1993 plot to assassinate former president Bush. However, Bush mostly focused on Hussein's refusal to cooperate with UN weapons inspectors or to provide accurate information on any of Iraq's programs to develop biological, chemical, and nuclear weapons.

Bush said the United Nations and the world faced a test. "Are Security Council resolutions to be honored and enforced, or cast aside without consequence? Will the United Nations serve the purpose of its founding, or will it be irrelevant?" He then issued an ultimatum: if Iraq wishes peace, it must comply with all Security Council resolutions. This included the immediate and unconditional disclosure, removal, and destruction of all weapons of mass destruction. Iraq must also cease persecution of its ethnic minorities, account for all personnel from the Gulf War whose fate is unknown, accept liability for the invasion of Kuwait, and police the corrupt oil-for-food program. Bush warned Hussein not to doubt his determination. "The Security Council resolutions will be enforced—the just demands of peace and security will be met—or action will be unavoidable."

•••

In October 2002, Congress passed a joint resolution authorizing the president to use force against Iraq. On the island of Bali in Indonesia, terrorists bombed two nightclubs, killing more than two hundred. In November, the UN Security Council approved a resolution requiring Saddam Hussein to disarm or face the consequences. In November, several Central and East European nations, including Bulgaria, Estonia, Latvia, Lithuania, Romania, Slovakia, and Slovenia joined NATO.

In his 2003 annual message, Bush announced creation of the Department of Homeland Security. He reported on the liberation of Afghanistan, and restated his pledge "to seek peace between a secure Israel and a democratic Palestine." He reported thousands of terrorists with al-Qaeda connections were arrested, including one who directed logistics for the 9/11 attack and another who planned the *Cole* attack. The greatest danger facing us now, he said came from outlaw regimes, such as Iran and North Korea that could use weapons of mass destruction to blackmail, terrorize, and threaten us, or give or sell them to terrorists. However, he did not provide any details about what his policy would be except to say, "Different threats require different strategies."[14]

Bush did say the United States was working with countries in East Asia to find a peaceful, multilateral solution to the problem on the Korean peninsula, but this was just a way to change the subject to Iraq. "Our nation and the world must learn the lessons of the Korean Peninsula and not allow an even greater threat to rise up in Iraq. A brutal dictator, with a history of reckless aggression, with ties to terrorism, with great potential wealth, will not be permitted to dominate a vital region and threaten the United States," he said. Bush then recounted Saddam Hussein's alleged pursuit of weapons of mass destruction, and his well-known contempt for UN resolutions.

Bush reminded his audience it was three months since the United Nations gave Hussein his last chance to disarm, and then repeated allegations—that we now know to be untrue—Hussein possessed tens of thousands of liters of biological weapons and hundreds of tons of chemical agents. Bush also relayed erroneous information—received from a variety of unreliable sources—Hussein had several mobile biological weapons labs that produced germ warfare agents and evaded weapons inspectors by moving around the country. Convinced Hussein had an ambitious nuclear weapons development program, Bush said, "Our intelligence sources tell us that he has attempted to purchase high-strength aluminum tubes suitable for nuclear weapons production."

Before the 9/11 attacks, he said, many people believed containment was the best policy option for Iraq. Actually, many people believed containment was the best policy after 9/11 too, but Bush was unwilling to take the risk. "Imagine those 19 hijackers with other weapons and other plans—this time armed by Saddam Hussein," he said, "It would take one vial, one canister, one crate slipped into this country to bring a day of horror like none we have ever known." Although he did not specifically use the phrase *preemptive action*, he did issue an ultimatum: if Saddam Hussein refused to disarm, the United States would disarm him.

•••

In February 2003, Secretary of State Colin Powell delivered an address to the United Nations presenting evidence, which later proved to be false, that Saddam Hussein possessed chemical and biological weapons. In mid-March, Bush addressed the nation to present another ultimatum: "Saddam Hussein and his sons must leave Iraq within 48 hours. Their refusal to do so will result in military conflict, commenced at a time of our choosing." Bush restated his rejection of appeasement, and recounted the diplomatic effort to resolve the situation in Iraq, including more than a dozen UN resolutions since the 1991 Gulf War. "Intelligence gathered by this and other governments leaves no doubt," said Bush, "that the Iraq regime continues to possess and conceal some of the most lethal weapons ever devised."[15] Regrettably, this was false. In addition to charging Iraq with possessing and concealing weapons of mass destruction, Bush also said Iraq trained and harbored members of the al-Qaeda terrorist organization, which if not true at the time, would be soon enough.

Bush reminded his audience Congress already passed a joint resolution in October 2002 authorizing him to use force. Speaking directly to the Iraqi people through a translator, Bush again described the limited objectives of the military campaign; the target was not the Iraqi people, but the "lawless men" who ruled the country. Bush believed the Iraqi people were capable of self-government—and establishing democracy in Iraq would set a good example for the whole region. "In a free Iraq, there will be no more wars of aggression against your neighbors, no more poison factories, no more executions of dissidents, no more torture chambers and rape rooms," he said, "The tyrant will soon be gone. The day of your liberation is near."

Meanwhile the forty-eight hour deadline passed and neither Saddam Hussein nor his two sons complied with Bush's demand to leave. The president addressed the nation again, this time to announce the launch of military operations. In the president's brief remarks, he stressed the United States had no ambitions in Iraq other than "to remove a threat and restore control of that country to its own people."[16]

•••

Shortly after the March 20 deadline passed, U.S. forces launched air attacks in Baghdad against Saddam Hussein and other high-level Iraqi officials, hoping to produce a "shock and awe" effect and decapitate Iraq's government. Coalition forces consisted of approximately three hundred thousand troops, mostly American and British. Using Kuwait as a staging area, coalition ground forces moved northwest into Iraq toward Baghdad, securing the southern oil fields and infrastructure as they went, fighting engagements near Basra, Nasiriya, and Najaf on their way toward the capital.

As Iraq's military forces began to disintegrate, widespread looting broke out in many parts of Baghdad and other cities. In Northern Iraq, coalition forces—along with Kurdish allies—captured Kirkuk and then Tikrit, Saddam Hussein's hometown. With the collapse of Iraq's military forces and government, coalition troops would begin hunting down key members of Hussein's regime, but Hussein's whereabouts remained unknown for the time being. When coalition forces helped topple a large statue of Saddam Hussein in Baghdad's Freedom Square, it symbolized the end of Hussein's ruthless dictatorship—and the beginning of the occupation.

In early May 2003, Bush landed on the aircraft carrier USS *Abraham Lincoln* off the coast of Southern California. Standing in front of a large banner that said *Mission Accomplished,* he announced the end of major combat operations in Iraq. "In the battle of Iraq, the United States and our allies have prevailed," he said. Bush specifically said "battle" rather than "war" several times not because the combat was brief, but to emphasize the Battle of Iraq was one conflict in the war on terror:

> In the images of falling statues, we have witnessed the arrival of a new era. For a hundred of years of war, culminating in the nuclear age, military technology was designed and deployed to inflict casualties on an ever-growing scale. In defeating Nazi Germany and Imperial Japan, Allied forces destroyed entire cities, while enemy leaders who started the conflict were safe until the final days. Military power was used to end a regime by breaking a nation. Today, we have the greater power to free a nation by breaking a dangerous and aggressive

regime. With new tactics and precision weapons, we can achieve military objectives without directing violence against civilians.[17]

As Bush said, new tactics and precision weapons (supported by special forces providing reconnaissance, intelligence, and target designation) gave the United States the ability to achieve military its objectives while minimizing civilian casualties. The invasion of Iraq signaled the end of one brutal regime, but also symbolized the convergence of limited war and advanced military technology. This convergence explains why the seventeenth century presumption of state sovereignty is obsolete.

Bush then restated the principles he would follow in the war on terror. (Unfortunately, the big banner upstaged Bush and everything he said, which is why it is good to reread the primary documents.) Although he presented these principles in previous speeches, the speech on the deck of the *Abraham Lincoln* was his clearest explanation. First, any person who plans or commits a terrorist attack is an enemy of the United States. Second, any person, organization, or government who supports or protects or harbors terrorists is no different from a terrorist. Third, the United States will confront any outlaw regime with ties to terrorist organizations, or possesses or seeks to possess weapons of mass destruction. Fourth, the United States will support anyone in the world—including anyone in the Arab world—who cooperates with us.

●●●

Following the swift military victory, coalition forces killed or captured many senior officials from Hussein's regime, and killed his two sons Uday and Qusay during a July 2003 raid in the city of Mosul in northern Iraq. In the early weeks and months of the occupation, insurgents launched an aggressive guerrilla war, particularly in the area between Baghdad and Tikrit, and around Fallujah, west of Baghdad. The insurgents—largely Baathist Party holdouts loyal to Hussein—often ambushed small numbers of coalition troops with roadside or suicide bombings, or targeted police stations and Iraqi police trainees with car or truck bombs.

In early September 2003, Bush addressed the nation to provide an update on the situation in Iraq.[18] He said the spate of recent terrorist attacks had one goal: to drive coalition forces out before the job was finished and Iraq's transition to self-government was complete. According to Bush, terrorists claimed any time you inflicted harm on Americans they ran from a challenge—and cited Somalia and Beirut as examples. Of course, Bush was referring to the 1993 firefight in Mogadishu and the 1983 suicide bombing in Lebanon. Bush's insinuation that Ronald Reagan ran away from Beirut is beside the point. On a previous occasion, Bush said the single most important lesson from the Gulf War is the futility of appeasement. Harry Truman called this the lesson of Munich: "Appeasement leads only to further aggression and ultimately to war."[19]

At this stage, Bush's strategy consisted of three objectives. First, hunt down the terrorists and kill or capture them. Second, enlist the support of other nations in Iraq's reconstruction and transition to self-government. Third, expedite transfer of sovereignty to the Iraqi people as quickly as possible. Iraq had a Governing Council with cabinet ministers at the national level, while dozens of towns and cities around the country had newly installed governments at the local level. The coalition was training Iraqi civil defense and police forces, border guards, and a new Iraqi army, and would encourage the Governing Council to draft a constitution and schedule elections.

•••

In December 2003, American troops captured Saddam Hussein hiding in a "spider hole" near a farmhouse outside of Tikrit. Bush made the announcement in a brief message. Bush cautioned people even though it was the end of the road for Hussein, his capture would neither end the violence in Iraq nor end the war on terror. Speaking directly to the Iraqi people, Bush restated his goals: "sovereignty for your country, dignity for your great culture, and for every Iraqi citizen, the opportunity for a better life."[20]

•••

In his 2004 annual message, Bush noted it was more than two years since the 9/11 attack. Despite terrorist attacks that killed hundreds in Bali, Jakarta, Casablanca, Riyadh, Mombassa, Jerusalem, Istanbul, and Baghdad, he also noted it was more than two years since the last attack on American soil. He reported armed forces from the United States, United Kingdom, Australia, and Poland enforced UN Security Council resolutions and ended the regime of Saddam Hussein and the Baathist Party. Bush reported the Iraqi Governing Council was making progress drafting a basic law in preparation for transfer of sovereignty to an interim Iraqi government by the end of June. As that date drew nearer, he predicted—rightly so—insurgents would do everything they could to disrupt the transfer and intimidate the new government. As pundits and academics argued over the definition of "sovereignty," the Coalition Provisional Authority took a subtle form of preemptive action by transferring sovereignty two days ahead of schedule.

Bush also reported Libya agreed voluntarily to disclose and dismantle all its weapons of mass destruction. Bush commented on the irony that nine months of negotiation with Muammar al-Qaddafi worked while twelve years of diplomacy with Saddam Hussein did not. "Different threats require different strategies," he said, repeating verbatim something from his 2003 annual message. The greatest threat facing the country, he said, came from outlaw regimes that could use weapons of mass destruction against us, or give or sell them to terrorists. He said his administration was "insisting" North Korea eliminate its nuclear program and "demanding" Iran meet its commitments and not develop nuclear weapons. Once again, he pledged to keep "the world's most dangerous weapons out of the hands of the world's most dangerous regimes."

In response to critics who did not support invading Iraq, Bush asked them to consider the alternative. If we left Hussein in power, "Iraq's torture chambers would still be filled with victims." To those who doubted democracy was a realistic possibility in the Middle East, he said, "it is mistaken, and condescending, to assume that whole cultures and great religions are incompatible with liberty and self-government."[21] Critics of Bush's Iraq policy should reread Ronald Reagan's 1982 speech to British parliament or Bill Clinton's 1993 speech to South Korea's legislature. Reagan observed democracy flourished in many countries and cultures with different historical experiences and said it would be condescending or worse to suggest any people would prefer dictatorship to democracy.[22] In Clinton's speech in South Korea, he said, "Korea proves that democracy and human rights are not western imports. They flow from the internal spirit of human beings because they reflect universal aspirations."[23] Reagan, Clinton, and Bush are right, at least about this facet of practical idealism. It is condescending—or worse—to suggest any people would choose dictatorship over democracy.

•••

While there was never any doubt the Republicans would renominate George W. Bush, the field for the Democratic nomination was crowded. After the capture of Saddam Hussein, it became increasingly risky for presidential candidates to criticize a sitting wartime president—even though the occupation of Iraq would prove to be more difficult than the invasion as suicide bombs became an almost daily occurrence and insurgents attacked occupation troops in Najaf, Sadr City, Basra, and elsewhere.

In April 2004, news broke about numerous cases of prisoner abuse at the U.S.-controlled Abu Ghraib Prison in Baghdad. The Pentagon's investigation confirmed reports of numerous instances—including digital photographs—of humiliation and criminal abuse of Iraqi prisoners. With these events setting the stage for the 2004 presidential election, the Democrats nominated John Kerry, Vietnam War veteran and protestor, former lieutenant governor and senator from Massachusetts. Although the Central Intelligence Agency confirmed there were no weapons of mass destruction in Iraq, and the violent occupation of Iraq eclipsed other important foreign and domestic policy issues, George W. Bush won reelection, narrowly but convincingly.

Epilogue

George W. Bush's second term began on January 20, 2005. In his inaugural address, he said the 9/11 attacks marked the beginning of a new chapter in American history. Echoing Woodrow Wilson who said, "The world must be made safe for democracy," Bush said the survival of liberty in America depended on the success of liberty in other countries. Pledging to promote human rights, encourage political reform, and promote democracy around the world, Bush said, "The best hope for peace in our world is the expansion of freedom in all the world."[1]

In his 2005 annual message, Bush proposed a comprehensive energy strategy to promote conservation and development of alternative energy sources because—as Jimmy Carter said in 1979—America is too dependent on foreign oil. In his 2006 annual message the following year, Bush proposed solving the problem by increasing government investment in alternative energy sources, such as "clean, safe nuclear energy." He also said, "America is addicted to oil."[2] In the lexicon of chemical dependence and alcoholism, an addiction is a physiological or psychological dependency on a habit-forming substance, an uncontrollable compulsion that causes the addict to repeat behavior regardless of its consequences.

In late February 2006, Bush addressed members of a large veteran's organization whose motto is *for God and Country*. His goal, he said was nothing less than ending tyranny in the world. Accomplishing this "historic long-term goal" required disrupting the status quo in the Middle East and transforming the entire region "from an arc of instability into an arc of freedom."[3] As democracy took root in Iraq—according to this unusual version of the domino theory—other countries would follow suit and the responsibilities of governing would somehow produce a *moderating influence* rather than a corrosive influence on those in power.

•••

One lesson from 9/11 is that weak states can be as dangerous as strong states. To prove the point, the al-Askari Mosque lay in ruins in the ancient city of Samarra, north of Baghdad. Destruction of the mosque sparked sectarian reprisals, attacks on other mosques, more killing and anarchy. Insurgents killed Iraqi civilians and coalition forces with impunity, often using improvised explosive devices made from artillery shells or other munitions, detonated from a safe distance. As the third anniversary of the invasion came and went, Bush remained optimistic, insisting he would settle for "nothing less than complete victory."[4] In his words, "Victory will come when the terrorists and Saddamists can no longer threaten Iraq's democracy, when the Iraqi security forces can provide for the safety of their citizens on their own, and when Iraq is not a safe haven for terrorists to plot new attacks against our nation."[5]

During a speech in West Virginia, Bush listed other lessons from 9/11, and explained the theoretical foundations and policy implications of preemptive action. Lesson One: Americans have an attention deficit, and as 9/11 recedes into the past, some people will begin to forget. Lesson Two: the best way to preempt another attack from organizations such as al-Qaeda is to deny them safe haven. Lesson Three: the greatest threat to our national security is if terrorists obtain weapons of mass destruction. We must take this threat seriously, and do everything in our power to eliminate it.[6] Meanwhile, as kidnappings, assassinations, and atrocities committed against unarmed civilians, women, and children took place in Iraq on a daily basis, Bush continued to argue the world was better off with Saddam Hussein out of power. In one speech, he blamed Hussein for the whole fiasco even as he tried to reassure his audience Iraq had not descended into civil war.[7]

In March 2006, the White House released an updated version of the *National Security Strategy*.[8] Like the 2002 version, the new version addresses a wide range of initiatives, including military power, homeland defense, law enforcement, intelligence, diplomacy, and foreign aid. Presented as a "wartime national security strategy," the new version proposes a range of policies designed to strengthen alliances to defeat global terrorism, alleviate regional conflicts, remove weapons of mass destruction, stimulate global economic growth, promote democracy, and restructure America's national security institutions. The document calls nuclear proliferation "the greatest threat to our national security," and specifically cites Iran and North Korea, two members of the so-called axis of evil.

In September 2006, the White House released a new *National Strategy for Combating Terrorism*. The document predicts a long war and outlines a variety of short-term objectives in support of a single long-term goal: advancing effective democracy. This new goal is considerably less ambitious than ending tyranny in the world, Bush's goal from seven months earlier. The strategy lists Iraq as both a success story and a challenge; the United States is "aggressively prosecuting the war" despite "twisted...terrorist propaganda." This document also rests on the theory that democracy is contagious.

•••

On the fifth anniversary of the 9/11 attacks, Bush addressed the nation. "On this solemn anniversary, we rededicate ourselves to this cause," he said, using a phrase Lincoln probably would have crossed out and rewritten. Without admitting any specific mistakes, Bush said withdrawing from Iraq before democracy was firmly established would be "the worst mistake." However, with Hussein deposed and Iraq disarmed, most Americans remained skeptical. According to Bush, people in the Middle East had one question for us: "Do we have the confidence to do in the Middle East what our fathers and grandfathers accomplished in Europe and Asia?"[9]

Given the scope of this book, Bush's question merits geopolitical analysis, not psychoanalysis. As such, we should look past the two world wars to the Spanish-American War, when the United States redefined and expanded the geographic scope of the Monroe Doctrine beyond the Western Hemisphere to include every region of the world. In 1898, American forces crushed Spain's naval power in the Pacific and occupied the Philippines. Many Filipinos thought the occupation was nothing more than one colonial power replacing another and launched a war of independence against the American occupation forces. From 1899 to 1902, thousands of Americans, Filipino guerillas, and civilians died until Theodore Roosevelt issued a blanket amnesty to anyone who participated in the insurrection.[10]

In 1901, Roosevelt said, "We hope to do for them [Filipinos] what has never before been done for any people of the tropics—to make them fit for self-government after the fashion of the really free nations." During the first two bloody years of insurrection, Roosevelt refused to withdraw because he feared the Philippines would "fall into a welter of murderous anarchy. Such desertion of duty on our part would be a crime against humanity."[11] The United States could not withdraw, permitting the situation to deteriorate into anarchy and chaos, nor could the United States accelerate the process of democracy building.

Of course, this argument reappeared during the American occupation of Iraq. In Bush's 2004 message, he said, "We have not come all this way—through tragedy, and trial, and war—only to falter and leave our work unfinished." Even though the American occupation of the Philippines resulted in the deaths of tens of thousands of Americans and Filipinos, Roosevelt also refused to admit the occupation was a mistake. He said if the United States made *any mistake* in the Philippines, it was in moving too fast toward democracy and self-government.[12]

In Theodore Roosevelt's 1905 annual message, he said anyone who wages a war of aggression is a demagogue of war. Anyone who "inflames a perverse and aggressive national vanity" and excites his people "against foreigners on insufficient pretexts" is a demagogue of war.[13] However, just as there are demagogues of war, there are also demagogues of peace. A demagogue of peace is anyone who would allow all of our interests to go undefended so that one of our principles could go uncompromised. A demagogue of peace advocates *peace at any price*.

Roosevelt said this more than a hundred years ago, so he could not have been referring to the current incumbent. Not that it matters, because practical idealism has not changed all that much in a hundred or even two hundred years. Then as now, it requires balancing our interests and ideals, standing up for our principles and standing by our friends. As John Kennedy said, it requires paying equal attention to the arrow and the olive branch. As we face the future, and face the world, we should let this simple but powerful image be our guide.

Notes

PREFACE

1. John Kennedy, *Annual Message,* January 30, 1961.
2. Bill Clinton, *Speech by President to Iowa State Legislature,* April 25, 1995.

INTRODUCTION

1. George W. Bush, *Annual Message,* January 29, 2002.
2. George W. Bush, *2002 National Security Strategy of the United States of America,* September 17, 2002. Almost two years before George W. Bush took office, Bill Clinton said "...the real challenge of foreign policy is to deal with problems before they harm our national interests," which is the principle underlying pre-emptive action. (Bill Clinton, *Speech by President on Foreign Policy,* February 26, 1999.)
3. *Treaty of Westphalia,* October 24, 1648.
4. George W. Bush, *President Commemorates 60th Anniversary of V-J Day,* August 30, 2005.
5. George W. Bush, *President Discusses War on Terror at National Endowment for Democracy,* October 6, 2005.
6. George W. Bush, *President Outlines Strategy for Victory in Iraq,* November 30, 2005; Bush, *President Discusses War on Terror and Rebuilding Iraq,* December 7, 2005; Bush, *President Discusses War on Terror and Upcoming Iraqi Election,* December 12, 2005; Bush, *President Discusses Iraqi Elections, Victory in War on Terror,* December 14, 2005; Bush, *President's Address to the Nation,* December 18, 2005. *National Strategy for Victory in Iraq,* U.S. National Security Council, November 2005.
7. George W. Bush, *President's Address to the Nation,* December 18, 2005. During a March 2006 press conference, a reporter asked Bush if there would come a day when all American troops would be withdrawn from Iraq. In response, Bush said the matter would be "decided by future Presidents and future governments of Iraq." (George W. Bush, *Press Conference of the President,* March 21, 2006.)

This stands in contrast to Bill Clinton's response following the October 1993 Battle of Mogadishu. Four days after the firefight in which eighteen Americans died Clinton ordered all American combat troops withdrawn from Somalia, announced the exact date and said, "We'll do what we can to complete the mission before then." (Bill Clinton, *Address to the Nation on Somalia*, October 7, 1993.)

8. George Washington, *Proclamation of Neutrality*, April 22, 1793.

9. *Jay Treaty*, November 19, 1794.

10. George Washington, *Farewell Address*, September 19, 1796.

11. *Treaty of San Ildefonso*, October 1, 1800.

CHAPTER 1

1. *Act to Suspend the Commercial Intercourse Between the United States and France, and the Dependencies Thereof*, June 13, 1798; *Act to Authorize the Defense of the Merchant Vessels of the United States Against French Depredations*, June 25, 1798; *Act to Declare the Treaties Heretofore Concluded with France, no Longer Obligatory on the United States*, July 7, 1798.

2. *Convention of 1800*, September 30, 1800.

3. Thomas Jefferson, *Inaugural Address*, March 4, 1801.

4. Treaty of Peace and Friendship between the United States and the Bey and subjects of Tripoli of Barbary, signed at Tripoli November 4, 1796, ratified by the U.S. Senate on June 10, 1797. (Italics added.)

5. Thomas Jefferson, *Annual Message*, December 15, 1802.

6. *Louisiana Purchase Treaty*, April 30, 1803.

7. *Treaty of Ghent*, December 24, 1814.

8. James Monroe, *Annual Message*, December 2, 1823.

9. James Monroe, *Inaugural Address*, March 4, 1821.

10. *Adams-Onís Treaty*, February 22, 1819.

11. John Quincy Adams, *Annual Message*, December 6, 1825.

12. Ibid., December 2, 1828.

13. Andrew Jackson, *Inaugural Address*, March 4, 1929.

14. Andrew Jackson, *Annual Message*, December 8, 1829.

15. The Supreme Court overturned the Indian Removal Act in 1832, but Andrew Jackson ignored the court's opinion.

16. Jackson, *Annual Message*, December 8, 1829.

17. John Tyler, *Annual Message*, December 3, 1844.

18. James Polk, *Annual Message*, December 8, 1846.

19. Ibid., December 7, 1847.

20. Ulysses Grant, *Annual Message*, December 5, 1870.

21. Ibid., December 5, 1876.

22. Grover Cleveland, *Annual Message*, December 2, 1895.

CHAPTER 2

1. *Treaty of Peace Between the United States and Spain*, December 10, 1898.

2. William McKinley, *Annual Message*, December 5, 1899.

3. *Convention for the Construction of a Ship Canal* (Hay-Bunau-Varilla Treaty), November 18, 1903.

4. Theodore Roosevelt, *Annual Message,* December 3, 1906.

5. Ibid., December 5, 1905. (Italics added.)

6. Ibid., December 6, 1904.

CHAPTER 3

1. Woodrow Wilson, *Annual Message,* December 2, 1913.

2. Ibid., December 8, 1914.

3. Woodrow Wilson, *Strict Accountability: President Wilson's First Warning to the Germans,* February 10, 1915.

4. Woodrow Wilson, *First Lusitania Note to Germany* (sent under the signature of Secretary of State William Jennings Bryan), May 13, 1915.

5. Wilson, *Annual Message,* December 7, 1915. (Italics added.)

6. Ibid., December 7, 1915.

7. *Sykes-Picot Agreement,* May 15–16, 1916.

8. *Zimmerman Note to the German Minister to Mexico,* January 19, 1917.

9. Woodrow Wilson, *Address to the Senate,* January 22, 1917.

10. Woodrow Wilson, *Message to Special Session of Congress,* April 2, 1917.

11. On May 16, 1918, Wilson signed the Sedition Act, which amended the Espionage Act and made it a crime to incite insubordination or mutiny in the armed services, to support any country with which the United States was at war, or even to display the flag of a foreign enemy.

12. *Balfour Declaration,* November 2, 1917.

13. Wilson, *Annual Message,* December 4, 1917.

14. Woodrow Wilson, *Fourteen Points,* January 8, 1918.

15. *Peace Treaty of Brest Litovsk,* March 30 and April 2, 1918.

16. Wilson, *Annual Message,* December 2, 1918.

17. *Peace Treaty of Versailles,* June 28, 1919. (Italics added.)

18. Wilson, *Annual Message,* December 7, 1915.

19. Wilson, *Annual Message,* December 7, 1920. The U.S. Government formally recognized the independence of the Republic of the Philippines on July 4, 1946.

CHAPTER 4

1. *Treaty Between the United of States of America, Belgium, the British Empire, China, France, Italy, Japan, the Netherlands, and Portugal,* February 6, 1922.

2. Calvin Coolidge, *Annual Message,* December 6, 1923.

3. Ibid.

4. Calvin Coolidge, *Inaugural Address,* March 4, 1925. (Italics added.)

5. *Treaty of Mutual Guarantee Between Germany, Belgium, France, Great Britain, and Italy (The Locarno Pact),* October 16, 1925.

6. *Kellogg-Briand Pact,* August 27, 1928.

7. Herbert Hoover, *Inaugural Address,* March 4, 1929.

8. Herbert Hoover, *Annual Message,* December 3, 1929.

CHAPTER 5

1. Congress would later amend the Neutrality Act, and in 1939 revise it again to permit "cash-and-carry" purchases of weapons and war materiel. The January 1941 Lend Lease policy would undo the Neutrality Act legally, while the December 1941 attack on Pearl Harbor would nullify it politically.

2. *Treaty of Nonaggression Between Germany and the Union of Soviet Socialist Republics,* August 23, 1939.

3. Franklin D. Roosevelt, *Fireside Chat,* May 26, 1940.

4. *Three-Power (or Tripartite) Pact,* September 27, 1940.

5. Roosevelt, *Fireside Chat,* December 29, 1940.

6. Franklin Roosevelt, *Annual Message,* January 6, 1941.

7. Roosevelt, *Fireside Chat,* September 11, 1941.

8. *Master Lend-Lease Agreement,* February 23, 1942.

9. Roosevelt, *Fireside Chat,* February 23, 1942.

10. Franklin Roosevelt, *Annual Message,* January 7, 1943.

11. Roosevelt, *Fireside Chat,* July 28, 1943. (Italics added.)

12. Ibid., *Fireside Chat,* December 24, 1943.

13. Franklin Roosevelt, *Annual Message,* January 11, 1944.

14. Ibid., January 6, 1945.

15. Franklin Roosevelt, *Address to Congress on the Yalta Conference,* March 1, 1945.

16. Harry Truman, *Radio Address to the American People after the Signing of the Terms of Unconditional Surrender by Japan,* September 1, 1945.

CHAPTER 6

1. Harry Truman, *Annual Message,* January 21, 1946.

2. Harry Truman, *Message to the Congress of the United States on Greece and Turkey,* March 12, 1947.

3. *Executive Order 9981: Establishing the President's Committee on Equality of Treatment and Opportunity in the Armed Services,* July 26, 1948.

4. George W. Bush gave Truman most of the credit for the United States' victory in the cold war. "By the actions he took, the institutions he built, the alliances he forged and the doctrines he set down, Truman laid the foundations for America's victory in the Cold War," Bush said. "His leadership paved the way for subsequent Presidents from both political parties—men like Eisenhower and Kennedy and Reagan—to confront and eventually defeat the Soviet threat." (George W. Bush, *President Delivers Commencement Address at the United States Military Academy at West Point,* May 27, 2006.)

5. *North Atlantic Treaty,* April 4, 1949.

6. Truman, *Annual Message,* January 4, 1950.

7. Harry Truman, *Radio and Television Address to the American People on the Situation in Korea,* July 19, 1950.

8. Truman, *Annual Message,* January 8, 1951.

9. Harry Truman, *Report to the American People on Korea and on U.S. Policy in the Far East,* April 11, 1951.

10. Truman, *Annual Message,* January 9, 1952.

11. Ibid., January 7, 1953.

12. Ibid., January 7, 1953.

13. Harry Truman, *President's Farewell Address to the American People,* January 15, 1953.

CHAPTER 7

1. Dwight Eisenhower, *The Chance for Peace,* April 16, 1953.

2. *Text of the Korean War Armistice Agreement,* July 27, 1953.

3. *Mutual Defense Treaty Between the United States and the Republic of Korea,* October 1, 1953.

4. Dwight Eisenhower, *President's News Conference,* April 7, 1954.

5. *Southeast Asia Collective Defense Treaty,* September 8, 1954.

6. *Pacific Charter,* September 8, 1954.

7. In 1999, the U.S. Information Agency was shut down and some of its operations transferred to the Department of State.

8. Dwight Eisenhower, *Special Message to the Congress on the Situation in the Middle East,* January 5, 1957.

9. Dwight Eisenhower, *Annual Message,* January 9, 1958.

10. *Antarctic Treaty,* December 1, 1959.

11. Eisenhower, *Annual Message,* January 12, 1961.

12. Dwight Eisenhower, *Farewell Radio and Television Address to the American People,* January 17, 1961.

13. Ronald Reagan, *Annual Message,* February 6, 1985.

14. Washington, *Annual Message,* December 3, 1793.

CHAPTER 8

1. John Kennedy, *Inaugural Address,* January 20, 1961.

2. John Kennedy, *Radio and Television Report to the American People on the Berlin Crisis,* July 25, 1961.

3. John Kennedy, *Address in New York City Before the General Assembly of the United Nations,* September 25, 1961.

4. John Kennedy, *Radio and Television Report to the American People on the Soviet Arms Buildup in Cuba,* October 22, 1962.

5. Kennedy, *Annual Message,* January 14, 1963.

6. John Kennedy, *Commencement Address at American University in Washington,* June 10, 1963.

7. John Kennedy, *Remarks in the Rudolph Wilde Platz, Berlin,* June 26, 1963.

8. *Treaty Banning Nuclear Weapon Tests in the Atmosphere, in Outer Space and Under Water,* August 5, 1963.

9. Lyndon Johnson, *Address Before a Joint Session of the Congress,* November 27, 1963.

10. Lyndon Johnson, *Special Message to the Congress on U.S. Policy in Southeast Asia,* August 5, 1964.

11. *Joint Resolution of the Congress,* August 7, 1964.

12. Lyndon Johnson, *Annual Message,* January 4, 1965.

13. Lyndon Johnson, *Address at Johns Hopkins University: "Peace Without Conquest,"* April 7, 1965. The title of Johnson's speech resembles Woodrow Wilson's January 1917 vision of "peace without victory."

14. Lyndon Johnson, *President's Address to the Nation Announcing Steps to Limit the War in Vietnam and Reporting His Decision Not to Seek Reelection,* March 31, 1968.

15. Lyndon Johnson, *President's Address to the Nation Upon Announcing His Decision to Halt the Bombing of North Vietnam,* October 31, 1968.

CHAPTER 9

1. Richard Nixon, *Address to the Nation on Vietnam,* May 14, 1969.

2. Richard Nixon, *Informal Remarks in Guam with Newsmen,* July 25, 1969.

3. Richard Nixon, *Address Before the 24th Session of the General Assembly of the United Nations,* September 18, 1969.

4. Nixon, *War in Vietnam,* November 3, 1969.

5. Richard Nixon, *Address to the Nation on Progress Toward Peace in Vietnam,* December 15, 1969.

6. Richard Nixon, *Annual Message,* January 22, 1970.

7. Nixon, *Progress Toward Peace in Vietnam,* April 20, 1970.

8. Richard Nixon, *Address to the Nation on the Situation in Southeast Asia,* April 30, 1970.

9. Richard Nixon, *Address to the Nation About a New Initiative for Peace in Southeast Asia,* October 7, 1970.

10. Nixon, *Situation in Southeast Asia,* April 7, 1971.

11. Richard Nixon, *Address to the Nation Making Public a Plan for Peace in Vietnam,* January 25, 1972.

12. Richard Nixon, *Joint Statement Following Discussion with Leaders of the People's Republic of China,* February 27, 1972.

13. Nixon, *Vietnam,* April 26, 1972.

14. Nixon, *Situation in Southeast Asia,* May 8, 1972.

15. *Treaty Between the United States of America and the Union of Soviet Socialist Republics on the Limitation of Anti-Ballistic Missile Systems,* May 26, 1972.

16. Richard Nixon, *Inaugural Address,* January 20, 1973.

17. Richard Nixon, *Address to the Nation Announcing Conclusion of an Agreement on Ending the War and Restoring Peace in Vietnam,* January 23, 1973.

18. Richard Nixon, *Address to the Nation About Vietnam and Domestic Problems,* March 29, 1973.

19. *War Powers Resolution,* November 7, 1973.

CHAPTER 10

1. Jimmy Carter, *Inaugural Address,* January 20, 1977.

2. Jimmy Carter, *Address before the UN General Assembly,* March 17, 1977.

3. Jimmy Carter, *Address at Commencement Exercises at the University of Notre Dame,* May 22, 1977.

4. Jimmy Carter, *Annual Message,* January 19, 1977.

5. In September 1977, the United States and Panama signed a treaty agreeing to relinquish control of the Panama Canal by the year 2000. The U.S. Senate would ratify the treaty in April 1978.

6. *Camp David Accords; Framework for Peace in the Middle East,* September 17, 1978.

7. *Camp David Meeting on the Middle East Remarks of the President, President Anwar al-Sadat of Egypt, and Prime Minister Menachem Begin of Israel at the Conclusion of the Meeting,* September 17, 1978.

8. Jimmy Carter, *Address Before a Joint Session of the Congress,* September 18, 1978.

9. Carter, *Annual Message,* January 23, 1979.

10. *Treaty Between the United States of America and the Union of Soviet Socialist Republics on the Limitation of Strategic Offensive Arms (SALT II),* June 18, 1979.

11. Jimmy Carter, *Energy and National Goals Address to the Nation,* July 15, 1979. Critics later nicknamed it the "malaise" speech despite the fact that word did not appear in it.

12. Carter, *Annual Message,* January 23, 1980.

13. Reagan, *Annual Message,* January 26, 1982.

14. This is remarkably similar to an observation Lyndon Johnson made seventeen years earlier: "In this period no new nation has become Communist, and the unity of the Communist empire has begun to crumble." Johnson, *Annual Message,* January 4, 1965.

15. Truman, *Radio and Television Address,* July 19, 1950.

16. Ronald Reagan, *Address to Members of the British Parliament,* June 8, 1982.

17. George W. Bush, *Address to a Joint Session of Congress and the American People,* September 20, 2001.

18. George W. Bush, *Annual Message,* January 20, 2004.

19. National Security Decision Directive (NSDD-17) *Cuba and Central America,* January 4, 1982.

20. Ronald Reagan, *Address Before the Bundestag in Bonn,* June 9, 1982.

21. Reagan, *Annual Message,* January 25, 1983.

22. Paraphrasing Matthew 7:3-5, Roosevelt said, "There must be no effort made to remove the mote from our brother's eye if we refuse to remove the beam from our own." Theodore Roosevelt, *Annual Message,* December 6, 1904.

23. Ronald Reagan, *Remarks at the Annual Convention of the National Association of Evangelicals in Orlando, Florida,* March 8, 1983.

24. Johnson, *Annual Message,* January 4, 1965.

25. Ronald Reagan, *Address to the Nation on Defense and National Security,* March 23, 1983.

26. Ronald Reagan, *Address to the Nation on the Soviet Attack on a Korean Civilian Airliner,* September 5, 1983.

27. Ronald Reagan, *Address to the Nation on Events in Lebanon and Grenada,* October 27, 1983.

28. Reagan, *Annual Message,* January 25, 1984.

29. Ronald Reagan, *Inaugural Address,* January 21, 1985.

30. Reagan, *Annual Message,* February 6, 1985.

31. Ibid., February 4, 1986.

32. Reagan, *Annual Message,* January 27, 1987.

33. Ibid.

34. Ronald Reagan, *Address to the Nation on the Iran Arms and Contra Aid Controversy,* March 4, 1987.

35. Ronald Reagan, *Remarks on East–West Relations at the Brandenburg Gate in West Berlin,* June 12, 1987.

36. Reagan, *Annual Message,* January 25, 1988.

37. Ronald Reagan, *Farewell Address to the Nation,* January 11, 1989. The original source of the metaphor is the Bible (Matthew 5:14–16) and a sermon by Governor John Winthrop of the Massachusetts Bay Colony in 1630.

CHAPTER 11

1. George Bush, *Address on Administration Goals Before a Joint Session of Congress,* February 9, 1989.

2. George Bush, *Remarks of the President and Soviet Chairman Gorbachev and a Question-and-Answer Session with Reporters in Malta,* December 3, 1989.

3. George Bush, *Address to the Nation Announcing United States Military Action in Panama,* December 20, 1989.

4. George Bush, *Annual Message,* January 31, 1990.

5. George Bush, *Address to the Nation Announcing the Deployment of United States Armed Forces to Saudi Arabia,* August 8, 1990.

6. George Bush, *Address Before a Joint Session of Congress on the Persian Gulf Crisis and the Federal Budget Deficit,* September 11, 1990.

7. George Bush, *Address to the United Nations General Assembly,* October 1, 1990.

8. George Bush, *Radio Address to the Nation on the Persian Gulf Crisis,* January 5, 1991.

9. *Persian Gulf War Resolution,* "Use of United States Armed Forces Pursuant to United Nations Security Council Resolution 678," January 12, 1991.

10. George Bush, *Address to the Nation Announcing Allied Military Action in the Persian Gulf,* January 16, 1991.

11. George Bush, *Annual Message,* January 29, 1991.

12. George Bush, *Address to the Nation on the Suspension of Allied Offensive Combat Operations in the Persian Gulf,* February 27, 1991.

13. George Bush, *Address Before a Joint Session of the Congress on the Cessation of the Persian Gulf Conflict,* March 6, 1991.

14. George Bush, *Remarks to the Supreme Soviet of the Republic of the Ukraine in Kiev, Soviet Union,* August 1, 1991. (Italics added.)

15. George Bush, *Address to the United Nations General Assembly,* September 23, 1991

16. George Bush, *Address to the Nation on Reducing United States and Soviet Nuclear Weapons,* September 27, 1991.

17. George Bush, *Annual Message,* January 28, 1992.

18. George Bush, *Address to the Nation on the Situation on Somalia,* December 4, 1992.

19. George Bush, *Remarks at Texas A&M University in College Station,* December 15, 1992.

20. George Bush, *Remarks at the United States Military Academy in West Point,* January 5, 1993.

CHAPTER 12

1. Bill Clinton, *Address Before a Joint Session of Congress on Administration Goals,* February 17, 1993.

2. Bill Clinton, *Address to the Nation on the Strike on Iraqi Intelligence Headquarters,* June 26, 1993.

3. Bill Clinton, *Remarks on Endorsements of the North American Free Trade Agreement,* November 2, 1993.

4. Bill Clinton, *Annual Message,* January 25, 1994.

5. Bill Clinton, *Statement on the Deaths of Leaders of Rwanda and Burundi,* April 7, 1994; Clinton, *Letter to Congressional Leaders on Evacuations from Rwanda and Burundi,* April 12, 1994; Clinton, *Remarks on the Situation in Rwanda,* April 30, 1994; Clinton, *Executive Order 12918,* May 26, 1994; Clinton, *Statement by the President on the Closing of the Embassy of Rwanda,* July 15, 1994; and Clinton, *Memorandum on Assistance to Refugees of Rwanda and Burundi,* July 17, 1994.

6. Bill Clinton, *Address to the Nation on Somalia,* October 7, 1993. (Italics added.)

7. Bill Clinton, *Address to the Nation on Haiti,* September 15, 1994.

8. Bill Clinton, *Remarks to the United Nations General Assembly,* September 26, 1994.

9. Bill Clinton, *Address to the Nation on Iraq,* October 10, 1994.

10. Clinton, *Annual Message,* January 24, 1995.

11. Bill Clinton, *Speech by President at 50 Years After Nuremberg Symposium,* October 15, 1995.

12. *Dayton Peace Accords,* November 21, 1995.

13. Clinton, *Annual Message,* January 23, 1996.

14. Bill Clinton, *Remarks by the President to the People of Detroit,* October 22, 1996.

15. Clinton, *Annual Message,* February 4, 1997

16. Bill Clinton, *Remarks by the President in Address on China and the National Interest,* October 24, 1997.

17. Clinton, *Annual Message,* January 27, 1998.

18. Bill Clinton, *Remarks by President to Genocide Survivors, Assistance Workers, and US and Rwanda Government Officials,* March 25, 1998.

19. Bill Clinton, *Address to the Nation Announcing Military Strikes on Iraq,* December 16, 1998. Britain also launched coordinated air strikes.

20. Clinton, *Annual Message,* January 19, 1999.

21. *Wye River Memorandum,* October 23, 1998.

22. Bill Clinton, *Address to the Nation on the Military Technical Agreement on Kosovo,* June 10, 1999. In an earlier speech, Clinton also listed as objectives continued cooperation with Russia and political and economic stability in the Balkans after the conflict. (Bill Clinton, *Speech by President at Air Force Academy Commencement,* June 2, 1999.)

23. Clinton, *Annual Message,* January 27, 2000.

24. Bill Clinton, *Foreign Policy for the Global Age,* University of Nebraska, December 8, 2000.

CHAPTER 13

1. George W. Bush, *Annual Message,* January 31, 2006.

2. *Protocol for the Prohibition of the Use in War of Asphyxiating Gas, and of Bacteriological Methods of Warfare,* February 8, 1928.

3. Franklin Roosevelt, *Annual Message,* January 3, 1936; Truman, *Annual Message,* January 21, 1946; Eisenhower, *Annual Message,* January 6, 1955; John Kennedy, *Address Before the Irish Parliament in Dublin,* June 28, 1963; Johnson, *Annual Message,* January 4, 1965; Johnson, *Annual Message,* January 12, 1966; Richard Nixon, *Address to the UN General Assembly,* September 18, 1969; Carter, *Annual Message,* January 23, 1979; Ronald Reagan, *Address to British Parliament,* June 8, 1982; Reagan, *Annual Message,* January 25, 1982; George Bush, *Address to the UN General Assembly,* September 25, 1989; Bill Clinton, *Public Law No: 103-150;* George W. Bush, *Address to the Nation,* March 17, 2003; George W. Bush, *President Outlines Strategy for Victory in Iraq,* November 30, 2005; and George W. Bush, *Annual Message,* January 31, 2006.

4. George W. Bush, *President Addresses the Nation,* March 19, 2003. Bush repeated the phrase a few days later. See *President Discusses the Beginning of Iraqi Freedom,* March 22, 2003.

5. George W. Bush, *Inaugural Address,* January 20, 2001.

6. George W. Bush, *Address Before a Joint Session of the Congress on Administration Goals,* February 27, 2001.

7. George W. Bush, *Statement by the President in His Address to the Nation,* September 11, 2001.

8. George W. Bush, *Remarks by the President in Photo Opportunity with the National Security Team,* September 12, 2001.

9. George W. Bush, *Radio Address of the President to the Nation,* September 15, 2001.

10. George W. Bush, *Remarks by the President at Islamic Center of Washington, DC,* September 17, 2001.

11. George W. Bush, *Address to a Joint Session of Congress and the American People,* September 20, 2001.

12. George W. Bush, *Annual Message,* January 29, 2002.

13. George W. Bush, *President's Remarks at the United Nations General Assembly,* September 12, 2002. (The United States withdrew from UNESCO in 1984.)

14. George W. Bush, *Annual Message,* January 28, 2003.

15. George W. Bush, *President Says Saddam Hussein Must Leave Iraq Within 48 Hours,* March 17, 2003.

16. George W. Bush, *Address to the Nation on Iraq,* March 19, 2003.

17. George W. Bush, *Remarks by the President from the USS Abraham Lincoln,* May 1, 2003.

18. George W. Bush, *President Addresses the Nation,* September 7, 2003.

19. Truman, *Radio and Television Address,* July 19, 1950.

20. George W. Bush, *President Bush Addresses Nation on the Capture of Saddam Hussein,* December 14, 2003. The Iraqi Special Tribunal tried and convicted Hussein and executed him in December 2006.

21. George W. Bush, *Annual Message,* January 20, 2004.

22. Ronald Reagan, *Address to Members of the British Parliament,* June 8, 1982.

23. Bill Clinton, *Speech by President to Korean National Assembly,* July 10, 1993.

EPILOGUE

1. George W. Bush, *Inaugural Address,* January 20, 2005.

2. George W. Bush, *Annual Message,* January 31, 2006.

3. George W. Bush, *President Addresses American Legion, Discusses Global War on Terror,* February 24, 2006.

4. George W. Bush, *President's Radio Address,* March 18, 2006.

5. George W. Bush, *President Discusses War on Terror and Operation Iraqi Freedom,* March 20, 2006.

6. George W. Bush, *President Discusses War on Terror, Progress in Iraq in West Virginia,* March 22, 2006.

7. George W. Bush, *President Discusses Democracy in Iraq with Freedom House,* March 29, 2006.

8. George W. Bush, *National Security Strategy of the United States of America,* March 16, 2006.

9. George W. Bush, *President's Address to the Nation,* September 11, 2006.

10. Theodore Roosevelt, *Proclamation Formally Ending the Philippine Insurrection and Granting of Pardon and Amnesty,* July 4, 1902.

11. Theodore Roosevelt, *Annual Message,* December 3, 1901.

12. Ibid., December 3, 1906.

13. Ibid., December 5, 1905.

Bibliography

My research has focused almost exclusively on primary documents, particularly the public statements of presidents. The American Presidency Project and the Avalon project were particularly valuable resources. The American Presidency Project (at the University of California, Santa Barbara) has collected and cataloged thousands of documents, including every inaugural and annual message of every American president. The American Presidency Project Web site also has links to presidential libraries and the national archives. The Avalon Project (at Yale University Law School) has collected numerous documents, including treaties relevant to the fields of law, history, politics, diplomacy, and government.

President George W. Bush's addresses, proclamations, press releases and other news items are located on the official White House Web site: http://www.white house.gov/. The proclamations of previous presidents and the text of every other document described or quoted in this study—unless otherwise noted—is located at one or more of the following locations:

American Presidency Project, John Woolley and Gerhard Peters, Department of Political Science, University of California, Santa Barbara, California 93106 • http://www.presidency.ucsb.edu/

Avalon Project at Yale Law School, The Lillian Goldman Law Library in Memory of Sol Goldman, 127 Wall Street, New Haven, Connecticut 06520 • http://www. yale.edu/lawweb/avalon/

George Bush Presidential Library and Museum, 1000 George Bush Drive West, College Station, Texas 77845 • http://bushlibrary.tamu.edu/

Jimmy Carter Library and Museum, 441 Freedom Parkway, Atlanta, Georgia 30307 • http://www.jimmycarterlibrary.org/

William J. Clinton Presidential Center, 1200 President Clinton Avenue, Little Rock, Arkansas 72201 • http://www.clintonlibrary.gov/

Dwight D. Eisenhower Library and Museum, 200 Southeast Fourth Street, Abilene, Kansas 67410 • http://www.eisenhower.archives.gov/

Gerald R. Ford Library, 1000 Beal Avenue, Ann Arbor, Michigan 48109 • http:// www.fordlibrarymuseum.gov/

John Fitzgerald Kennedy Library, Columbia Point, Boston, Massachusetts 02125 •
    http://www.jfklibrary.org/
Library of Congress, American Memory Collection, 101 Independence Avenue, SE,
    Washington, DC 20540 • http://memory.loc.gov/ammem/
Library of Congress, Thomas: Legislative Information for the Public, 101 Independ-
    ence Avenue, SE, Washington, DC 20540 • http://thomas.loc.gov/
Lyndon Baines Johnson Library and Museum, 2313 Red River Street, Austin, Texas
    78705 • http://www.lbjlib.utexas.edu/
William McKinley Memorial Library and Museum, 40 North Main Street, Niles,
    Ohio 44446 • http://www.mckinley.lib.oh.us/
United States National Archives and Records Administration, 700 Pennsylvania
    Avenue, Northwest, Washington, DC 20408 • http://www.archives.gov/
Richard Nixon Library and Birthplace, 18001 Yorba Linda Blvd, Yorba Linda,
    California 92886 • http://www.nixonfoundation.org/
Ronald Reagan Presidential Library and Museum, 40 Presidential Drive,
    Simi Valley, California 93065 • http://www.reaganlibrary.net/• http://www.
    reaganlibrary.com/
Franklin D. Roosevelt Presidential Library, 4079 Albany Post Road, Hyde Park,
    New York 12538 • http://www.fdrlibrary.marist.edu/
Harry S. Truman Library and Museum, 500 W. US Highway 24, Independence,
    Missouri 64050 • http://www.trumanlibrary.org/

Because presidents frequently refer to events or other developments that took place
since their last statement, I wrote numerous "bridge" paragraphs to maintain precise
chronology. I used the following Web sites as resources:

Internet Public Library, a public service organization and learning/teaching
    environment at the University of Michigan, School of Information, Ann Arbor,
    Michigan 48109 • http://www.ipl.org/
George C. Marshall Foundation, a library and archive which houses thousands of
    documents on American military and diplomatic history, P.O. Drawer 1600,
    VMI Parade, Lexington, Virginia 24450 • http://www.marshallfoundation.org/
Public Broadcasting Service (PBS), a comprehensive companion Web site for
    PBS television programs and original web content, 1320 Braddock Place,
    Alexandria, Virginia 22314 • http://www.pbs.org/
University of Michigan Government Documents Center, a reference center for
    government information, University of Michigan Library, 203 Hatcher Gradu-
    ate Library North, Ann Arbor, Michigan 48109 • http://www.lib.umich.edu/
    govdocs/
Wars for Viet Nam, a Web site for Robert Brigham's seminar at Vassar College
    which includes numerous official documents from the Vietnamese Archives in
    Hanoi, Vassar College, Box 711, 124 Raymond Avenue, Poughkeepsie, New
    York 12604 • http://vietnam.vassar.edu/
World War I Document Archive, an archive of treaties and other official primary
    documents from WWI, Brigham Young University, Harold B. Lee Library,
    Provo, Utah 84602 • http://www.lib.byu.edu/~rdh/wwi/

Index

About the Author

JACK GODWIN is a political scientist with extensive experience in business, government, and higher education spanning more than two decades and dozens of countries. He currently serves as Chief International Officer at California State University, Sacramento. He has a doctorate in political science from the University of Hawaii and degrees from San Francisco State University and the University of California, Berkeley. He is a member of the Pacific Council on International Policy. He was a Fulbright Scholar in Japan, Germany, and Hungary, and a Peace Corps Volunteer in Gabon.